C000246621

The Illustrated Guide to
TROPICAL AQUARIUM FISHES

The Illustrated Guide to TROPICAL AQUARIUM FISHES

IVAN PETROVICKÝ

Illustrated by
LADISLAV PROS

Translated by Marie Hejlová
Graphic design by Ladislav Pros

Previously published in Great Britain by The Hamlyn Publishing Group
Designed and produced by Aventinum

This 1993 edition published by
Chancellor Press
an imprint of Reed Consumer Books Limited
Michelin House, 81 Fulham Road, London SW3 6RB
and Auckland, Melbourne, Singapore and Toronto

ISBN 1 85152 356 1

A CIP catalogue record for this book is available at the British Library

Printed in Slovakia by Neografia, Martin
3/15/07/51-04

Contents

Introduction

The oldest records on aquaristics concerned with rearing the 'goldfish' date back to 1163 and come from China. Nevertheless, it was not until the 1850s that the history of modern aquaristics began. The first aquarium with plants and fish was set up by the English naturalist S. H. Ward in 1841. In 1855 it was, by coincidence, another Englishman and naturalist, P. H. Goss, who in his publication used the word 'aquarium' for the first time. The Frenchman Carbonnier, a pioneer in this area, was the first breeder: in 1869—1870 he succeeded in breeding and rearing the Paradise Fish *(Macropodus opercularis).* During the last two decades, a factual aquaristic explosion has taken place all over the world, resulting in an increasing flow of information on the subject, but simultaneously also a merciless devastation of natural habitats. It is in fact easier to take a fish from the wild than to breed it. The demand for fish is immense, their production is insufficient and the resources of nature are much too easily exhaustible. The solution to this problem, which has become more than pressing, lies in mastering the artificial breeding of fish in captivity, so as to leave nature as a laboratory, a place of study and a fish reservoir.

The reader who takes up a book about nature is sure to be interested also in its preservation. This small book is intended primarily for those who have become so fascinated by the mysterious kingdom of fish that they devote their leisure time to the noble activity of aquaristics. In view of the fact that, with the aquarium, we also bring to our homes a small part of the remote tropical nature, it is necessary to acquaint ourselves, at least in brief, with the original dwelling place of the inhabitants of our aquariums.

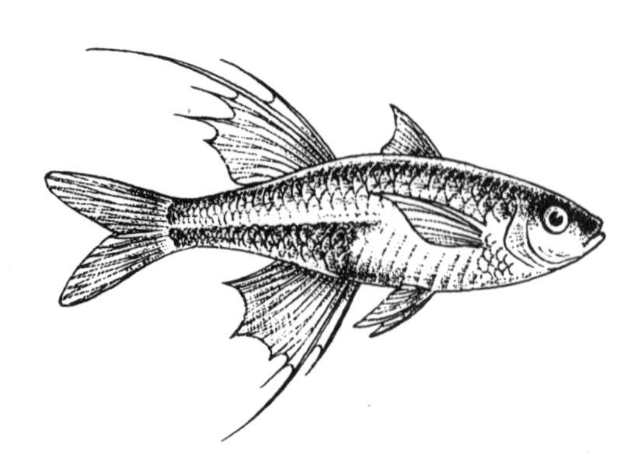

Waters of South America

The major waters of South America are three river systems affecting all life over a vast territory. In the north it is the Orinoco; to the south, the most powerful river, the Amazon, flows across nearly all the continent, and still further south is the Paraná—Paraguay river system. The Amazon is fed by mighty rivers as well as by a number of smaller rivers and brooks. This great network of meanders, inlets and tributaries alternately filled with tropical rain torrents and flooded with tropical sun, has made it possible for the richest and most variegated ichthyofauna of the Earth to develop on the South American continent. Ichthyologists estimate that there are up to 2,500 fish species living here. The variety of fish communities is made still greater by the differences in chemical composition of the waters, from soft, slightly or very acid clean ones—the so-called black waters, the Río Negro—to muddy ones called white waters. Many kilometres below the confluence of the Río Negro and the Amazon, one part of the river remains black and the other white: no substantial fusion is taking place.

South America is the home of 6 m long sawfish, Amazon sharks, predatory catfish called *'pirabiá'* attaining a length of 3 m and electric eels generating electricity with a current of as much as 650 volts. Also, minute parasitic fish of the genus *Stegophilus* live here, burrowing in the gills of large fish, and the no less tiny, very dangerous, small catfish of the genus *Vandellia* which penetrate the urinary system of bathing mammals. Shoals of piranhas with strong jaws equipped with many teeth as sharp as scalpels inspire terror. Besides these ichthyological dainties, there is a great variety of species of small fish, many of which, e.g. tetras of the family Characidae, adorn our aquariums.

Waters of Central and North America

The region of Central America also includes the territory of the West Indies stretching from the peninsula of Florida as far as the mouth of the Orinoco and the island group of the Greater Antilles. Central America is certainly interesting from the ichthyological point of view, for here lies the borderline along which fish typical of both South and North America are living side by side. Mexico with the Californian peninsula in the northwest and Yucatan in the east is a predominantly mountainous country with a large number of still active volcanoes. The coastal regions of Mexico are mostly covered with mangrove swamps leading to stretches of savannas and, towards the south and southeast, jungles overgrow the eastern slopes of the mountains. The mountainous character of the region gives the rivers a steep gradient.

Among those having a structure characteristic of Central American fish is first and foremost the family Poeciliidae (live-bearing tooth carps), and also the family Cyprinodontidae (tooth carps). Many spe-

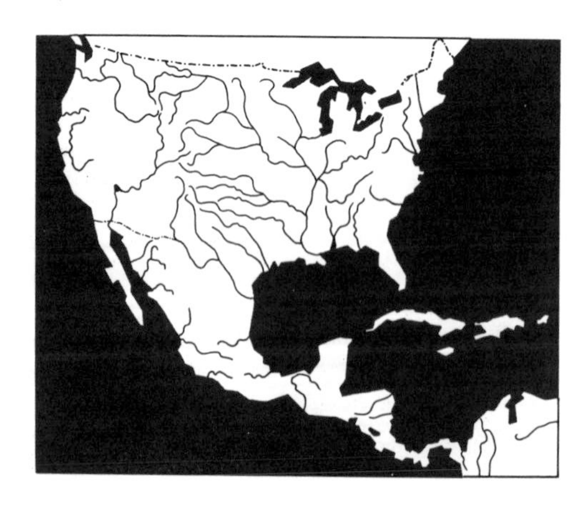

cies belonging to these families are not only much-sought-after aquarium fish, but also useful aids in fighting malaria because they destroy mosquito larvae. Another characteristic family of this area is Goodeidae. Representatives of some characin and cichlid species are found here in small numbers.

As to North America, it is the western Californian coast and also the lowlands bordering the eastern shores of Texas up to South Carolina that have aroused the aquarists' attention. In the state of Luisiana, the river Mississippi flows into the Appalachian Gulf. This is the home of predatory fish of the family Lepisosteidae (gars). These are often on view in large public aquariums. The nature of Florida is especially noteworthy and in the south is the Everglades National Park. Here the climate, considerably influenced by the Gulf Stream, has contributed to the rise of a naturally tropical scenery. Streams and rivers flow through groves of royal palms, forming many swamps and pools, and there is both fresh and salt water harbouring a rich ichthyofauna, e.g. Sunfish of the family Centrarchidae.

Waters of Australia

Australia, the smallest continent, is largely arid and inhospitable. Scattered islands and Oceania, with its most important islands of New Guinea, New Zealand and Tasmania, form part of this continent. Australian nature is entirely different from that of other continents. A number of animals living there are relics which died out many million years ago everywhere else on Earth. Among the fish this applies to is the Australian Lungfish, *Neoceratodes forsteri.*

With the exception of the largest rivers, the Murray and the Darling,

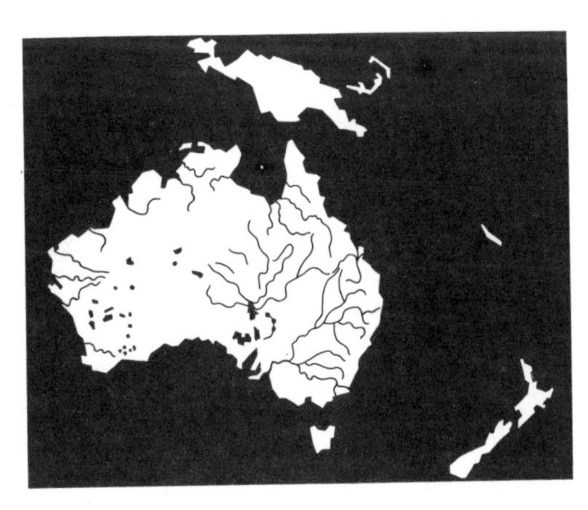

only periodic streams flowing into basins without outlets drain the interior of the continent. The longest river is the Darling, covering 2,800 km, but even this sometimes dries out in as much as its bed is transformed into so-called billabongs or bow lakes. The Western Australian plateau is almost entirely devoid of flowing water and there are only short rivers on the eastern, western and northern coast. The 180 species of Australian freshwater fish include only two species that are primarily freshwater; all the others originated in the sea.

Waters of Africa

The landscape most characteristic of Africa is the savanna, overgrown with high grass interspersed with groups of trees or single trees, particularly with umbrella-like acacias. Both to the north and south, the savanna gives way to forest steppe which in turn becomes desert. The only rivers found here at all are no more than dried-out river beds for the greater part of the year. A periodic alternation of summer rain and winter drought is typical of the African savanna and the bush-overgrown steppe. It gives rise to the so-called periodic waters, the wellknown habitat of egg-laying tooth carps (genera *Aphyosemion, Nothobranchius).* The tropical rain forest abounding in rivulets and creeks or shallow lakes and pools stretches from the coast of Guinea almost 5,000 km west to east and about 1,600 km north to south to the wooded basin of the river Congo. The rivers rise at mountain sources and swamps; as rapids and waterfalls they rush through narrow canyons to the lowlands where they change into broad, deep, sluggishly flowing waters. The waters are rich in fish — there are numerous species of aquarium fish as well as of those important for local fisheries (genera *Tilapia, Synodontis, Labeo).*

Especially in the last decade, aquarists have been strongly attracted by the eastern part of Africa where the lakes of the Great Rift Valley are situated, the main ones being Lakes Tanganyika and Malawi. The water in these lakes is alkaline. A number of experts in African ichthyofauna have agreed on the hypothesis that an ichthyological 'miracle' is under way in the lakes: an extraordinarily rapid evolution of fish belonging to the family Cichlidae. The cichlids living here are represented mostly by mouthbreeders. Single mouthbreeder groups form closely related strains called 'generic swarms'. (Thus, for example, lake Malawi is inhabited by a genus of the family Cichlidae which comprises more than a hundred closely related species developing from a single common ancestor.) Beside the cichlids there

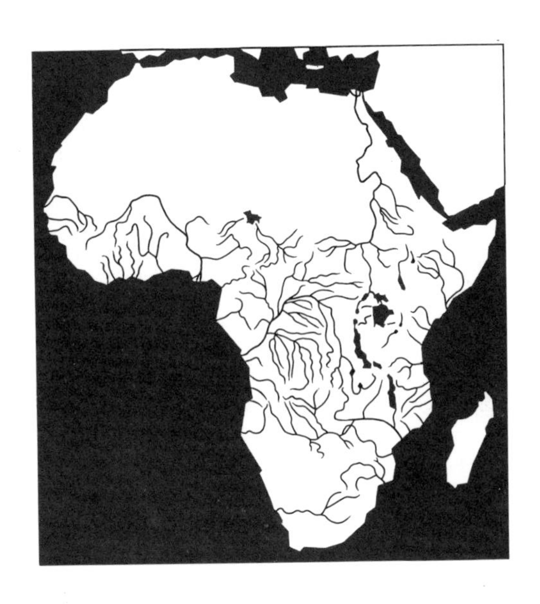

are many other fish species, very often endemic ones (i.e. their distribution is restricted to this particular region).

According to present thought, twenty million years ago the island of Madagascar was isolated from the African continent. Its isolation caused it to become an independent zoogeographic region. There is an outstanding difference between the island's animals and the African fauna. Madagascar is poor in fish. The development of the species living here took place in the sea, and it was only in the course of time that the fish acclimatized themselves to fresh water. Their double dorsal fin and their capacity for living in brackish coastal waters betray their origin.

Waters of Tropical Asia

From the aquaristic point of view, the most interesting parts of the largest continent are the tropical south and southeast, known also under the name of Monsoon Asia and including the adjacent islands. This is a region of extensive, but diminishing rain forests. The waters abound in small tropical fish. The low-country water systems lie at the foot of massive mountains in the southern and southeastern parts of the continent, as well as in island groups of the Pacific and Indian Oceans. The climate is influenced by dry winds coming from the mainland and by regular wet monsoons. The monsoons accompanied by tropical rains are vital for this area, though they simultaneously

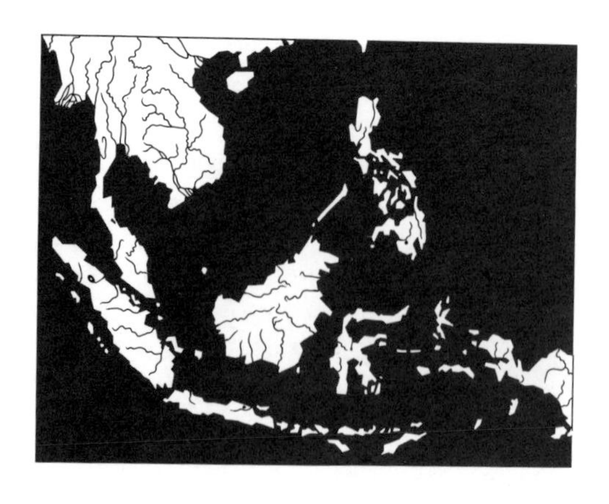

cause destructive floods. The parched and arid soil eagerly absorbs moisture, nature puts on a brilliant green cloak, half-desiccated river-beds are quickly refilled with water. Southwards from the Malay Peninsula, however, rains continue to fall almost all the year round and strongly affect the character of nature in these parts.

A great many aquarium fish come from the waters of Sri Lanka, Thailand, Malaya, from the neighbourhood of Singapore, from Sumatra and Java. Here the period of vegetation growth and fish spawning starts with the onset of rains. Of course, in various localities this period is affected by considerable differences in altitude.

From the slopes of mountain ranges situated along the western coast of Sumatra, swift-running mountain rapids gush out into the Indian Ocean. On the opposite side of the island facing the Malay Peninsula there are lowlands rich in rivers and swamps. Stagnant waters are relatively warm: 25—39° C. In frequently inundated areas the natives build their dwellings on piles above the level of the water. The water near such villages is contaminated by refuse which attracts huge numbers of fish belonging to a variety of species. Pits, holes and ditches filled with dirty water are inhabited predominantly by labyrinth fish (family Belontiidae). In the region of Sumatra, mountain streams offer quite different biotopes with a specific fish structure. Representatives of labyrinth fish found here are, for instance, *Trichopsis vittatus* and *Trichogaster trichopterus*. The waters of Sumatra are usually soft, slightly acid, and are brown-coloured due to decaying plants at the bottom. Mangrove jungles stretching along the shores of almost all tropical Asia represent a world of their own. The water is predominantly brackish; hence the structure of fish is again different. Fish of the genus *Periophthalmus* (mudskippers) belonging to the family Goobiidae are characteristic of this region.

Setting up an Aquarium

It is frequently said that wage earners have no time left for maintaining an aquarium. If their work entails their leaving the house for a number of days, this opinion may be justified. Even if this is the case, however, modern techniques are now available that offer a solution to problems of this kind. Adequately equipped aquariums, well-overgrown with plants and, particularly important, not overcrowded with a chaotic miscellany of fish, are sure to prosper with even the minimum of care and attention. In principle, the following points must be observed:

a) The permanent location of the aquarium should make it tastefully complement the interior furnishings.
b) The larger the aquarium, the less work it requires and the more success may be expected.
c) The time reserved for maintenance and feeding must be taken into account, for only a well-maintained aquarium and healthy fish can fulfil their aesthetic purpose. For one aquarium it is necessary to reckon on spending approximately 5—10 minutes daily on feeding, and one hour weekly for maintenance.
d) The financial aspect is not negligible: an aquarium is by no means a cheap affair.

In the beginning it is unlikely that everything will go right; experience and a vast amount of patience are needed to make an aquarium the showpiece of a home.

One must not expect to set up an aquarium, spend a lot of money and then become merely a spectator. It is necessary to supply the fish with suitable food once a day or, in smaller quantities, twice a day; to wipe the glass both inside and outside, suck off the mulm from the bottom and clean the filter once a week; and to drain a quarter of the old water and replace it by fresh tapwater of the same temperature every fortnight. Yet this need not put an end to holidays: if the fish are carefully fed throughout the year, they will survive without food and without harm as long as three weeks (that is, of course, only adult fish). Storing food in the tank for future use is inadmissible because of the rapid decomposition of organic matter in warm water. As regards volume, an aquarium holding 50 l or more should be chosen, and only exceptionally a smaller one. Small aquariums should in fact be regarded as auxiliary containers only. If an aquarium is to be purely ornamental, it is better to select one larger tank (100—500 l). If the intention is to make some species reproduce, it is necessary to reckon on buying more tanks and spending more time on this hobby.

As has been mentioned previously, the aquarium must be given a permanent location; one exposed to plenty of diffused daylight is ideal. Yet such a place is not a precondition. The aquarium may occupy the darkest corner of the house. In this case, of course, natural light must be replaced by artificial illumination switched on for twelve hours a day.

Aesthetic and Breeding Aquaristics

There are very great differences between aesthetic and breeding aquaristics.

Ornamental tanks should tastefully complement the interior of both living and public rooms. The following ornamental freshwater tanks can be distinguished:

1. Aquariums of the Dutch type
2. Biotopical aquariums
3. Paludariums
4. Others

1. The Dutch school works on the idea that the aquarium should be a tastefully arranged water garden complemented by fish, or without them. This implies that well-organized and healthy plants are the main attraction of the aquarium. The Dutch aquarium should be sufficiently large; it should blend perfectly with the interior furnishings; it should tastefully and perfectly conceal the technical equipment; the plants should be grouped with the highest at the back and the lowest at the front of the aquarium. The groups should differ in colour, shape of leaves and in height. In no case should a group contain more than a single plant species. The number of suitable fish is limited; their only purpose is to complement the overall picture.

The bottom of the tank is covered with coarse-grained, rinsed sand of a darker hue; adequate rocks are placed on the bottom or piled up in terraces. Petrified wood obtained from peat bogs may be added. The background is usually arranged so as to create the impression of a natural waterside. The most important constituent of the technical equipment is illumination: only optimal light conditions can guarantee perfect growth of the plants. An invariable and accomplished appearance of the tank is achieved by constantly adjusting the plants to make the separate groups merge without intertwining and overlapping on the surface.

2. Ornamental biotopical tanks should represent in miniature parts

of nature according to biotopes. It is, however, difficult to harmonize certain fish and plant species. In a number of natural localities inhabited by fish there are either no plants at all or a single plant species. And again, the occurrence of a rich plant community does not necessarily lead to the presence of suitable aquarium fish. Biotopical aquariums need to be stocked with combinations of fish and plants indigenous to a certain territory. Thus, for example, there are South American aquariums of the virgin-forest type, African aquariums of the rocky type, etc. The tanks should never be overstocked with fish. Overcrowded tanks provide no adequate environment for successful plant growth, and obscure many interesting aspects of piscine life. The bottom covering is similar to that in the Dutch tanks, and an adequate background will complete the general picture of the tank.

3. Paludariums are a combination of freshwater aquariums and terrariums or flower-boxes, and are intended to represent also the waterside overgrown with moisture-loving plants. A combination of fish and amphibians, aquatic and marshland plants and orchids can help to endow the paludarium with the genuine character of a tropical shore. Appropriate light, warmth and moisture are the basic conditions for life in a paludarium. Large paludariums are, as a rule, expensive and require the owner to possess at least a basic knowledge about the life of plants, fish and amphibians. Only well-managed paludariums can fulfil their purpose and offer a fascinating sight. Increased demands laid on maintenance and breeding experience are seemingly the cause of the reduced occurrence of paludariums in homes.

4. Other ornamental aquariums are also called community aquariums. They are connected with the history of modern aquaristics and have become so popular that they substantially contribute to the world-wide popularity of aquaristics. They are inhabited by fish and stocked with plants regardless of the geographical distribution of species. They would approximate the aquariums of the Dutch type but for the less strict demands laid on them. However, the underlying principle of community aquariums is to keep together only piscine species having the same requirements and size. Even here it holds true that 'less is greater than more'.

The technical equipment of modern ornamental tanks includes an adequate illumination meeting the requirements of the plants, motor-driven forced-circulation filters, a thermostat provided with a radiator and, in some cases, an ozonizer or an ultraviolet lamp supplying ultraviolet rays. In addition, a reliable thermometer and aids, such as nets, catchers, etc., are used.

Breeding aquaristics is aimed at obtaining, through intensive breeding of fish or cultivation of plants, the greatest possible number of young specimens corresponding to the original type on the one hand, and of new colour and shape mutations or hybrids on the other. The breeding establishment is based on a unified series of medium- to large-sized aquariums, a system of reservoirs or a combination of both. The whole breeding complex, including the technical equipment, must fulfil the basic purpose, i.e. simplicity and accessibility facilitating easy control of the fish as well as quick maintenance. With private breeders, breeding and aesthetic aquaristics are closely linked because the installations form an integral part of the home. Greater possibilities are available when the breeding complexes can be located in a separate room.

There exist practically no instructions about how to become a good breeder. This is conditioned, in the first place, by the love of the activity itself. Fish breeding on a large scale is a very exacting, time-consuming work requiring self-denial and sacrifice. Only intensive perseverance and an accumulation of knowledge will in time result in the experience and routine needed to make the work easier. It is best to take any opportunity to see other breeding establishments or to visit tropical countries. Another important source of information is the professional literature, which gives a global survey of developments. The rewards for this work are the knowledge of most aspects of piscine life as well as the satisfaction that comes from the results obtained. The contemporary breeder may derive no less pleasure from the feeling that he is contributing to the protection of the already much devastated nature by making reared specimens partly supply the demand for fish, thus cutting down the excessive depletion of natural resources. It would not be appropriate to practise intensive fish rearing together with the cultivation of plants: besides light, plants need quiet for their growth. Breeding tanks overcrowded with fish, and consequently necessitating intensive maintenance and care, fail to fulfil this condition—apart from the fact that they almost never have a founded bottom. Maintenance, fresh water and effective filters keep the living environment of fish within the bounds of tolerability.

Water

Fish coming from various regions and biotopes make different claims on the composition of the water. The closest possible approximation to their natural needs is often essential for successful breeding and especially rearing of aquarium fish. The properties of water important for aquarism are temperature, oxygen content, reaction (pH), general hardness (dGH), carbonate hardness (dCH), and the content of nitrogen compounds.

The optimal temperature for rearing most tropical fish is 24°C. Higher or lower variations are mentioned in discussing the individual species.

The amount of oxygen dissolved in water decreases with rising temperatures. Although tropical fish living in warm waters can be considered undemanding as regards water-oxygen content, they cannot do without it. A sufficient supply of oxygen is secured by introducing air into the water over porous stones, and in the case of well-illuminated tanks, by stocking these abundantly with plants.

Fish are very sensitive to water reaction. This reaction is measured by the amount of hydrogen ions in the solution and is indicated as pH. It can be neutral (pH = 7), or alkaline (pH is higher than 7), or acid (pH is lower than 7). The pH range within which the majority of aquarium fish can live is between 5.5 and 9.0.

acid		neutral		alkaline
5.5	6.8	7.0	7.2	9.0

The optimal pH for rearing young fish is quoted under each species.

The hardness of water is determined by the content of salts of calcium (Ca), magnesium (Mg) and their compounds. The general hardness expressed in German degrees is designated as dGH, the carbonate hardness, which is of utmost importance for the development of eggs, as dCH.

The general hardness of water may be divided into the following groups:

0— 5° dGH = very soft water
5—10° dGH = soft water
10—20° dGH = medium-hard water
20—30° dGH = hard water
30° dGH = very hard water

Water hardness can also be expressed in other units. Conversions of units used in various countries are given in the following table:

Hardness unit	mval/l	dGH	TH	English	American	
millival/l	1	2.80	5.00	3.50	2.91	
1°dGH	0.36	1.00	1.79	1.25	1.04	German degrees
1°TH	0.20	0.56	1.00	0.70	0.58	French degrees
1°A	0.29	0.80	1.43	1.00	0.83	English degrees
1°Am	0.34	0.96	1.72	1.20	1.00	American degrees

Measurements of both general and carbonate hardness are made with the aid of colour-change indicators.

A very harmful factor in the aquarium, often overlooked by aquarists, is the presence of nitrogenous substances. The decomposition of organic matter (excrement, decaying food, etc.) leads to an accumulation of proteins in the water. These proteins are continually being decomposed by bacterial processes to form peptides and amino acids and then ammonia which, in this case, can assume two forms: the loose, strongly toxic form (NH_3) or the bound form (NH_4OH). Through further action by microorganisms, the ammonia is oxidized into poisonous nitrogen dioxides (NO_2), and then into less poisonous nitrates (NO_3). These chemical processes are called biological self-purification of water. An oversaturation of water with nitrogen dioxides and nitrites causes the reverse process (reduction) to take place—from NO_3 via NO_2 to NH_3—and hence there is a recurrent danger of poisoning the fish. As a matter of fact the once exalted old water is in fact poisonous water, especially in overfilled breeding tanks without plants. It is important, therefore, to replace about 25% of the water regularly every fortnight; in overfilled tanks 75—100% should be changed once a week depending on the species of fish concerned. For detecting poisonous nitrites, reagents undergoing a colour change in response to the content of NO_2 in mg/l are produced.

Adjustment of Water

Optimal water is hardly ever readily available; it is therefore necessary to mix waters of various degrees of hardness, by boiling, by demineralization, with the aid of plant extracts and chemicals, and by filtration. Such water-adjustment methods, described below, are designed chiefly for breeders. In ornamental aquariums the condition of plants and the behaviour of fish or slugs are sufficient indicators. In unsatisfactory water the fish contract their fins, gasp for air at the surface and become discoloured; slugs retreat to the surface endeavouring to escape from the water; plants turn yellow and fade away. As a rule, however, these phenomena never occur in well-maintained aquariums.

The simplest adjustment is effected by mixing waters of various degrees of hardness. Before doing so, the aquarist must find out the hardness values of the waters, determine the required value, and calculate how much of each type of water is needed.

Boiling the water brings about the decomposition of acid carbonates and the precipitation of the normal calcium carbonate ($CaCO_3$) and magnesium carbonate ($MgCO_3$) into a 'boiler encrustation'.

Distilled water is very suitable for fish breeding, but it must be further adjusted according to requirements. Distillation must take place in glass distillation columns, for the water from copper apparatuses might be toxic.

Increasingly in recent years water has been adjusted by demineralization in columns filled with ion exchangers. Since there exist a great number of trade marks under which these are available, it is advisable to consult an expert about the most suitable trade mark as well as about the details involved in the regeneration procedure.

Rainwater, distilled and demineralized water and even raw water are further adjusted with the help of certain substances and chemicals. These usually involve peat extracts, protective colloidal solutions, citric acid, sodium hydroxide, etc. Recently it has become increasingly popular to keep endemic African fish from sodium lakes in aquariums; for this reason, sodium hydrocarbonate (acid carbonate) ($NaHCO_3$—edible soda) is often made use of in adjusting water. It is applied to regulate the pH of excessively acid waters.

Filtration is effected by making aquarium water circulate through a filtration substance attracting or absorbing particles or dissolved substances; on the other hand, it can introduce suitable water-adjusting substances so as to make the living environment of the reared fish optimal. Some types of filters aerate the water sufficiently, thus avoiding the need for aeration over a porous stone.

Mechanical, absorbent and biological filters can be distinguished by their packing.

Mechanical packings attract floating particles; filtration materials involved here are sand, glass wool, nylon yarn, etc. They can also enrich the water with valuable substances, or with substances adjusting the chemistry of water, especially the pH reaction. In such cases peat, brown coal, or various pH stabilizers are applied as filtration packings.

Activated coal can serve as absorbent packing. Besides its mechanical function it is capable of absorbing dissolved protein compounds,

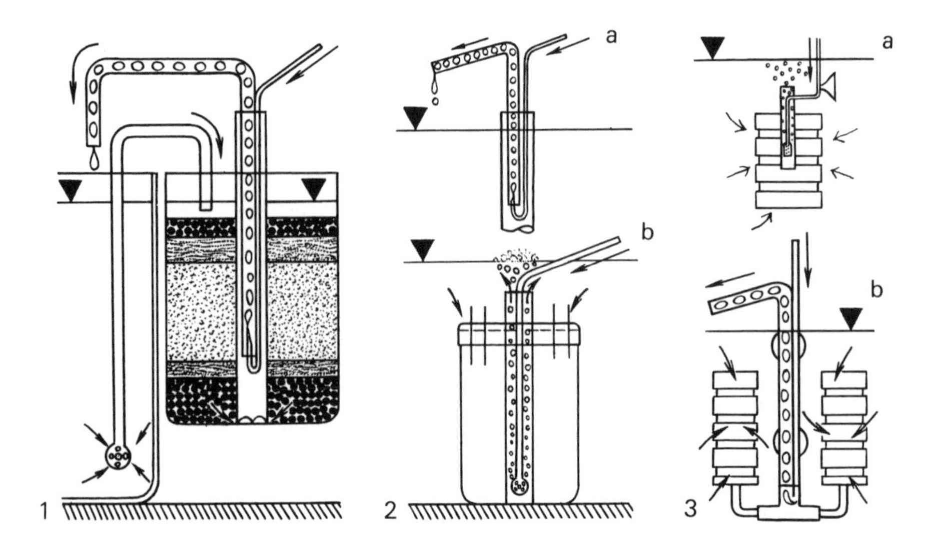

pigments and other macromolecular substances. These filters are absolutely indispensable in marine aquaristics.

In biological filters water flows through an intensively illuminated tank densely overgrown with algae; from here it returns to the aquarium. Sometimes also aerial roots of some tropical terrestrial lianas *(Monstera, Philodendron, Syngonium)* are put to use: these aerial roots are led directly down into the tank where they are covered with water. When in water, these roots form a dense network of fine rootlets. Algae as well as the liana root systems absorb nitrogenous substances contained in aquarium water.

Outside, inside, under-gravel and forced-circulation filters are distinguished according to their make.

In the table, several types of filters are schematically represented. Most of the filters are air-driven with the help of an air compressor. The inflow of air is marked by arrows, and the flow of water by full triangles. Filters using forced water circulation are provided with an independent electric pump. The water surface is indicated by black triangles.

1. An older type of glass outside filter. Water flows in on the principle of joint vessels and is driven back into the tank by air. The packing can be exchanged arbitrarily, as required.

2. Two types of inside filters (a) making use of ejection—the riser tube must always protrude above the surface; (b) with the aid of an

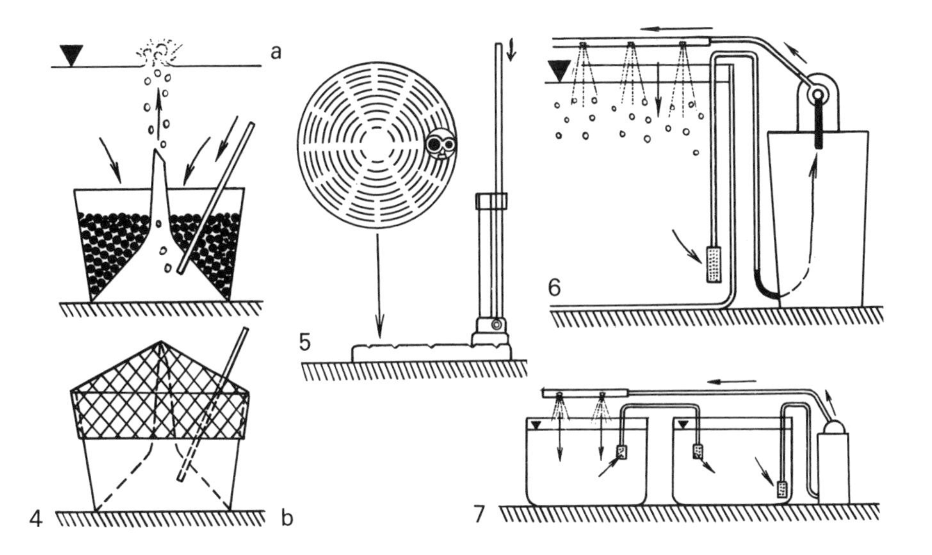

aerator stone, the riser tube is submerged. The filter packing is arbitrary.

3. Two types of easily handled and frequently used inner filters. Filtration is mechanical and effected by means of a glass-wool packing; (a) with the aid of a stone, the riser tube is submerged; (b) on the basis of ejection, the outflow tube rises above the surface.

4. An amateurish, inexpensive inside filter used in large professional establishments all the world over. Its advantages include the fact that it is very cheap and demands little attention. It is unsuitable for ornamental aquariums. The most usual packing is coarse gravel or peat—type a). In type b) the filter is covered with a nylon net to prevent excavating fish from throwing out the contents of the filter.

5. An under-gravel filter designed primarily for ornamental aquariums. Here the bottom of the aquarium itself acts as the filtration layer. From time to time the detritus accumulating below the filter is sucked out with the aid of a hose fixed to the riser tube. Plants are placed in vessels sunk into the bottom. One of the disadvantages of this filter is the necessity to dismantle the whole tank to see if the ejection is blocked.

6. Filters with forced circulation where the water is driven by a pump through the filter packing and forced back again into the

tank. These filters are indispensable for large ornamental aquariums. Having a high filtration capacity, they supply the tank with abundant oxygen. Filters must be cleaned regularly, including the driving unit, which must be freed from dust from time to time and lubricated with oil where indicated.

7. The scheme shows the connection of a circulation filter to more tanks. These tanks must necessarily be joined in series, and the connecting tube must be large enough to make the flow match the inflow. Suction is effected in the first tank, inflow in the last. The number of tanks may be arbitrary. The flow tubes must never get blocked. Protective baskets are applied to prevent the fish from being sucked in.

COLOUR ILLUSTRATIONS

The fish are classed according to
the continents they come from.
In the continents the fish are classed systematically.

Bronze Catfish or **Aeneus Catfish**
Corydoras aeneus (GILL, 1858)

In the family Callichthyidae there are a great number of small catfish of the genus *Corydoras* inhabiting the waters of South America. A characteristic feature of these fish is a short, high-backed body covered with bony plates arranged in two rows (with each plate overlapping the next), hence their generally used name 'armoured catfish'. One of them is the Bronze Catfish whose range extends throughout the water systems of Venezuela, Trinidad and to the south as far as the La Plata basin. The more robust females grow to a length of 7 cm. The males are slimmer and somewhat smaller in size. These fish are bottom-dwellers intensively turning over the ground when foraging for food. In captivity they accept food of all kinds.

Spawning often takes place after either sudden fall in atmospheric pressure or rainfall. If ripe breeders are available at this time, spawning can be encouraged by adding fresh, cool water so as to make the temperature of water in the tank drop by approximately 5° C. The fish are accommodated in spacious tanks holding about 100 l, always in larger groups and with a higher proportion of males. The requisite water temperature is 20—22° C. The composition and quality of water make almost no difference. During the act of spawning the female is pursued by several males at the same time (1,2). Eggs are deposited by the female into a pouch formed by her ventral fins (3) and subsequently anchored on a previously cleaned, firm substrate (4). Immediately after spawning, the adults are removed and several drops of methylene blue are added to the tank. The fry hatch after 60 hours and learn to swim freely in a few days. An ideal food for the young fry is brine shrimps. Later they are fed on finely chopped tubifex.

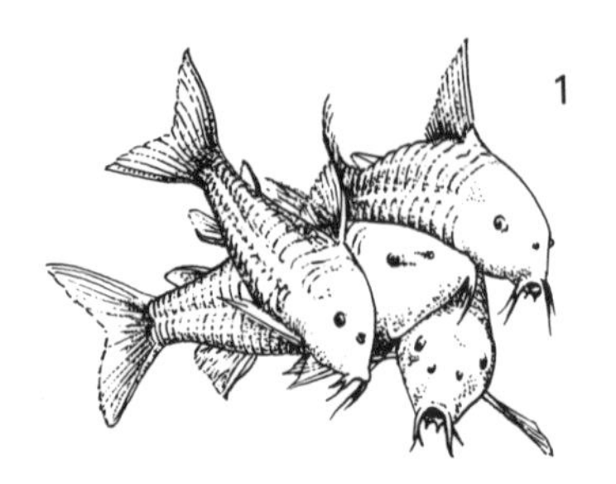

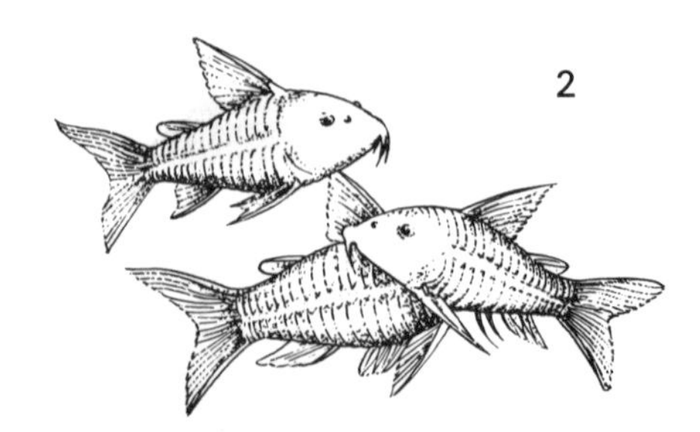

The Bronze Catfish and the other representatives of this genus provide a suitable complement to all larger community aquariums. In consideration of the fact that it is the natural instinct of these fish to excavate the bottom, it is advisable to use only purely washed sand and to prevent the detritus from accumulating at the bottom of the tank. The Bronze Catfish is a relatively cold-loving species, the right temperature for adult fish being 18—22° C.

If the catfish have spawned in a community tank, to save the eggs it is necessary to scrape them carefully off the substrate with a razor blade and transfer them to a clean tank containing water of the same composition. Here they will continue to develop.

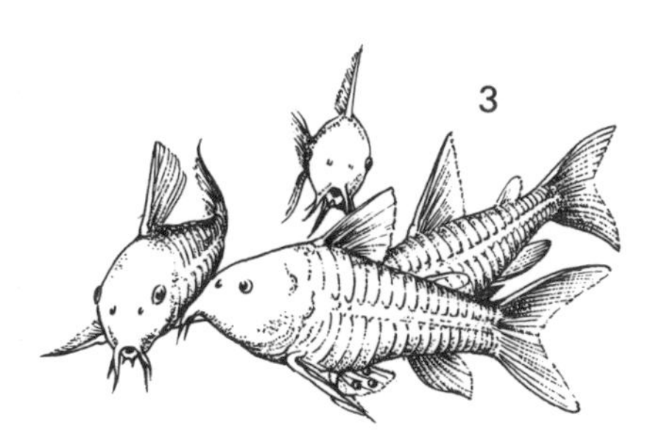

Peppered Catfish

Corydoras paleatus (JENYNS, 1842)

Callichthyidae

The Peppered Catfish belongs to the scanty group of fish bred in aquariums for more than a hundred years. In 1878 the well-known breeder Carbonnier in Paris was the first to induce this small catfish to reproduce. It comes from southeastern Brazil and the La Plata basin and grows to a length of 7 cm. The females are more robust. The dorsal fin in the slimmer males is supported by an elongated pectoral ray.

The manner of setting up the fish and spawning is similar to that prevalent in the species *C. aeneus.* The admixture of cool, fresh water and a simultaneous fall in atmospheric pressure may serve as a stimulus to spawning. It has been proved that there is a relationship between the behaviour of the fish and atmospheric pressure. The manner of spawning has been disputed by many people, the most likely method being that described by Knaak, an expert in these fish: 'After a tempestuous prelude in the initial phase of wooing, the male uses one of his pectoral fins to get hold of the female's barbels and simultaneously presses her against his belly. The motion of fins and gills helps the spermatozoa to reach the eggs which, in the meantime, have been expelled into a pouch formed by the ventral fins. The female then swims to the place she has found adequate and cleaned in advance, cleans it again, and sticks the eggs thereon. And everything starts again from the beginning'. This species closely resembles the Bronze Catfish also in the development of eggs and brood care.

The Peppered Catfish is a peace-loving fish well suited to community tanks. It prefers dim light and cool water from 19° to 23° C. In this species, an albinotic form (1) with red eyes has been produced. Albinism is hereditary in thoroughbred individuals.

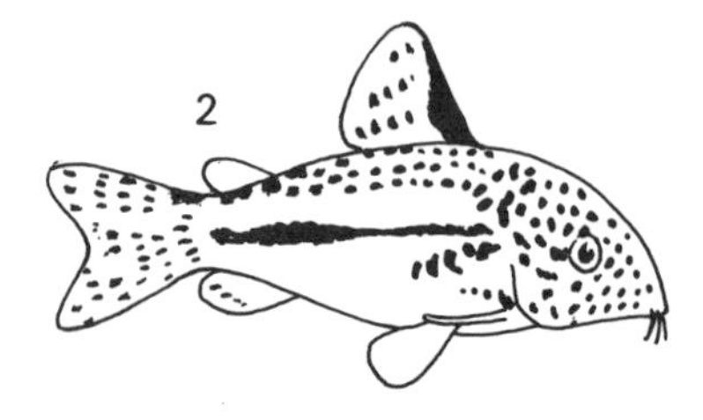

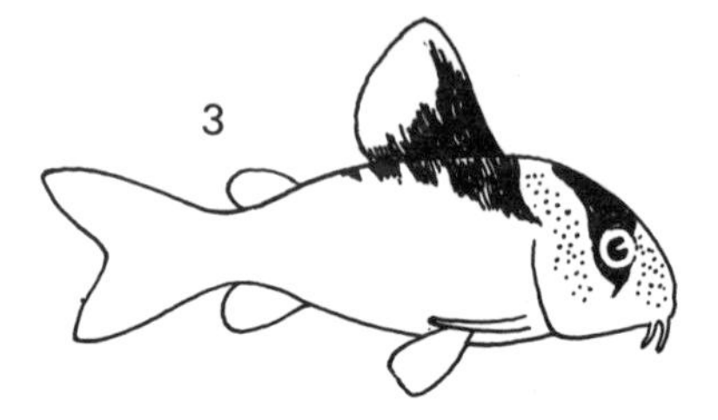

To date, aquarists are acquainted with a great number of catfish belonging to the genus *Corydoras*. Although the individual species are closely related in appearance, the demands they make on the living environment are different. This is why many species have not yet been bred in captivity. Major differences among the species mostly relate to size and colouring. *C. bondi coppenamensis* (2) and *C. bicolor* (3) most closely resemble the species *C. paleatus* in pattern.

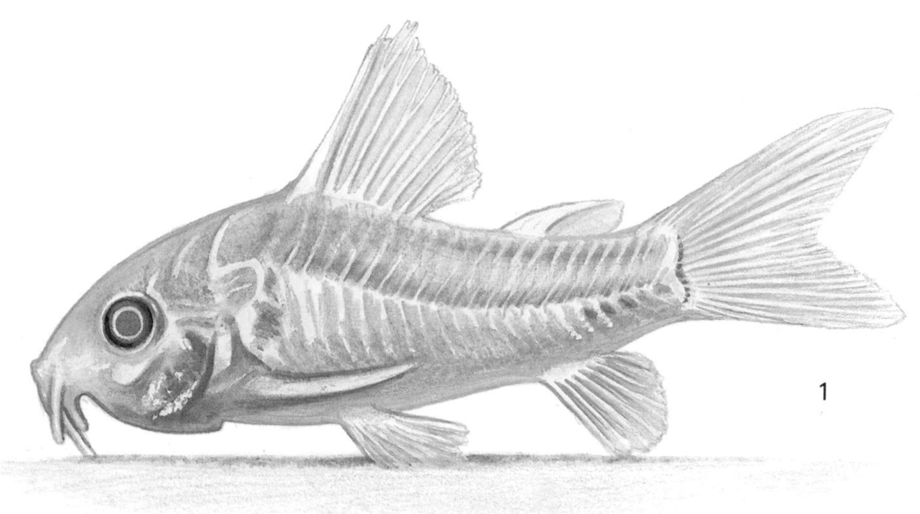

This catfish is abundantly distributed in the waters of the Amazon basin. It grows to a length of 9 cm. There is no pronounced sexual dimorphism; the males are slimmer and the first rays of their pectoral fins are only slightly elongated. When in the wild the *Dianema longibarbis* likes quiet waters and localities shaded by vegetation.

Males build bubble nests on the underside of broad-leaved plants. In captivity such spawning sites are replaced by hanging, inverted plastic plates, about 20 cm in diameter. The separate phases of the simple spawning process are shown in the line drawing (1—3). The female lays about 300 yellowish eggs, 1.5 mm across, in the nest. The bubble nest bearing the eggs is cared for by the male. The plates with the eggs are transferred into independent tanks. Water: 24° C; pH 7.0; 8—10° dGH; up to 2° dCH. The water is tinged slightly with methylene blue. The incubation of the eggs (i.e. the time interval between the fertilization of the egg and the hatching of the fry) takes five days. It may happen that some embryos are incapable of bursting the eggshell. They can be helped by gently tapping the eggshell with a goose quill. The absorption of the yolk sac takes 24 hours and the larvae immediately start taking food. Brine shrimps are most suitable as the first food. In their first days of life the fry are extremely sensitive to dissolved protein substances and any fall in temperature. They are often attacked by mildew and perish. This makes it necessary to filtrate the water over activated coal and frequently to replace about one half of the tank's content by fresh water. In the course of time, the sensitivity of the fry becomes minimal.

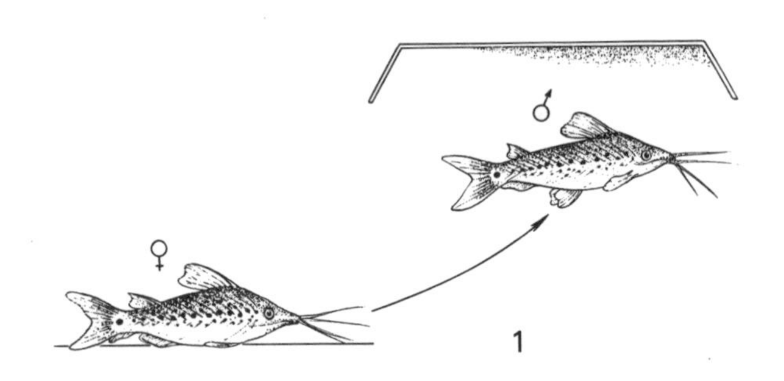

D. longibarbis is an absolutely peaceful fish. In foraging for food it likes to burrow in the bottom of the aquarium. Occasionally these fish may be found floating motionless in the middle layers of water. In this they differ from a vast number of other catfish species. They are reared in larger groups and in larger-sized aquariums. Being a twilight fish, the *D. longibarbis* (4) loves a dimly lit environment, and the bottom of the aquarium should be provided with sufficient shelter and with dark corners. In the wild it often coexists with the related species *D. urostriata* (5) whose caudal fin is markedly striped.

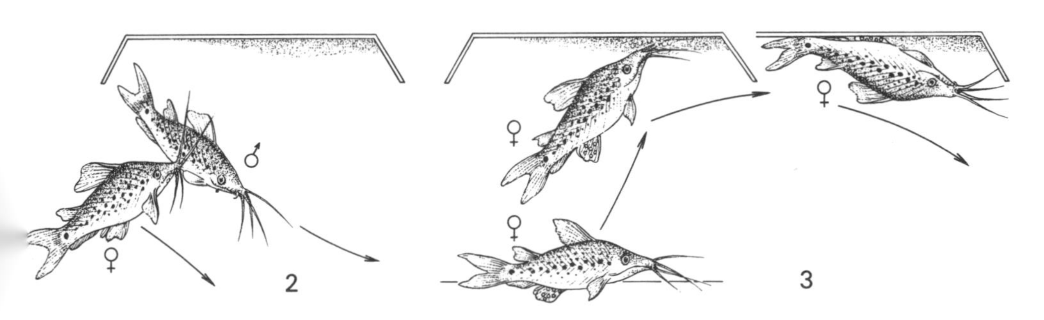

Port Hoplo or **Atipa** Callichthyidae

Hoplosternum thoracatum (CUVIER ET VALENCIENNES, 1840)

The Amazon basin, Guyana, Trinidad and Martinique are the habitat of the 18 cm long catfish Port Hoplo. As it is distributed over a vast territory, it forms a great number of ecotypes differing in colour and body shape. The lower part of the body is white in females and young fish, and violet-grey in adult males. It is a characteristic feature of the males that the first rays of their pectoral fins are transformed into a powerful spine covered with minute teeth.

In the period of spawning, the male builds a large bubble nest on the underside of broad paludal plant leaves floating on the surface. In aquarium breeding, the plant leaves are replaced by a synthetic plate turned upside down and firmly anchored at the surface (1). In a single act of spawning the female is capable of producing as many as 1,000 eggs. After spawning is over, the plate with the spawn is taken into another tank containing water at 24° C, with pH ranging from 6.5 to 7.0 and carbonate hardness up to 2° dCH. A trace of colour is added to this water by applying methylene blue. The first larvae appear after three days, yet the hatching may go on until the fifth day. The 6 mm long larvae have developed fins and barbels, and it takes them only a short time to consume the yolk sac. Forty-eight hours after hatching they are offered brine shrimps. The fry are light-sensitive and seek shelter. This is why it is advisable to insert several perforated flowerpots into the tank.

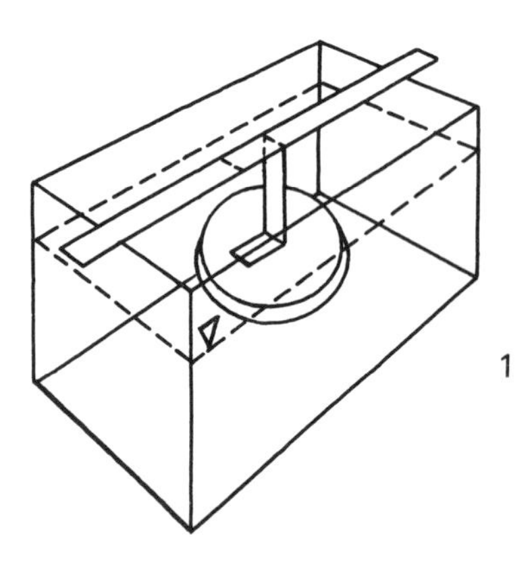

1

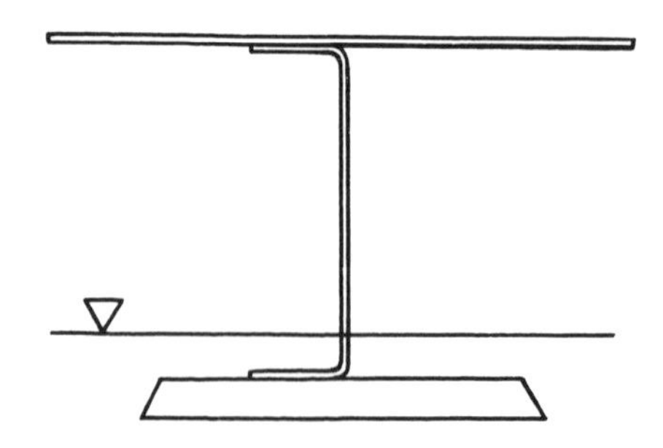

The Port Hoplo is a peaceful, twilight-loving catfish. It excavates the ground with zeal and likes roomy, dimly lit tanks full of hiding-places and with dark bottom areas. Good and seemingly natural shelters are provided by a tangle of aerial roots of tropical lianas which branch extensively in water *(Monstera, Philodendron, Syngonium).* Here the aerial roots change into assimilative ones supplying the plant with moisture and nitrogenous substances detrimental to the fish. The water temperature suitable for adult catfish ranges between 20° C and 24° C. The Port Hoplo takes both dry and live food, mostly at the bottom. Related catfish species of the genera *Dianema* and *Callichthys* have a similar way of life.

Whiptail or **Upper-whiptailed Catfish** Loricariidae

Rineloricaria filamentosa STEINDACHNER, 1878

One of the numerous, bizarre armoured-catfish species is the Whiptail inhabiting the northwest of South America (the river Magdalena basin). It grows to a length of 25 cm. The male can be recognized by the little 'brushes' on his pectoral fins. It is far from easy to draw a distinction among individual species of the genus *Loricaria;* the main clue is the arrangement of bone plates covering the ventral region. The uppermost ray of the Whiptail's caudal fin has developed into a thread-like extension; this provides a contrast with other species possessing two such filaments or lacking them altogether.

The fish become lively after dark. The main spawning period seems to coincide with the winter months and is followed by a long pause. The insertion of plastic tubes, approximately 30 mm in diameter, has proved an advantage: the fish spawn inside the tube. The male takes care of the eggs, literally sitting on them. He can easily be transferred in the tube, together with the whole clutch of eggs, to the nursery tank. The eggs are 2 mm in diameter. The young fish emerge in nine days, and when they are free-swimming, the male is removed and the tube is simultaneously taken away. At this stage the fry are 7 mm long and resemble the adult fish. Since even the smallest traces of protein substances are fatal for the alevins, it is absolutely necessary to introduce filtration over activated coal before the first feeding and to replace the water every other day with fresh water of the same composition and temperature. The water is not particularly relevant: ordinary tapwater will do. The most suitable foods are brine shrimps. The quickly growing fry gradually lose their sensitivity to water pollution.

These fish suitably complement the bottom layers of community tanks. They are absolutely peaceable and their life span is long. They are more or less unseen inhabitants of the tank, being visible in the daytime only spasmodically when they are searching for food on the bottom. Their flattened, elongated body shape and their mouth functioning as a sucking organ enable them to live in rapidly flowing waters. They take all the food available at the bottom, but can nimbly get hold of the plankton on the glass sides of the aquarium.

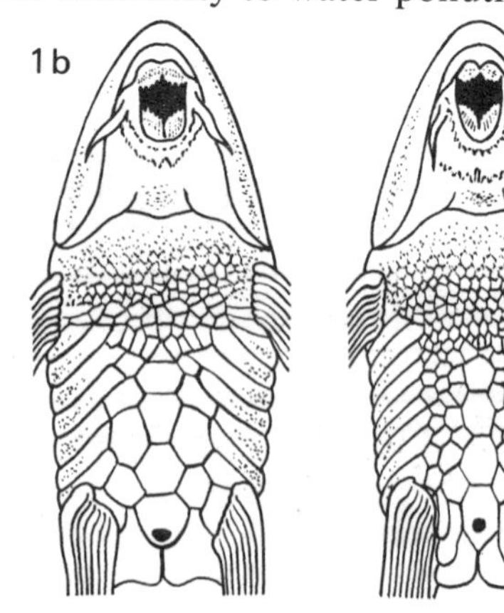

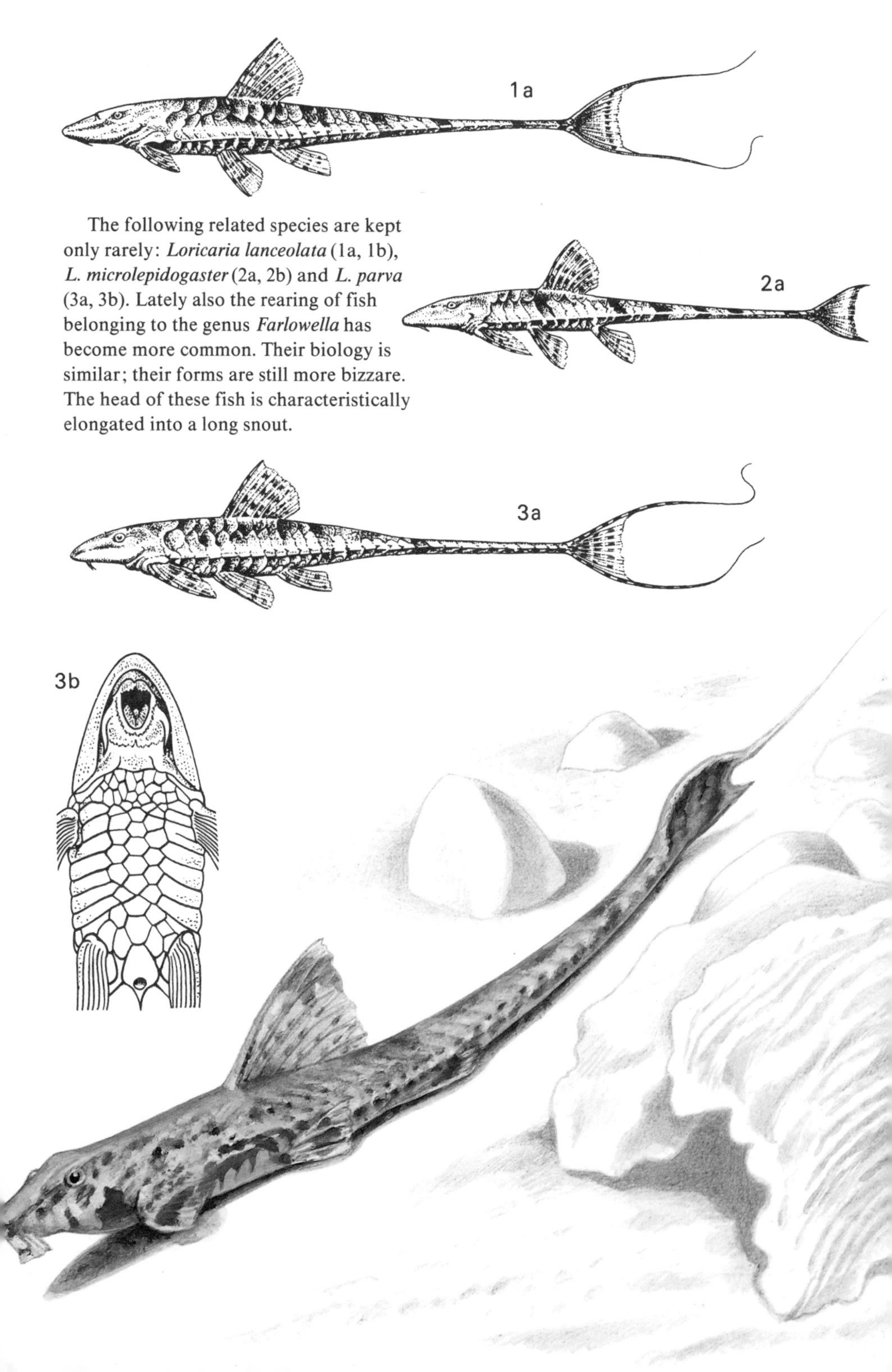

The following related species are kept only rarely: *Loricaria lanceolata* (1a, 1b), *L. microlepidogaster* (2a, 2b) and *L. parva* (3a, 3b). Lately also the rearing of fish belonging to the genus *Farlowella* has become more common. Their biology is similar; their forms are still more bizzare. The head of these fish is characteristically elongated into a long snout.

The genus *Ancistrus* includes armoured catfish inhabiting the swift-flowing waters and rapids of South America in the Amazon basin and in Guyana. Its typical features include a sucking mouth with horny papillae (1) located at the underside of the head, a flattened body shape and hard, sharp first fin rays (with the exception of the caudal fin). The sexes are easily distinguishable: the 15 cm long males have ramified projections, or tentacles (2), on their head and around the upper jaw, whereas in the females this feature is but little developed.

A. multispinnis seeks various fissures and cavities to hide in; these are also its spawning sites and are territories tenaciously defended by the males. Males also take care of eggs and larvae. Plastic tubes or hollow bricks are inserted into the breeding tanks and spawning takes place inside these. The male is ready to spawn with several females simultaneously. The females lay racemose clusters of 50—100 eggs. The eggs, with a diameter of 3 cm, are yellow and very sticky. In controlled breeding, the egg clusters are collected and transferred into a nursery tank containing fresh water of 24°C, pH 7.3, 8°dGH and 2°dCH. The larvae hatch on the sixth day after spawning. The 5 mm long larvae depend on the yolk sac for their nutrition. In eight days the fry attain a length of 15 mm. At this stage they are fed with brine shrimps and plant food.

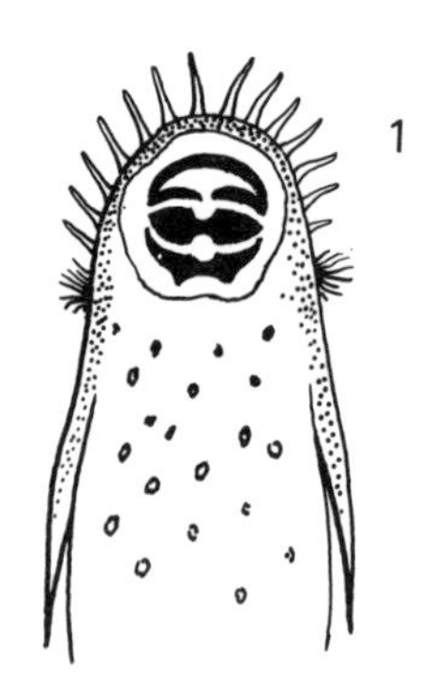

The fish are peaceable and may be kept in spacious community tanks. They flourish in a shady environment with a water temperature of 22—24°C. Their usefulness lies in their foraging for plant and animal remains at the bottom, and they scrape off algae growths. Their diet must also include plant food (spinach purée, scalded leaves of spinach, turnip-cabbage, lettuce, dandelion or algae).

The activity of adult fish intensifies in twilight or in daytime with falling atmospheric pressure. Related species reared in captivity include *A. cirrhosus* and *A. dolichopterus*.

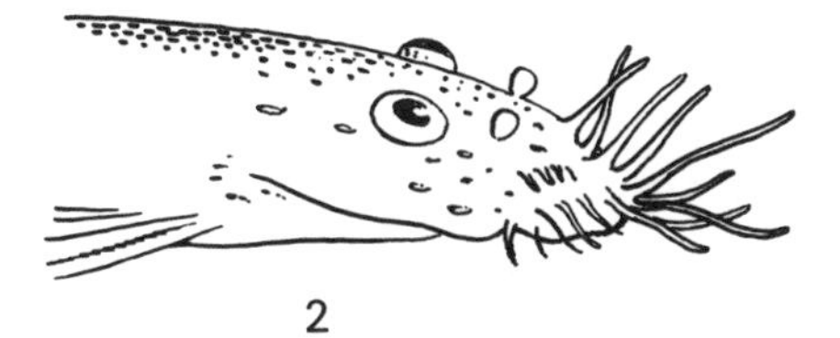

Bloodfin

Aphyocharax anisitsi EIGENMANN ET KENNEDY, 1903

Aphyocharax anisitsi, syn. *A. rubripinnis* (1), although bred in captivity since 1906, has not become particularly popular among aquarists until recently. These fish, with a length not exceeding 5 cm, are not difficult to breed and rear. As the fish love motion and sun, larger light-flooded tanks with a capacity for at least 20 l are considered best. The bottom of breeding tanks is covered with a spawning grid (2a, 2b), protecting the eggs against their parents' voraciousness. The development of eggs requires relatively soft water, 10° dGH, up to 2° dCH and with a pH of 6.0—7.0. The fish spawn either in pairs or in shoals at 22—24° C. Minute glassy eggs fall through the grid to the bottom. The fry need 24 hours to hatch, and several days afterwards they learn to swim freely. Being very shy, they welcome even the smallest shelter; thus they are easily overlooked. When they become free-swimming they start taking brine shrimps or copepods. Tanks for breeders as well as tanks for the growing fry must be covered with glass, for the slightest impulse may frighten the fish into jumping considerable distances. If supplied with sufficient natural food and fresh water rich in oxygen, the baby fish grow very quickly. They have a particular liking for running water which can be secured with the help of forced-circulation filters.

The Bloodfin can fully display its radiant beauty only in a bigger shoal, in a roomy tank, and especially in a peaceful, habitable environment. The tank should not be excessively plant-stocked, otherwise the plants might prevent the free movement of the fish. The fine, beautiful, vivid colours of the fish can be enhanced by a dark bottom.

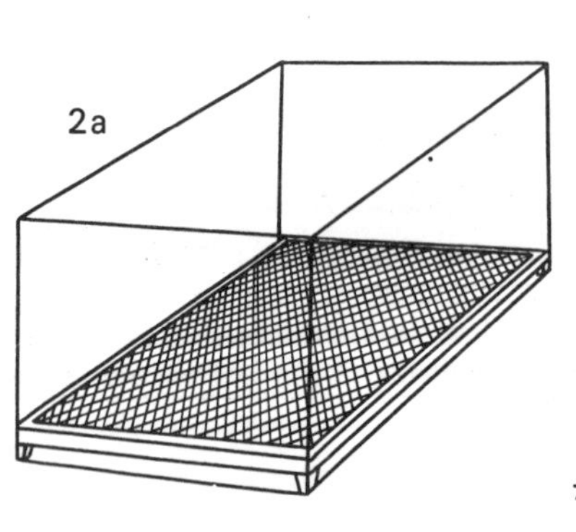

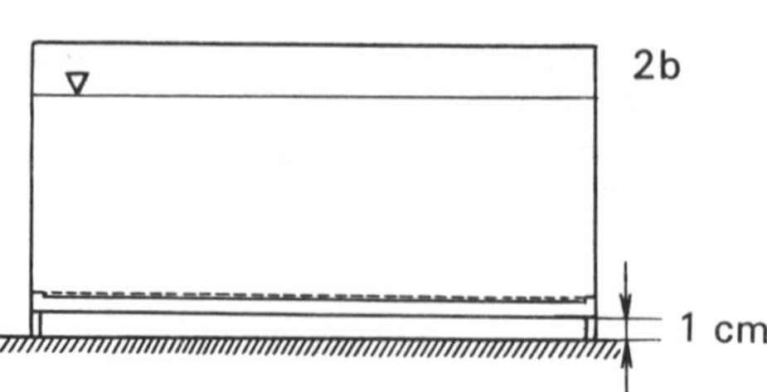

The probable reason why they are seldom asked for in shops is that there they find no peace, turn skittish and consequently their colouring becomes faint and inexpressive. The Bloodfin is a peace-loving fish; as such it can be kept in company with other small fish having similar requirements. The species *A. rathbuni* (3), *A. alburnus* and *Prionobrama filigera* (4) are related fish reared in captivity.

Yellow-banded Moenkhausia or **Red-eyed Moenkhausia**

Characidae

Moenkhausia sanctaefilomenae (STEINDACHNER, 1907)

The Yellow-banded Moenkhausia is an attractive tetra coming from the rivers of Paraguay and the Paranaiba. It made its first appearance in the tanks of European aquarists in about 1956. The length attained by this fish is 7 cm. The most reliable sexual differentiation characteristic is the fuller ventral region in females.

The maturing young females are separated from the males for about three weeks and richly supplied with food. As soon as they are ready to spawn, which can be seen by their rounded ventral region, they are paired off with the males and transferred into 10 l tanks provided with a protective grid. Plant tufts are inserted into the tanks. The water should be 24°C, pH 6.5—7.0 and up to 1°dCH. As a general rule such water is obtained by mixing boiled water with rainwater in equal quantities. Peat extract is added to the water. The Yellow-banded Moenkhausia is a very prolific fish. The incubation period is 24 hours. To start with, the fry are very small indeed and must consequently be fed on nauplii of the finest brine-shrimp sorts, the finest copepod nauplii, wheel-worms (Rotatoria), or infusorian monocultures *(Paramecium).* Even when they are fed carefully, the young fry take a long time to grow.

The Yellow-banded Tetra (1) is a peaceful fish kept in larger shoals in company with characins requiring similar conditions and having similar properties and size. These fish prosper in spacious tanks with a dark bottom covering. They eat predominantly live food, mostly zooplankton.

The 12 cm long Glass Tetra *(M. oligolepis)* (2) is a related and very similar species.

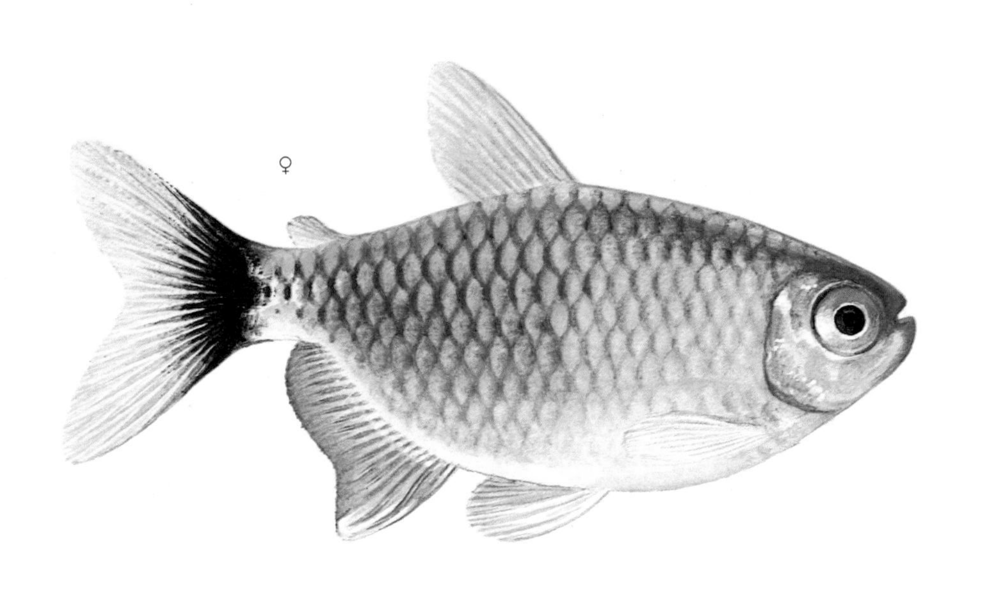

1

Emperor Tetra

Nematobrycon palmeri EIGENMANN, 1911

Although this superb fish was described as early as 1911, it was not included in European aquariums as a novelty until 1959. The Emperor Tetra lives in Colombia, in the San Juan river system. It grows to 5.5 cm long and can be distinguished from the other characins by the absence of the adipose fin. The sexes are easily discernible; in males the medium rays of the caudal fin are elongated, while in the somewhat smaller females the prolongation of these rays is merely indicated. The females also have a fuller ventral region and their colours are less vivid than in males. Successful breeding depends on the selection of suitable males because it would appear that not all of them are fertile.

The fish are set up in pairs in relatively roomy aquariums (about 10 l). Before spawning, the females are separated from the males for about a fortnight. Water taken from the breeding tanks, with peat extract added, has proved favourable for the development of eggs. The required temperature lies within the range of 24—26° C. Other values should be pH 7.0—7.5, 10° dGH and up to 2° dCH. Though there are no irregularities in the incubation of eggs in excessively acid and soft water, the embryos often suffer from dropsy. The fish are willing to spawn, especially if they have been separated prior to spawning, but their productivity is rather low. The larvae leave the eggshell in 24 hours and learn to swim freely five days thereafter. No difficulties arise when rearing the fry; their usual food is brine shrimps and, later, chopped tubifex worms.

The full beauty of the Emperor Tetra (1) comes to the fore in a larger shoal. The tanks should be spacious, with subdued light and a dark bottom. In polyculture, the Emperor Tetra is best kept in the company of small characins. Mosquito and midge larvae or high-grade oat-flake food constitute their favourite diet. As additional food, besides tubifex, they may be offered also fruit flies (genus *Drosophila).*

The name 'Emperor Tetra' probably arose due to the fact that it is always the strongest male who dominates over the group and forcefully chases away all other males, thus creating the impression that he is holding sway over the whole group. Of course, this behaviour can be observed in other piscine species as well.

Very similar species are *N. lacortei* (2) reared in aquariums only sporadically and the considerably smaller species *Inpaichthys kerri* (3).

Swordtailed Characin
Corynopoma riisei GILL, 1858

Characidae

The *Corynopoma riisei,* syn. *Stevardia riisei,* is native to the waters of Trinidad and northern Venezuela and was imported to Europe probably in 1932. It grows to a length of 7 cm. Its method of reproduction is interesting and unique. The male and the female join in the act of spawning but the female lays no eggs. The male places the milt enclosed in spermatophores near the female's sexual opening. After a certain interval the female lays eggs, one by one, among the plants. Before the eggs become ripe in the ovaries the female bears spermatophores encasing the spermatozoa in her oviducts. She is capable of spawning several times in the absence of the male. Whenever eggs are laid, a part of the sperm supply is released. The Swordtailed Characin is reared in larger shoals, the ratio being one male to two females. Fertilized females are placed in larger breeding tanks holding about 20 l. These are stocked with fine-leaved plants. Water: 24°C, pH 6.5—7.0, up to 2°dCH. The female lays her eggs unnoticeably while swimming among plants, and, from time to time, seemingly rubbing against them. This motion in fact helps her to attach a sticky egg to the plant. The larvae hatch in 20—36 hours depending on the water temperature. In their first days of free swimming the fry are given copepods or brine shrimps. Rearing is easy and the alevins grow quickly.

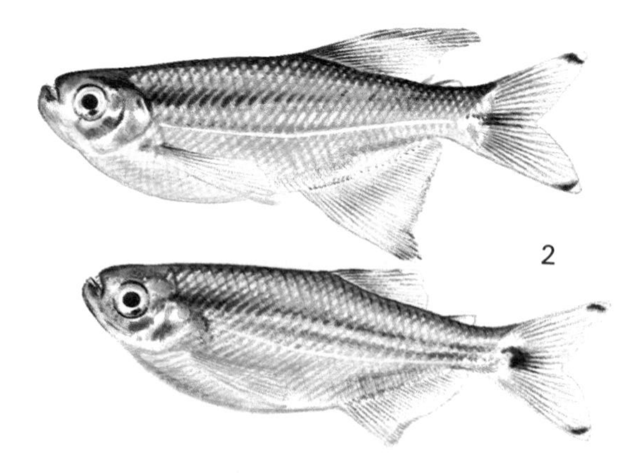

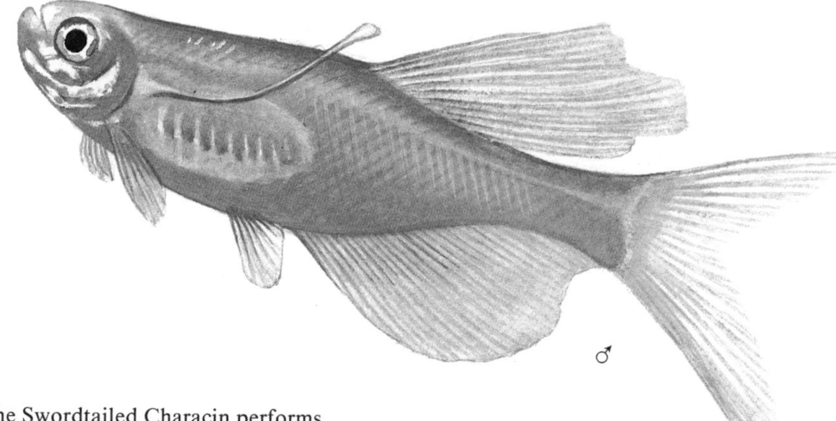

The Swordtailed Characin performs the most remarkable mating games. The males' opercula are greatly extended (1) and terminate in small dark surfaces. These extensions often reach beyond the dorsal fin. During courtship display the male directs the quivering surfaces towards the female, while the stem remains almost invisible. The female dashes out against the male and the act of spawning begins.

The Swordtailed Characin is a peace-loving fish well suited to a mixed aquarium community. It is an omnivore.

Much earlier than the Swordtailed Characin, in 1905, a similar fish, *Pseudocorynopoma doriae* (2), was brought to Europe by the Rossmäszler society in Hamburg. In the same year the firm Köppe and Siggelkow imported the same fish in large quantities, and the Dresden breeder P. Schäm was the first to rear it in captivity.

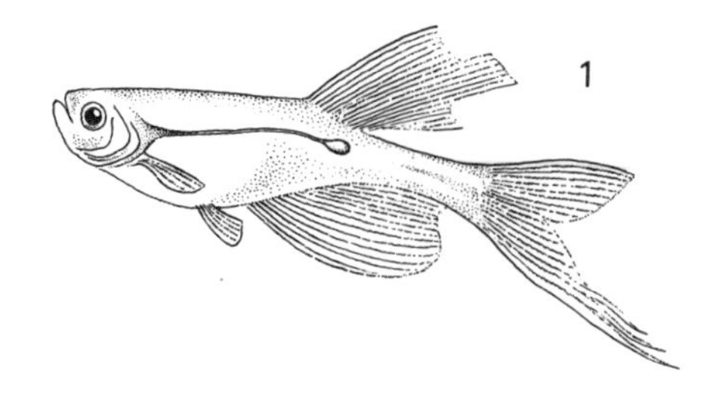

Black Tetra or **Blackamoor** *Gymnocorymbus ternetzi* (BOULENGER, 1895)

There are scarcely any special aquaristic shops which do not stock the Black Tetra, *Gymnocorymbus ternetzi,* both in its wild and its cultivated veil-finned strains. This species has acclimatized itself in captivity without any problems, spawns willingly and produces offspring in great abundance. The Black Tetra is distributed in South America in the Mato-Grosso region, as well as in the Río Paraguay and Río Negro basins. It was imported into Europe in 1935. The deep black juvenile colouring can be found later on only in males. The more robust females grow to be about 5 cm long; they are silvery with a smoky hue. Although it used to be a popular aquarium fish, nowadays it is somewhat less sought after owing to a deluge of other, more colourful novelties.

Breeding in captivity is easy. The breeding fish are set up in one or more pairs in tanks of about 50 l in volume. The bottom is covered with a spawning grid. The development of minute eggs does not have any attendant problems if it takes place in boiled tapwater at 20—24°C, with pH values ranging from 6.5 to 7.0 and carbonate hardness up to 2°dCH. Free-swimmers are fed first on brine shrimps and later on all kinds of traditional live and artificial foods. They grow quickly; however, because of the huge number of young produced, their growth is directly dependent on there being sufficient space in the tanks.

The Black Tetra (1) is at its best in a shoal and in roomy tanks affording sufficient space for free motion. Being a peaceful fish, it makes an appropriate companion to middle-sized fish with similar requirements. It prefers live food. Just like all the other aquarium-fish species, it has a particular liking for mosquito larvae (2a), pupae (2b) and imagos (2c) of the genus *Anopheles.*

Owing to the supraterminal position of its mouth it prefers to take food from the surface, as the collection of food from the bottom is only accomplished with some difficulty. In captivity, a strain with prolonged veil-shaped fins (3) was developed.

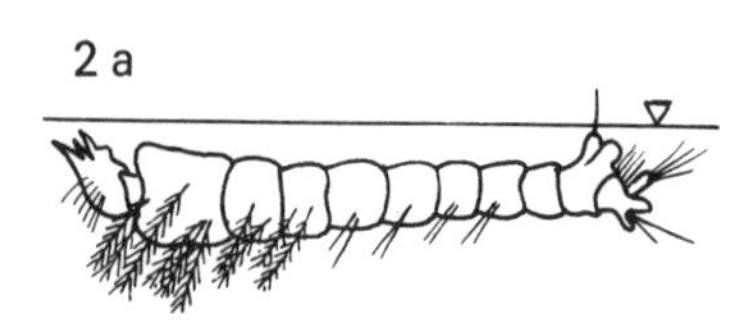

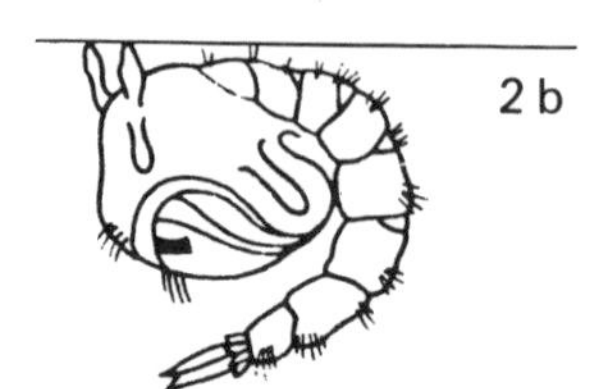

1
♂
♀
3
2 c

Cardinal Tetra

Cheirodon axelrodi SCHULTZ, 1956

In 1956 in the upper Río Negro, a 4 cm long characin was discovered which soon became an ornament of aquariums. After being scientifically catalogued, it was named after the well-known American ichthyologist and aquarist, Dr. Herbert R. Axelrod. Shortly after its discovery the Cardinal Tetra was successfully propagated. Later it was also found in some tributaries of the Orinoco. Almost all biotopes of this type are situated within the inaccessible jungle, in the permanent shade of the surrounding vegetation, in soft, brownish and considerably acid water.

This environment must be reproduced as far as possible in order to rear these fish in captivity. It is advisable to use water at a temperature of 24—26° C, with a pH ranging between 5.0 and 5.5 and a carbonate hardness of 0° dCH. The Cardinal Tetra is set up to spawn in pairs in larger, approximately 10 l tanks. A protective grid is placed at the bottom. Spawning usually does not take place until after several days; it usually coincides with a rising atmospheric pressure and occurs before daybreak. After all the spawn has been released, the breeding pair is removed and the tank is only dimly lit. The incubation time is 24 hours. The alevins are fed brine shrimps or copepods. A gradual addition of tapwater in the course of their growth helps the young fish to get used to the different environment in which they are going to grow and mature later on. When about 1 cm long, the young fry are given minced tubifex, which contributes to their quick growth. The females are fairly plump and their ventral region is markedly convex. The main spawning period lasts from October to April.

Since rearing in captivity fails to produce enough of the fish to meet the demand, the Cardinal Tetra is imported from Brazil to Europe and to the USA in huge quantities. Shaded tanks of the virgin-forest type with a dark bottom have proved suitable. The best colour effects are achieved by larger fish schools. Cardinal Tetras are reared in company with small South American characins. They eat both live and

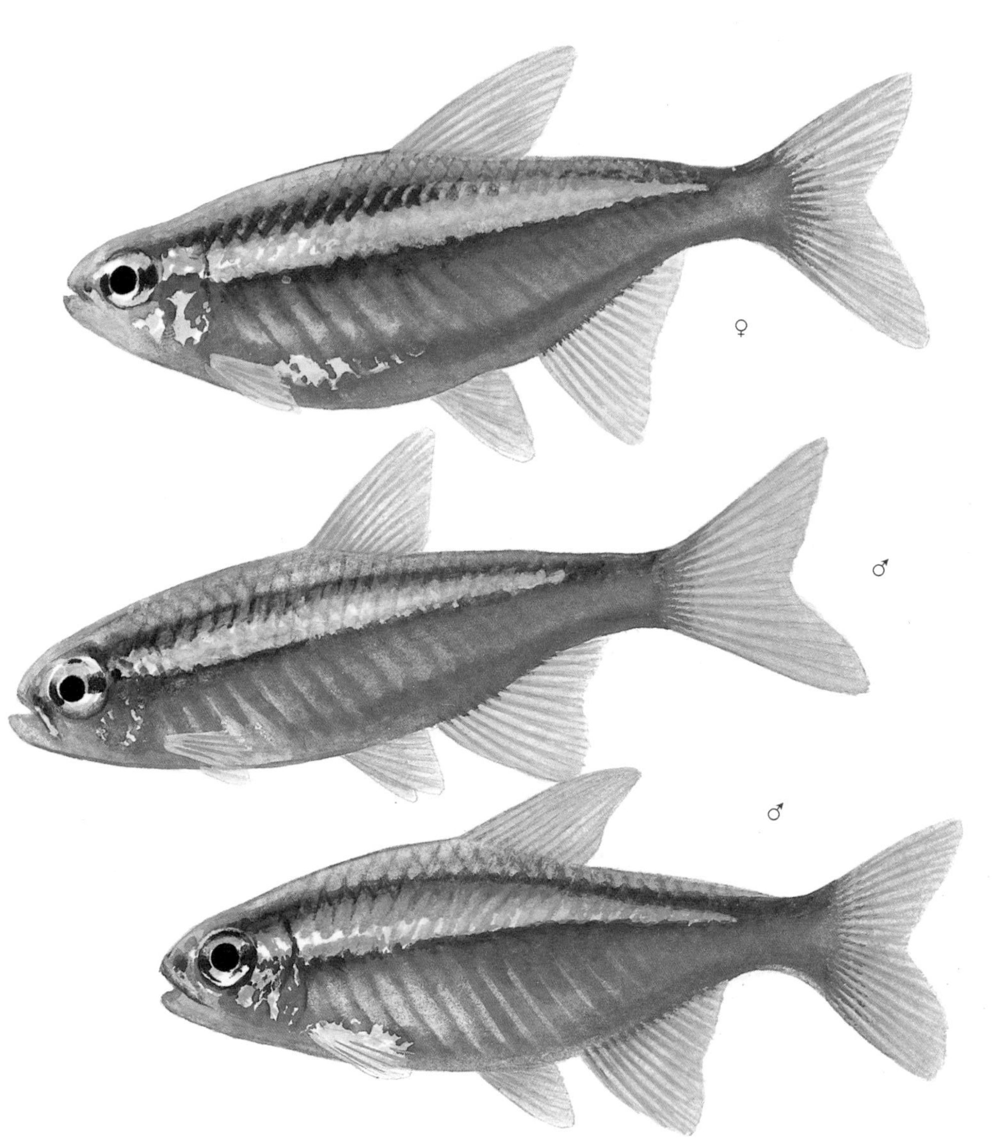

high-grade artificial food. The Cardinal Tetra is a typical representative of the lavish natural history of South America where the waters teem with richly coloured fish. Radiant flowers of numerous orchid species shine in the tops of trees. Even the stinging mosquitoes are coloured, and these in turn are hunted by no less coloured tree frogs, such as those belonging to the genus *Dendrobates* (1).

Neon Tetra

Characidae

Paracheirodon innesi (MYERS, 1936)

Since 1936, and even several years following World War II, aquarists tried in vain to induce this fish to reproduce. Step by step, however, the Neon Tetra (the name used all over the world) acclimatized itself. Nowadays many breeders reproduce it by the thousands. Its main habitat is the upper-Amazon region near the cities of Leticia and Tabatinga.

The Neon Tetra grows to a length of 4 cm. Small all-glass aquariums (6 l) are used for spawning and rearing. The bottom is covered with a spawning grid, and a tuft of Java moss or Willow moss (genus *Fontinalis)* is also included. Water: temperature 23—24° C, 0° dCH, pH 6.2. Before setting up the breeding pairs, aquarists should keep the sexes separately for a fortnight in somewhat cooler water (19—21° C). The females are more robust in comparison with the males, their ventral region being markedly rounded. The fish are set up in pairs. Spawning tanks are located in a place concealed from light and provided with subtle aeration. The breeding pairs are given no food. When spawning is over, the adult fish are removed. The fry hatch in 24 hours; they are light-sensitive. Having learned to swim freely, the alevins feed on a fine sort of newly hatched brine-shrimp nauplii. During the alevins' development, water from the tank into which they are to be transferred later to become free-swimming is added every other day (i.e. acclimatization of the fry to different water). The most harmful factors for the fish are protein substances in the water and an excessive amount of infusorians.

The Neon Tetra is a peace-loving fish well suited to life in community tanks. It is always kept in shoals, with other fish similar in size and requirements. The tank bottom should always be dark—only this can truly enhance the exquisite beauty of these fish.

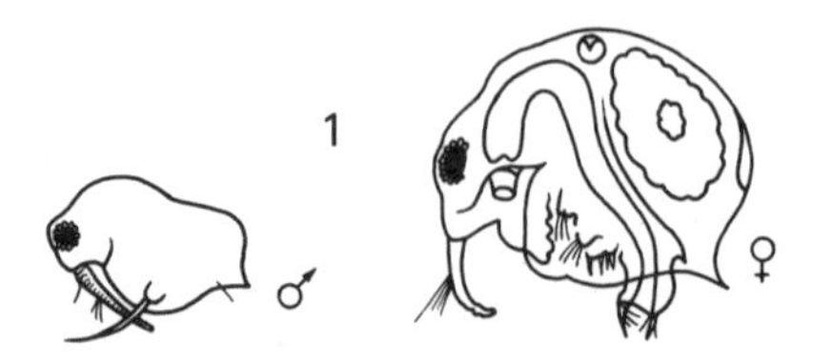

Neon Tetras are fed with dry food of high quality, as well as with live food. The live food, zooplankton, includes numerous crustaceans, such as *Bosmina longirostris* (1).

A very similar species is the 3 cm long 'Blue Neon Tetra' *(Hyphessobrycon simulans),* distinguished by a neon stripe stretching from the snout as far as the base of the caudal fin. It is indigenous to the Río Lufaris, a tributary of the Río Negro.

Glowlight Tetra

Hemigrammus erythrozonus DURBIN, 1909

Hemigrammus erythrozonus (syn. *Hyphessobrycon gracilis*) is a native of the waters of Guyana and was imported to Europe in 1939. It grows to a length of 4.5 cm. The females are larger than the males, with a markedly convex ventral region. Frequent breeding failures are atributed to the deep-rooted belief that soft, acid water is needed for the development of the eggs, as is the case in the species *Paracheirodon innesi.* It must be admitted that the development of eggs in soft, acid water presents no problems whatsoever and virtually all the fry hatch, but they are incapable of filling the gas bladder and die within a few days. Instead, water with pH values between 6.5 and 7.0, a general hardness of 10° dGH, and carbonate hardness up to 2° dCH should be used. The water temperature should be 24—26° C. Water of similar values can be obtained, for example, by mixing equal amounts of rainwater or distilled water with boiled tapwater. Water prepared in this way may be enriched by adding several drops of peat extract. Tanks holding 6 l and provided with a protective grid at the bottom will suffice for spawning. The fish are set up in pairs. A shaded, peaceful environment and a timely introduction of spawn-ripe females will contribute to successful breeding. The fry hatch in 24 hours, and, after learning to swim freely, they are offered live dust food. Recently more and more faintly coloured populations lacking the rich ruby stripe have made their appearance. This is why the once very popular species has become less attractive to aquarists.

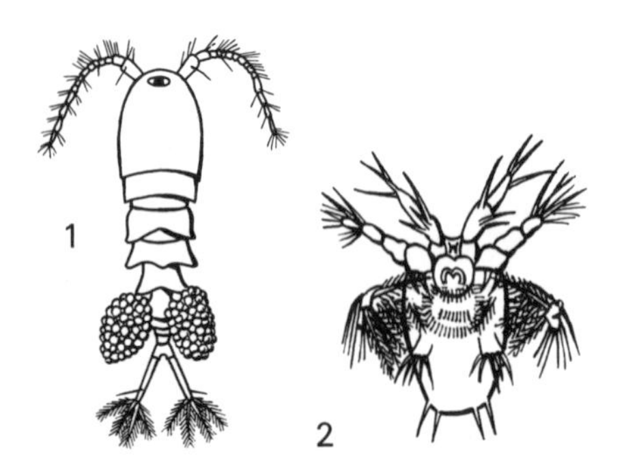

These fish make an excellent show in shoals comprising ten or more specimens. Tanks of the virgin-forest type with petrified wood and branches from peat bogs, provided with a dark bottom, have proved suitable. Such an environment brings out the brilliantly luminous, longitudinal band of these fish from which the commonly used name 'Glowlight Tetra' has beed derived. Tanks of this kind also enhance the beauty of other 'shining' fish, e.g. Neon Tetras. The superb colours have their source in pigment cells (chromatophores).

The Glowlight Tetra takes both dry and live food of an appropriate size. It favours copepods *(Copepoda),* e.g. *Cyclops strenuus landei* (1) and its larval (nauplius) stage (2). Copepod nauplii represent an ideal fry food. In aquaristic practice it is called 'live dust food' or, more simply, 'dust'.

Garnet Tetra or **Pretty Tetra** Characidae
Hemigrammus pulcher LADIGES, 1938

In 1938 the German importing firm Aquarium Hamburg organized an ichthyological hunting expedition to catch a large amount of Neon Tetras *(Paracheirodon innesi).* The fish were caught in the central parts of the Amazon basin, from the city of Tefé in Brazil as far as Iquitos in Peru. The expedition brought back a great many new species, including the 4.5 cm long Garnet Tetra from the Peruvian part of the Amazon River above Iquitos.

The reproduction of the Garnet Tetra in captivity was difficult, hence it was regarded as a problematic fish for many years. Consequently, the price of these fish was high. Successful breeding is based on the selection of compatible pairs. Females are larger and fuller. Many breeders recommend that successful pairs should remain together, since not every pair selected at random is able to spawn. The Garnet Tetra is set up in pairs in moderately illuminated tanks holding 6 l. Eggs are protected by spawning grids placed at the bottom. The incubation of eggs takes 24 hours at a water temperature of 26—28° C, with a pH of 6.5, and carbonate hardness of up to 1° dCH. Fresh free-swimmers are fed on brine shrimps and copepods.

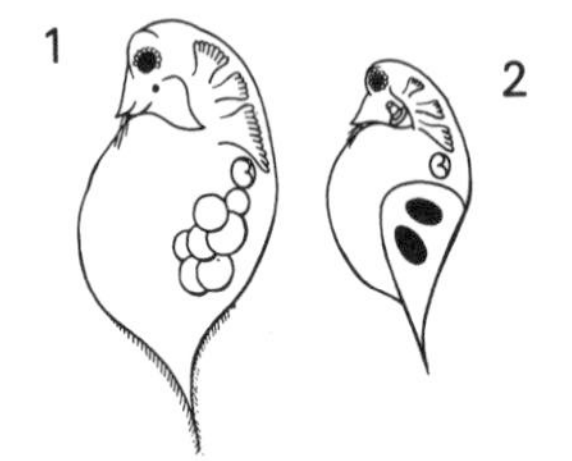

The Garnet Tetra is a peaceful fish well adapted for life in aquarium communities including various species of small tetras. Being a gregarious fish, it is always kept in shoals.

Its diet consists of both live and dry food. It favours zooplankton and tiny water-insect larvae. The cladoceran *Daphnia longispina,* with differently formed summer (1) and winter (2) females forms, is often part of the zooplankton. Water-fleas (Cladocera) are tiny, 0.25—10 mm long, phyllopodous crustaceans. In a special depression located in the front part of the head there is a single compound eye with its large pigment spot surrounded by a ring of minute, light-deflecting bodies.

Buenos Aires Tetra Characidae

Hemigrammus caudovittatus AHL, 1923

This 8—10 cm long fish is a native of the La Plata basin. In 1922 it was brought to Hamburg. Females have a convex ventral region, males are slimmer.

Spawning takes place in pairs or in groups in 50—200 l tanks with a protective grid at the bottom. Larger-sized tanks are advisable because of the size and mobility of the fish (spawning is fairly vigorous) as well as the large quantity of eggs produced. A mature female, separated from the male before spawning and given abundant food for a fortnight, is capable of laying several thousand eggs. This makes it an ideal species for fish-food production for those rearing predators. The development of eggs takes 24 hours in water of 20—24°C, with pH values ranging between 6.5 and 7.0 and carbonate hardness not exceeding 2°dCH. The greatest number of fertilized eggs is obtained from young, regularly spawning females. In fish that are two years old or more, with irregular spawning cycles, the percentage of fertilized eggs and living larvae drops to the minimum, the primary reason being the degeneration and excessive fattiness of the ovaries. The free-swimming fry are easily fed on dust food. However, conditions necessary for a successful and quick growth of fry are roomy aquariums, pure water and abundant food. After attaining a length of 2 cm, the fry may be kept in the open air, in garden pools, from the beginning of June until mid-September.

In recent years, a somewhat smaller (7 cm) albino strain (2) possessing the same properties as the wild form has made its appearance on the market.

The Buenos Aires Tetra (1) is well suited to large ornamental tanks. It is always kept in larger shoals, in combination with bigger and mobile species. The diet of these fish should also include plant food. This is why scalded cabbage or lettuce leaves, spinach purée and other, even dry, plant food should serve as a complement to the usual foodstuffs. Being herbivores these fish like to bite off frail aquarium plants. The tank accommodating such fish should therefore be planted with tough, solid plant species. The Java moss, *Vesicularia dubyana,* and the ferns *Microsorium pteropus* and *Bolbotis heudelotti* are left untouched.

Flame Tetra, Red Tetra, or **Tetra from Rio** Characidae
Hyphessobrycon flammeus MYERS, 1924

This fish lives in the vicinity of Rio de Janeiro, and has populated European aquariums since 1920. The slimmer males have blood-red ventral and anal fins; the latter are edged with black. In females the colours are less vivid, and their anal fin has no black edging. The fish grow to a length of 4 cm.

No problems arise in connection with spawning and rearing these fish. The females are separated from the males for about one week. In the meantime, small all-glass aquariums with a capacity for 3—6 l should be prepared, with a protective spawning grid at the bottom. These are filled with water having a pH of 6.5, 10° dGH and up to 2° dCH (boiled tapwater). The water temperature should be 24° C. The water may be enriched with several drops of peat extract. Each tank should be provided with a tuft of Java moss and an aerator, and the pairs are introduced to it in the evening. Spawning usually takes place on the following day. Small, sticky eggs get caught in the Java moss, among the grid meshes, but most of them fall through the grid to the bottom. After spawning is over, the breeding fish are removed, the water is slightly aerated and the eggs are protected from intense illumination. The embryos take 24 hours to hatch. Then the grid frames are carefully taken out and tapped gently against the surface to make all the embryos fall into the aquarium. The free-swimming alevins are shy and prefer to remain hidden. Their nourishment consists of fine dust food (copepod or brine-shrimp nauplii). After a fortnight the fry are carefully poured into a clean tank having a capacity for at least 100 l. The water level is gradually raised by adding small quantities of tapwater, which helps the fry to become accustomed to a new environment.

The Flame Tetra (1) is a peace-loving, gregarious fish enlivening community aquariums inhabited by characins of a similar size. It is hardy and capable of tolerating transient falls of temperature to below 20° C. It takes food of all kinds, but with a preference for live food. During the summer months the diet of these fish may be varied by adding aphids.

In 1957 the Dutch ichthyologist Hoedeman described a fish closely resembling the Flame Tetra: *H. griemi* (2) from the neighbourhood of Goyaz in Brazil. *H. griemi* is smaller and interbreeds with *H. flammeus*. A closely related, undemanding, but biting fish is *H. bifasciatus*.

♂
1
♀
♂
2
♀

Callistus Tetra or **Jewel Tetra**

Characidae

Hyphessobrycon callistus (BOULENGER, 1900)

It is more or less only by chance that an aquarist will own thoroughbred specimens of the species *Hyphessobrycon callistus,* coming from the Paraguay lowlands. The long-lasting hybridization of the so-called Callistus group has given rise to whole generations of prolific bastards closely resembling each other. The following species can be described in this way: *H. callistus* (1), *H. serpae* (2), *H. minor* (3), *H. hasemani* and *H. heraldschultzi* (4). These species interbreed in captivity very easily, as do *H. georgettae* (5) and *H. takesi* (6). Males are bright red in colour and are slimmer than the females, which have stouter ventral parts. The length attained by these fish is approximately 4 cm. It is not too complicated to breed and rear them. The fish are set up in pairs in larger elementary tanks holding 6—10 l, which are provided with a protective grid at the bottom. The best environment for the development of eggs is water of 24°C, pH 6.5—7.0, up to 2°dCH and 10°dGH (or more). This, in substance, corresponds to aged or distilled tapwater enriched with peat extract. There is a huge number of small greyish eggs. These should be protected against intense light and treated by adding a few drops of methylene blue. The young fry need 24 hours to burst the eggshells; as free-swimmers they are fed on live dust food (copepod or brine shrimp nauplii).

The Callistus Tetra is a gregarious fish. Some populations of these fish, however, are aggressive not only to other fish but also to members of their own species. Other populations are prone to various diseases, the most frequent

symptoms of disease being dropsy or cachexia. The cause of the disease can be revealed only by complex laboratory investigation. Some breeding fish are bearers of infections in a latent stage, without evident external symptoms. The disease may break out on a mass scale in the progeny.

As regards nutrition the Callistus Tetra is not difficult to feed and takes both live and artificial food.

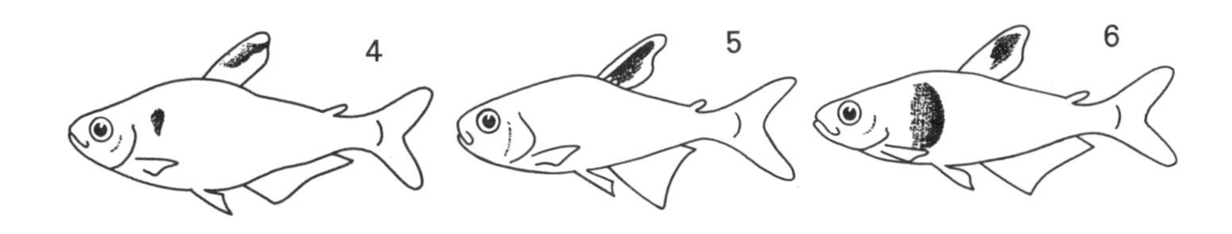

Lemon Tetra Characidae

Hyphessobrycon pulchripinnis AHL, 1937

This 5 cm long fish comes from the Pará region in Brazil. It was imported to Europe in 1932. The males are slimmer; their dorsal and anal fins are of a brilliant yellow rimmed with black.

Before spawning, the females are separated from the males for about a fortnight, and the fish are given an abundance of varied live food. Larvae of the genera *Culex, Chaoborus* and *Chironomus,* and grown-up forms of copepods, if included in the diet, may speed up the ripening of spawn in females. As soon as the females' ventral region becomes well rounded, the fish are set up in pairs in 6—10 l aquariums. Spawning should start within five days at the most; rising atmospheric pressure increases the chances of success. Water at a temperature of 24—26°C, with a pH value equal to 6.5, general hardness 10°dGH and carbonate hardness up to 1°dCH, fosters the optimal development of eggs. Protective grids and tufts of fine-leaved plants (Java moss) are placed on the bottom of breeding tanks. During the mating games the male lures the female above a plant thicket, his yellow and black colours shining on his arched body and quivering fins. When spawning is over, the fish are removed and the eggs are protected against strong light. The young fry need 24 hours to hatch. Fresh free-swimmers are best fed on copepods or brine shrimps. As the fry grow, ordinary water is gradually added into their tanks and, in due course, they are transferred into roomy tanks with a lowered water level. The water level is raised, step by step, as the young fish grow.

The Lemon Tetra is an ideal fish for community tanks. It always forms larger groups and complements the rich colour spectrum of the aquarium community. Males often attack each other, but their combats are harmless.

The fish consume both live and artificial food. Particularly prolific morsels are supplied by larvae (1a) and pupae (1b) of a midge belonging to the genus *Chaoborus* (imago-1c), known to aquarists under the name of glass larva or Corethra. However, since the larvae of this midge are voracious, they must not be allowed access to very young fry.

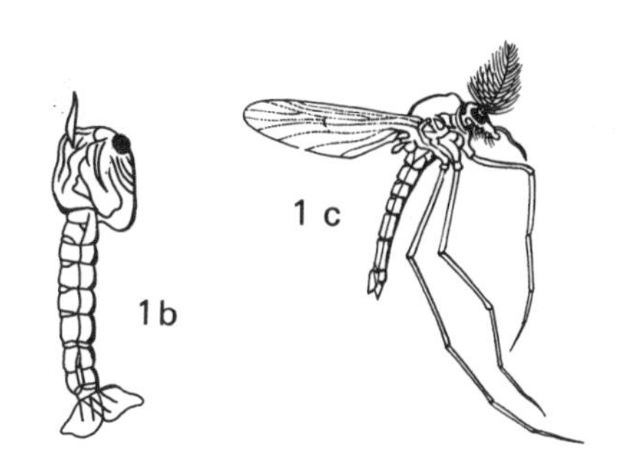

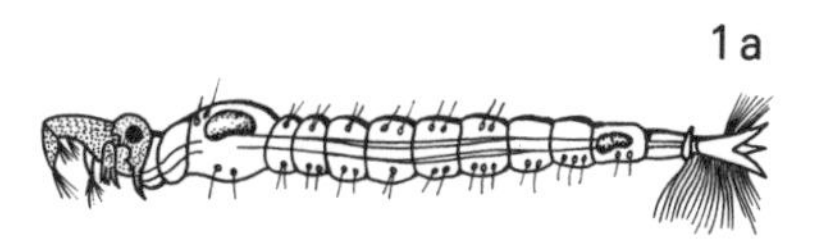

Tetra Perez or **Bleeding Heart Tetra** Characidae
Hyphessobrycon erythrostigma (FOWLER, 1943)

Hyphessobrycon erythrostigma (syn. *H. rubrostigma)* inhabits the rivers of Colombia and the frontier zone of Brazil and Peru. It grows to a length of 6 cm. This tetra has been known to aquarists since as early as 1943; from 1953 onwards it has been imported in growing numbers. In literature, reports about successful breeding of these fish are very scarce.

For a long time, however, nobody suspected that another, hitherto unknown species was often imported under the name of *H. erythrostigma.* In 1971, in a special aquaristic shop in Washington, the American ichthyologist Stanley H. Weitzman noticed fish that aroused his curiosity by exhibiting some unusual characteristics. In 1977 he described these fish as *H. socolofi.* The basic differences between these two species are in their dorsal, anal and ventral fins. These are shorter in the adult males of *H. socolofi* than in those of *H. erythrostigma. H. socolofi* is smaller, more brightly coloured and glistens with a blue sheen, while *H. erythrostigma* is paler and lacking the blue sheen. *H socolofi* was found to be more frequently imported and bred than *H. erythrostigma;* claims of success in breeding this species are possibly better substantiated.

The Tetra Perez is an impressive fish in large ornamental aquariums. It is so attractive by itself that it is advisable to keep it separately with more specimens. Nevertheless, it is a peaceful fish. In tanks with a dark bottom and diffused light it looks superb. Water should be crystalline pure, well oxidized, soft and enriched with peat extract.

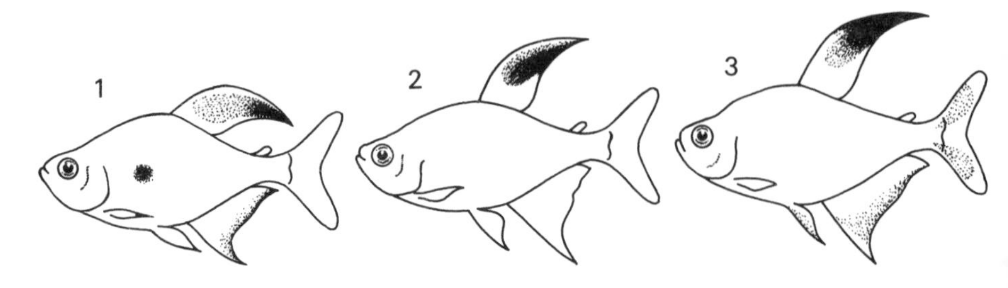

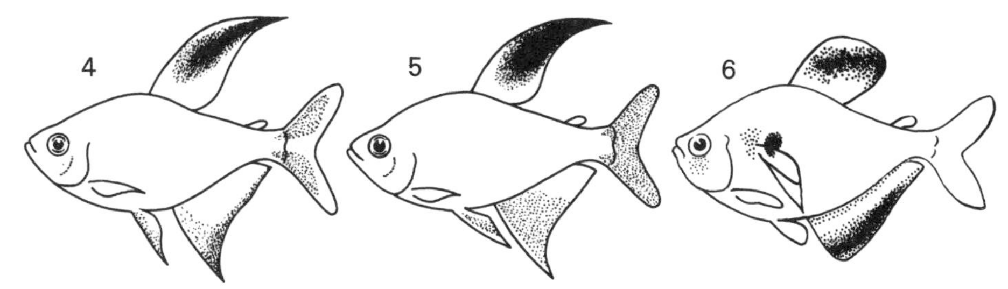

For ease of identification, linedrawings are introduced here indicating the differences between males of similar species: *H. erythrostigma* (1), *H. bentosi* (2), *H. ornatus* (3), *H. rosaceus* (4), *H. 'robertsi'* (5) and *H. socolofi* (6).

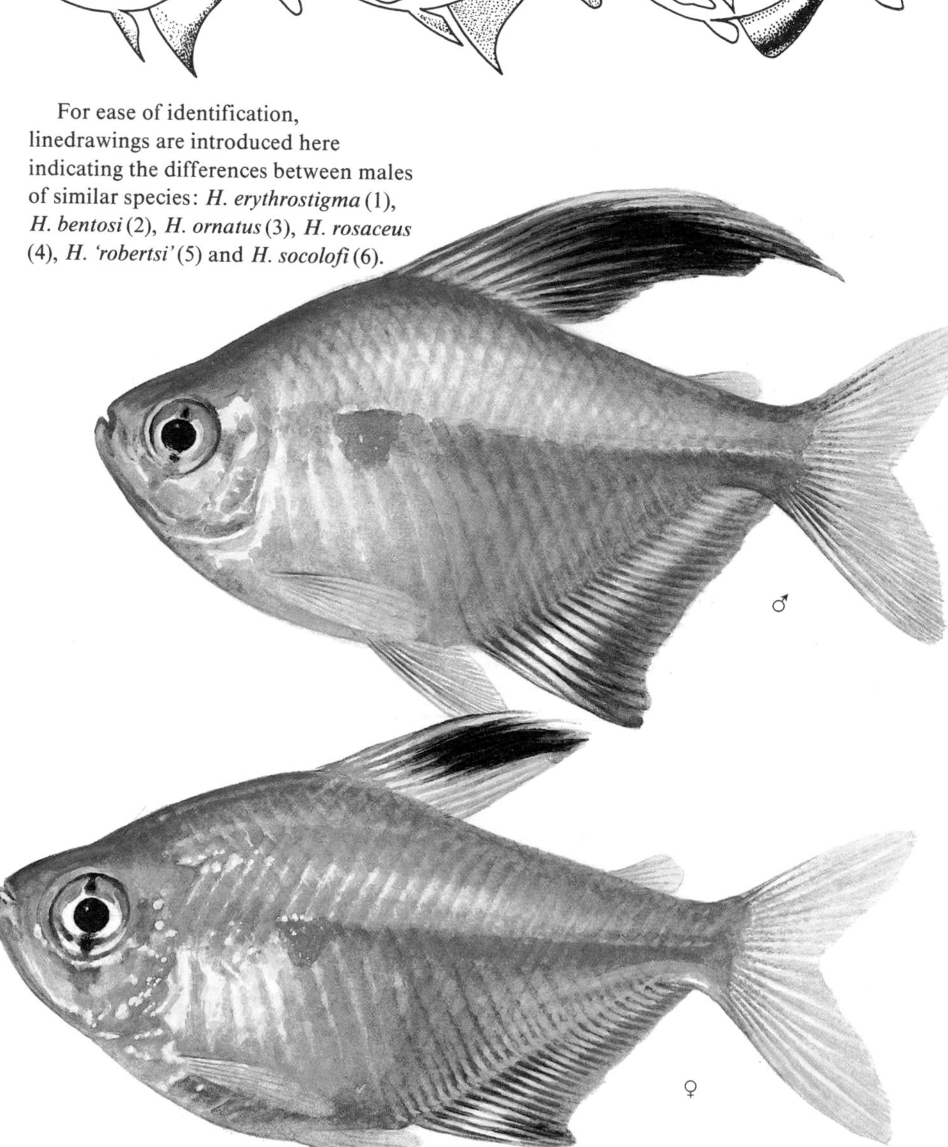

Splash Tetra, Jumping Characin

Lebiasinidae

Copella arnoldi (REGAN, 1912)

The waters of the lower Amazon and the Río Pará are inhabited by slender fish reminiscent of miniature sharks—Splash Tetras. European aquarists have been familiar with them since 1905. Males grow to a length of up to 8 cm, but the females remain smaller and have shorter fins.

The Splash Tetra has a peculiar manner of spawning which is unique in the kingdom of fish: outside water. The aquariums must be carefully covered with glass serving not only to prevent the fish from jumping out but also as a substrate on which the eggs can be deposited. The clearance between the glass and the water surface should range between 5 and 8 cm (1). In the act of spawning both the male and the female jump out together to the cover glass where mating takes place, accompanied by a release of several eggs. The whole process is repeated until all the spawn has been expelled. To prevent the desiccation of eggs in the course of their development, the male uses his caudal fin to splash them with water. During one spawning period the male may successively spawn with several females. The development of the eggs takes 36 hours; the male's care ends with the fall of hatched embryos into the water. In intensive breeding, eggs are regularly wiped off the cover glass by means of a goose quill into small nursery tanks with a water depth of about 1 cm. The water should range between 24 and 26° C, pH 6.0—7.0, 10° dGH and no more than 2° dCH. The nursery tanks are slightly aerated, and after the fry have learned to swim, the level of the water is raised to 5 cm. The fry, being very tiny, must be offered the finest possible food; thus they are fed microscopic Rotatoria or infusorians (genus *Paramecium)* bred in monoculture. Within a week the fry learn to catch brine-shrimp nauplii. Many young fish can be reared in this way.

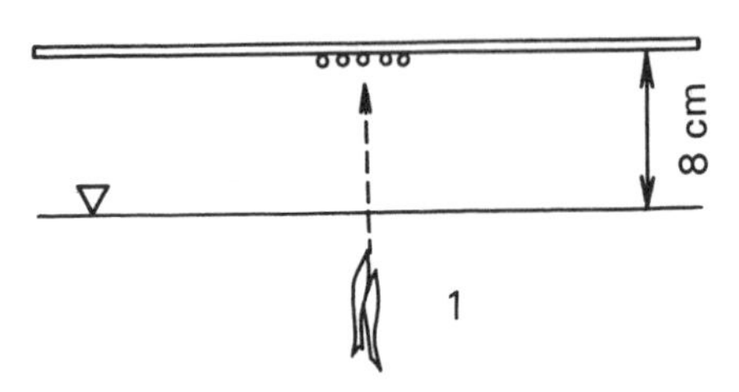

The Splash Tetra suitably complements mixed aquarium communities consisting of small fish from South America. The fish flourish in tanks of the virgin-forest type or in paludariums. They should be provided with sufficiently large open-surface areas,

adequate spawning sites, subdued light and a dark tank bottom. They are reared in larger shoals. Frequent skirmishes among males are harmless.

Copella vilmae and *C. metae,* representatives of the same genus with a similar body shape, are reared less frequently. The atypical manner of reproduction, however, is characteristic of the species *C. arnoldi* only; the other two species referred to above spawn on submerged leaves of aquatic plants.

Nannobrycon eques (STEINDACHNER, 1876)

The Pencilfish inhabits the Amazon and water systems of Guyana. The length it attains is 5 cm. It was brought to Europe in 1910. There are differences between its nocturnal and diurnal colouring: in the dark, the black lateral band gives way to oblique cross stripes.

The Pencilfish spawns on the underside of broad-leaved plants. The fish are set up in pairs in 6—10 l tanks containing seedlings of broad-leaved plants. The protective grid placed inside lets a great many eggs fall through, thus saving them from the cannibalism of their parents. The water should be 26—28°C, pH 6.0—6.5 and 0°dCH. Spawning is remarkable. The slimmer male, whose bright red anal fin is bordered with bluish white, slowly swims above the female; as the partners' mouths are kept close to each other, the fish form a kind of triangle. The female uses her mouth to examine a suitable leaf to which she subsequently presses herself and lays several eggs. These are simultaneously fertilized by the male. The eggs must not be exposed to intensive light. Minute, glassily transparent larvae with a large yolk sac emerge in 24 hours. On the sixth day the alevins assemble into a closed shoal. They are at least three times longer than at the moment of hatching and are immobile, resembling plant fragments.

In some publications the Pencilfish is described under the generic name *Nannostomus* or *Poecilobrycon*. In 1975 the separate genus *Nannobrycon* was established, involving two species: *N. eques* (1) and *N. unifasciatus* with the subspecies *N. unifasciatus ocellatus* (2).

All these fish require well-vegetated tanks with crystalline pure water. Their colouring is enhanced by a dark bottom and appropriate, subdued lighting.

The fish prefer live food; in spite of their small mouths they are capable of devouring even relatively large midge larvae. They can also be supplied with additional dry food of good quality.

Dwarf Pencilfish
Nannostomus marginatus EIGENMANN, 1909

The Essequibo basin in British Guyana is the home of the 3.5 cm long Dwarf Pencilfish. The fish *Nannostomus marginatus* and *N. beckfordi aripirangensis* were imported from this area in 1928, but it was not before 1931 that the German ichthyologist Dr Meinken identified them as being two different species. The sexual characteristics of the Dwarf Pencilfish are scarcely discernible, especially in young fish. Males are slimmer and their anal fin bears a marked black edge; the ventral fins are deep red. It is often possible to identify a spawn-ripe female by the throng of males following her.

For serious breeding and the rearing of the greatest possible quantity of young fish, it is necessary to separate the females from the males for about a fortnight before spawning. After attaining sexual maturity the fish go on spawning all the year round. The breeding tanks are only moderately lit, and protective spawning grids are placed on the bottom. The water is 26—28°C, pH 6.0—6.5 and 0° dCH. The number of eggs is small: 100 at the most. The incubation of eggs takes 24 hours. On hatching, the tiny and light-shy larvae are transparent, little developed and are supplied with a large yolk sac. Before this is consumed the fry grow to be 3.5 mm long, and their pigmentation is remarkable. Fed with brine shrimps or copepods they grow quickly, and at the age of five weeks their colouring resembles that of adult fish.

The Dwarf Pencilfish (1) is a small, peaceful, thermophilic fish. It may be kept separately even in smaller 30—50 l tanks. It is in larger shoals that the advantages of these fish can be fully appreciated.

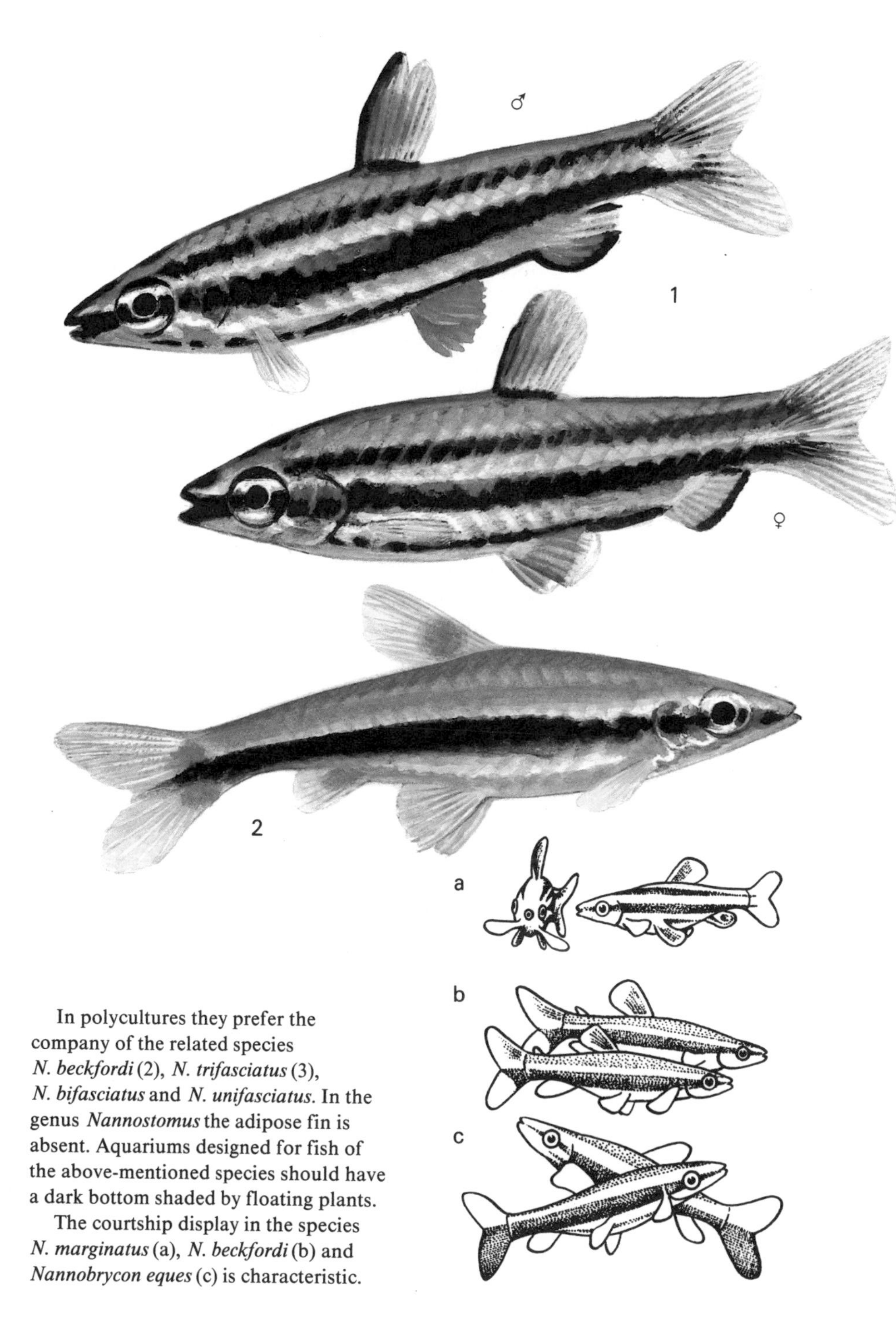

In polycultures they prefer the company of the related species *N. beckfordi* (2), *N. trifasciatus* (3), *N. bifasciatus* and *N. unifasciatus*. In the genus *Nannostomus* the adipose fin is absent. Aquariums designed for fish of the above-mentioned species should have a dark bottom shaded by floating plants.

The courtship display in the species *N. marginatus* (a), *N. beckfordi* (b) and *Nannobrycon eques* (c) is characteristic.

Black-tailed Piranha or **Naterer's Piranha** Serrasalmidae
Serrasalmus nattereri (KNER, 1859)

This 30 cm long fish (1) is reared in captivity only occasionally. It is one of the many feared piranhas whose shoals populate the Amazon basin. These fish are dangerous especially in the period of drought when the hungry shoals are confined to bow lakes. Under normal conditions they are very shy and timid. Their lower jaws are equipped with large, sharp teeth (2) enabling the fish literally to bite off large mouthfuls as if with a knife. The upper jaw is armed with no less sharp but smaller teeth. Sex distinctions are practically absent. The males are usually somewhat smaller, the keel of their belly viewed from the front is V-shaped, while that of the females is U-shaped. When excited or in spawning, the fish turn a dark, bluish black colour.

The male makes spawning pits in the bottom where 300—400 yellowish, transparent eggs, 1.5 mm in diameter, are deposited later by the female. Spawning is stimulated by sufficient space, fresh water at 24—26° C and, above all, adequate food in the form of live fish. The spawning site is guarded by the male. The larvae break the eggshell in 36 hours and stay at the edge of the hollowed-out pit. It is recommended that, at this moment, they be sucked out by a hose pipe and transferred into a separate aquarium. The fry need seven days to become free-swimmers. For their first nourishment they require brine shrimps; later they eat chopped tubifex and zooplankton and maybe also the fry of live-bearers. Having reached the length of 1.5—2 cm the young fish (3) will attack and injure each other. This can be partly avoided by reducing the number of fish, sorting them according to size frequently and by regular and sufficient feeding.

The Black-tailed Piranha and related species are kept only in the largest tanks able to hold 500 l or more. It must be borne in mind that the fish should always be very well fed. Hungry fish are aggressive and mutilate and kill each other. The most suitable foods are both live and dead fish. The piranhas, being clumsy hunters, mostly ignore small, swift fish.

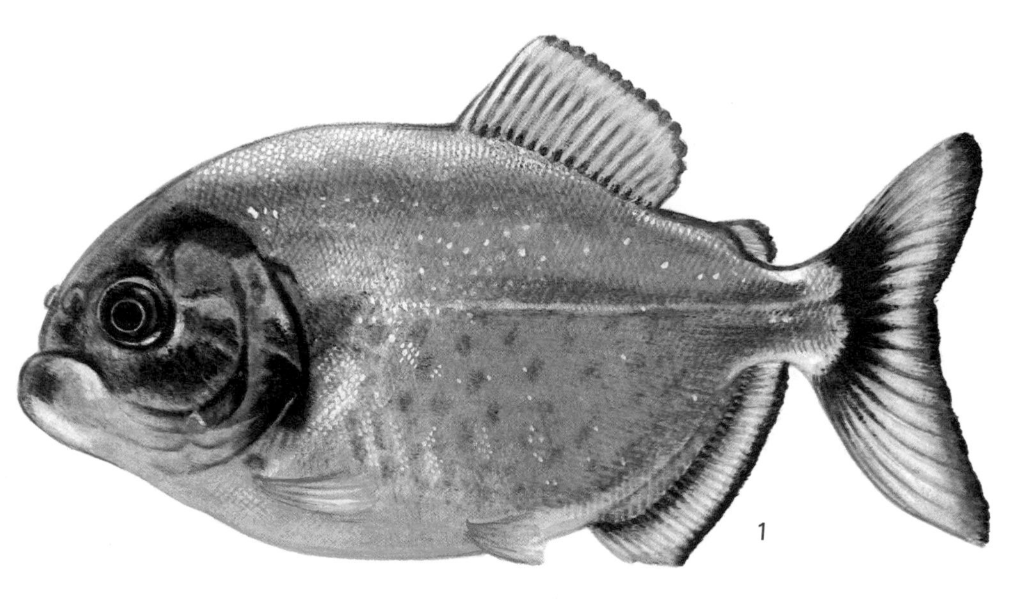

1

Adequate pieces of beef, heart, poultry meat, big earthworms, etc., serve as supplementary food. Due precaution should be exercised in keeping and handling these fish; their bite can cause a severe injury. Wire nets should be used for catching them; other nets will be bitten through in no time.

The species *S. rhombeus* is different in shape. Its juvenile stage is shown in Plate 4.

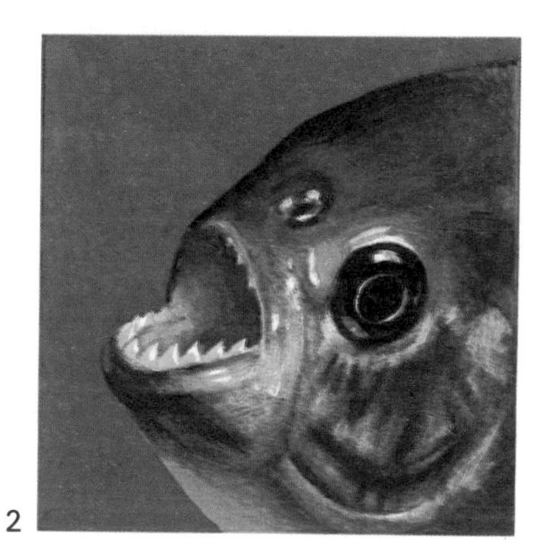

2

3

Marbel Hatchetfish or **Striped Hatchetfish** Gasteropelecidae

Carnegiella strigata (GÜNTHER, 1864)

This fish lives in the central and upper stretches of the Amazon as well as in the rivers of British Guyana, favouring small forest creeks with soft, slightly acid water at a temperature of 25°C. It grows to a length of 4.5 cm and is a surface-dweller. Making use of its large pectoral fins, this fish is capable of jumping several metres. The aquarium must, therefore, be well covered with a glass sheet. The Marble Hatchetfish has a characteristic hatchet-like body shape; hence its name. Although it was imported to Europe as early as 1912 it has not become particularly widespread. This can be ascribed to the fact that cases of successful breeding in captivity are sporadic and have not been given sufficient publicity in professional literature. There is practically no sexual dimorphism: only a view from above allows one to determine the sex; the female is somewhat fuller-bodied. In the opinion of several American authors these fish spawn right under the surface, and the eggs remain stuck among the plants. Before any attempts to breed this species are made, it must be remembered that, in the wild, the fish enjoys plenty of sunlight as it lives just below the surface (solar radiation fosters the formation of vitamin D). Another factor of importance is the large variety of flying insects included in the diet of these fish. This might provide the initial clue for successful breeding.

The Marble Hatchetfish flourish in roomy aquariums of the virgin-forest type filled with soft, slightly acid water and with peat roots alternating with plant thickets and open-surface areas. The Marble Hatchetfish (1) is always kept in larger shoals.

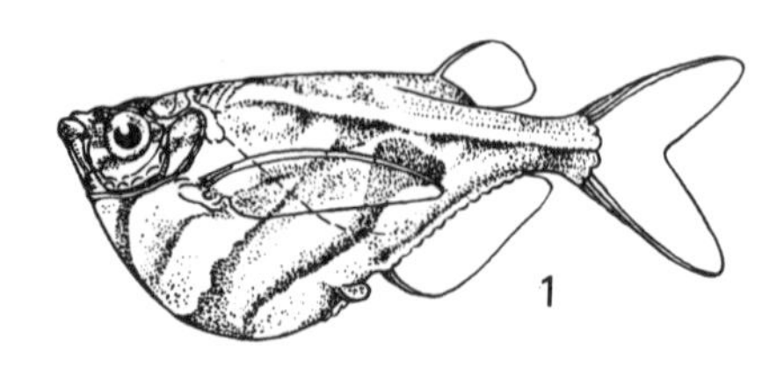

The fish prefer food floating on the surface or found in the middle layers of water. Besides zooplankton, excellent nutritional substances are provided by mosquito larvae, fruit flies, and small insects caught in a sweeping net. Food that sinks to the bottom remains unnoticed.

The species *Carnegiella strigata vesca, C. fasciata* (2) and *C. marthae* (3) are also occasionally reared in captivity. Small characins with similar requirements may be incorporated in such fish communities.

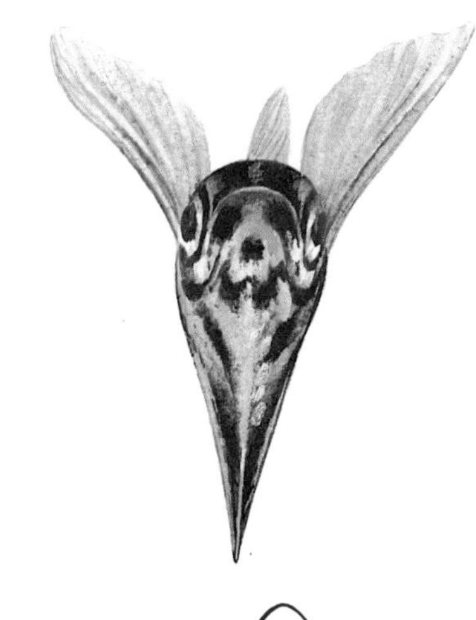

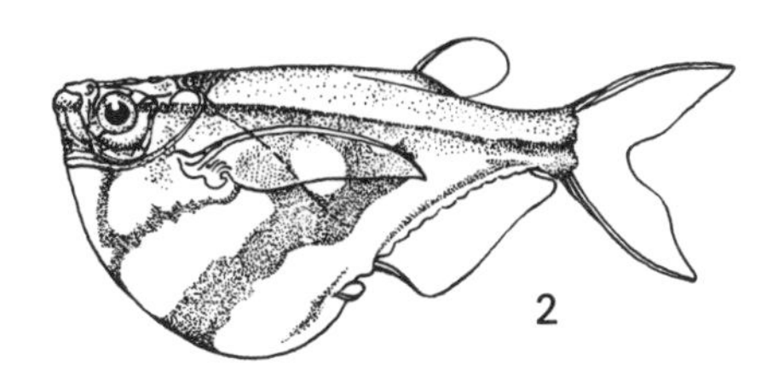

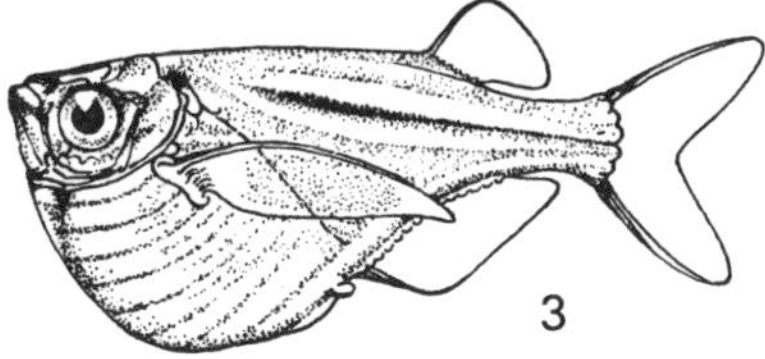

Black-finned Pearl Fish or **Black-finned Cynolebias**

Cyprinodontidae

Cynolebias nigripinnis REGAN, 1912

The development of fish in the occasional waters of the South American pampas was significantly influenced by the rough local climate. In the season of rains even tiny depressions are completely filled with rainwater and are enlivened with huge quantities of fish fry. Biotopes of this kind can be found e.g. in Argentina, in the neighbourhood of the cities of Buenos Aires and La Plata; this is the home also of the Black-finned Pearl Fish. The whole weather-linked spawning cycle is shown in the diagram worked out according to S. Haag (1). (A) Mature fish spawn in shallow waters in the soft bottom substrate. (B) The sun dries up the puddles; adult fish die, and eggs capable of surviving the unfavourable period remain buried in the moist substrate. The embryos inside the eggs pass through a diapause, i.e. their development is suspended for a certain period of time (according to some authorities they may survive a period of up to three years). (C) April comes with its ample rains, and the alevins emerge from the eggs; their growth is very quick. (D) Within two months they attain sexual maturity, spawn, and the whole process starts again from the beginning.

The Black-finned Pearl Fish grows to be 5 cm long. The fish are set up for spawning in greater numbers (20—30 with fewer males than females). Spawning boxes (2) (plexiglass vessels provided with a lid) containing crushed peat are placed at the bottom of the tank. After a week the peat content is gently squeezed in a dense net and put into polyvinyl sacs marked with the respective date of spawning. Refilled boxes are returned to the tank. In six weeks to five months, water at 18—20°C, with pH 6.5—7.0 and up to 2°dCH is poured over the peat. The young do not take more than one hour to emerge. The substrate can be stored and moistened several times. If the young fish are to grow quickly, they must be given ample quantities of large enough live food.

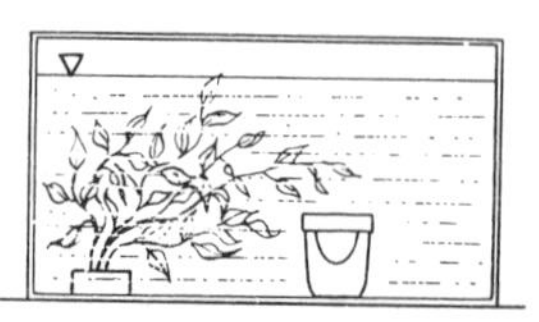

2

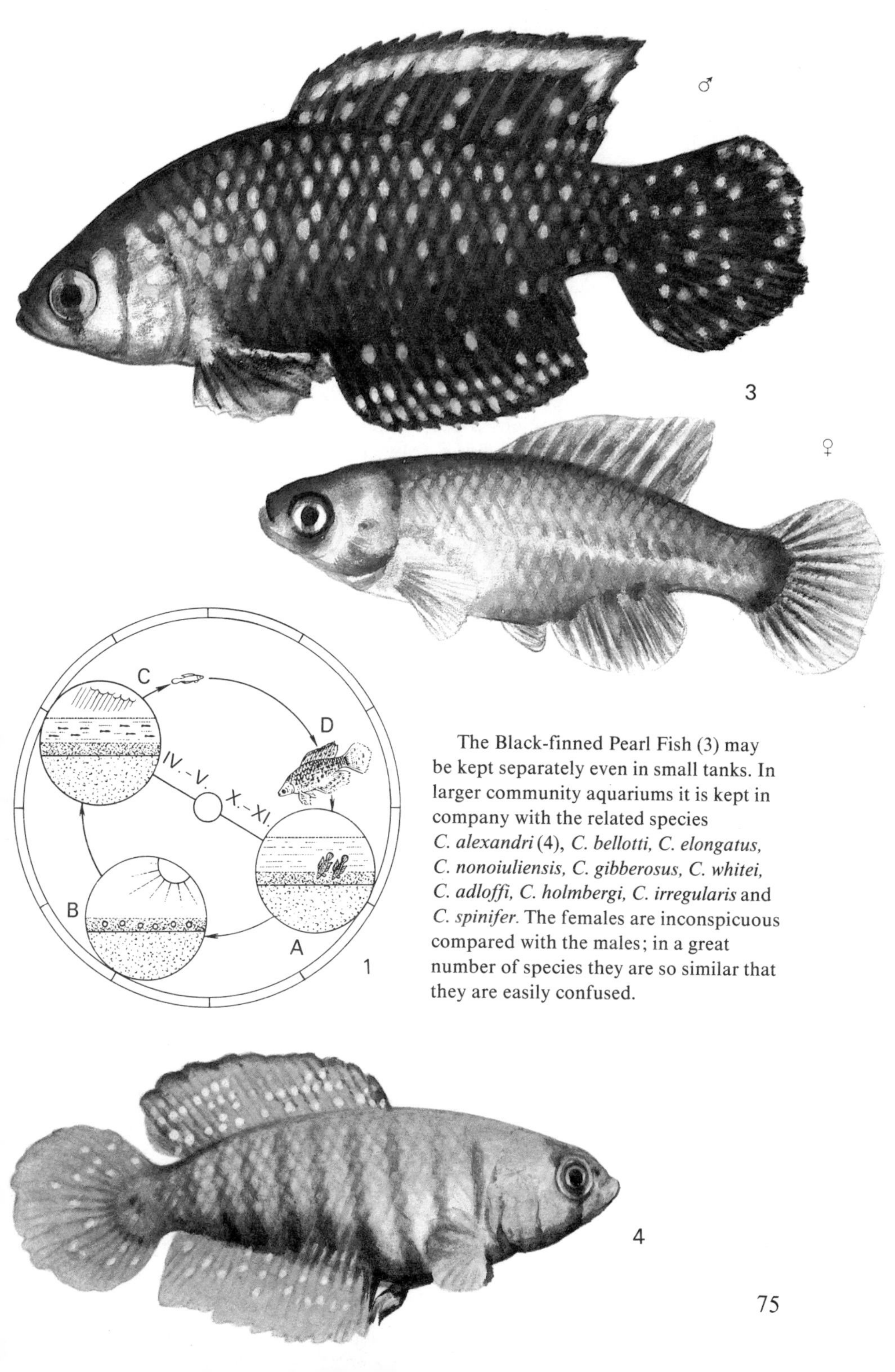

The Black-finned Pearl Fish (3) may be kept separately even in small tanks. In larger community aquariums it is kept in company with the related species *C. alexandri* (4), *C. bellotti, C. elongatus, C. nonoiuliensis, C. gibberosus, C. whitei, C. adloffi, C. holmbergi, C. irregularis* and *C. spinifer.* The females are inconspicuous compared with the males; in a great number of species they are so similar that they are easily confused.

American Flagfish

Cyprinodontidae

Jordanella floridae GOODE ET BEAN, 1879

In spite of its colouration and interesting way of life, the American Flagfish has not become too popular among aquarists. Its specific name indicates that it comes from Florida, particularly from the southern parts where it inhabits numerous swamps and pools. It was imported for the first time to Berlin in 1914. The greatest length attained by the fish is 6 cm. Males are more colourful with their red-green, glistening rows of scales. The females' colouring is less conspicuous.

The fish are set up for spawning in pairs in 20 l aquariums. Males take care of both the eggs and fry, tolerating neither members of their own species nor other fish in their territory. The breeding tanks should be densely vegetated and provided with abundant light. The water should be slightly alkaline (pH 7.5) and at a temperature of 24° C. Eggs are deposited in pits hollowed out by the male, but they are also scattered freely among plants or on nearby objects. These fish usually need five days for spawning. The number of eggs laid by the female per day amounts to several dozen. The female is removed when spawning is over. The incubation of eggs takes six days. As soon as the young fish start swimming freely they are given brine-shrimp dust (1) and the male is removed. After a fortnight the fry from the separate breeding tanks are transferred to a spacious aquarium and offered coarser foodstuffs. Supplementary plant food is added regularly. Sunlit tanks sufficiently stocked with algae are ideal. Under optimal conditions the fry need three months to attain sexual maturity.

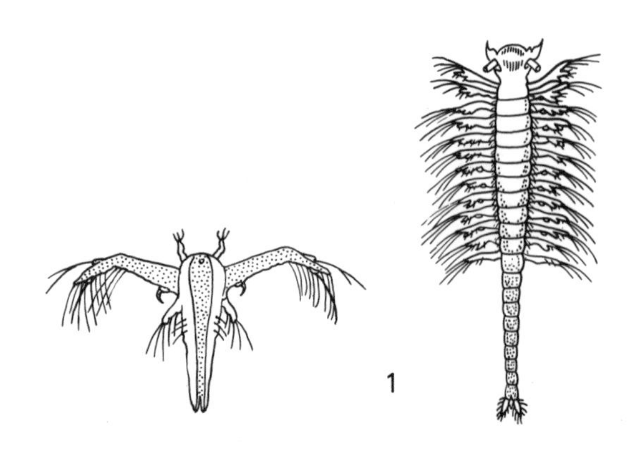

Fish of this species are kept separately. They require smaller but richly planted aquariums exposed to morning sunlight. Since the fish like to bite off fine-leaved plants, these must be supplied in large enough quantities, or else tough-leaved plants may be used. Additional plant foods are provided (spinach purée, scalded leaves of lettuce and vegetables of the turnip-cabbage type). Scalded and finely cut young nettle or dandelion leaves are suitable nutritive substances.

Red-tailed Goodeid

Goodeidae

Xenotoca eiseni RUTTER, 1896

The live-bearing Red-tailed Goodeid (1) inhabits inland waters of the upland plain of Mexico, particularly the Río Lerma water systems. It was imported to Germany in 1974. Females grow to as much as 9 cm; males are somewhat smaller. Members of the family Goodeidae differ from common live-bearers of the family Poecilidae in the morphology of their sexual organs and in their embryonal development. The male's mating organ (andropodium or pseudophallus [2]) was formed through a transformation of the anterior part of the anal fin, while its posterior part has remained unchanged. Ripe females may be recognized by their enlarged ventral parts and the swollen region adjacent to the sexual orifice. They are removed into breeding cages made of a network of meshes 5 × 5 mm in size. The water should be clean, medium-hard, with a neutral to slightly alkaline reaction and a temperature of 22—24° C. The number of young varies from 20 to 60, depending on the female's development level. The interval between the births of individual litters is six weeks, each birth being accompanied by a new insemination. The females are cannibalistic.

As the eggs of these fish contain only a small supply of nutritive yolk, the embryos draw nourishment from their mother's body by means of embryonic appendages, the so-called trophotaeniae, which are connected to the ovarial mucous membrane by villi. The trophotaeniae are observable in the young only shortly after birth; they are quickly absorbed.

The Red-tailed Goodeid likes to attack other piscine species, biting off their fins. This is why fish of this species should be kept separately. Their diet is miscellaneous.

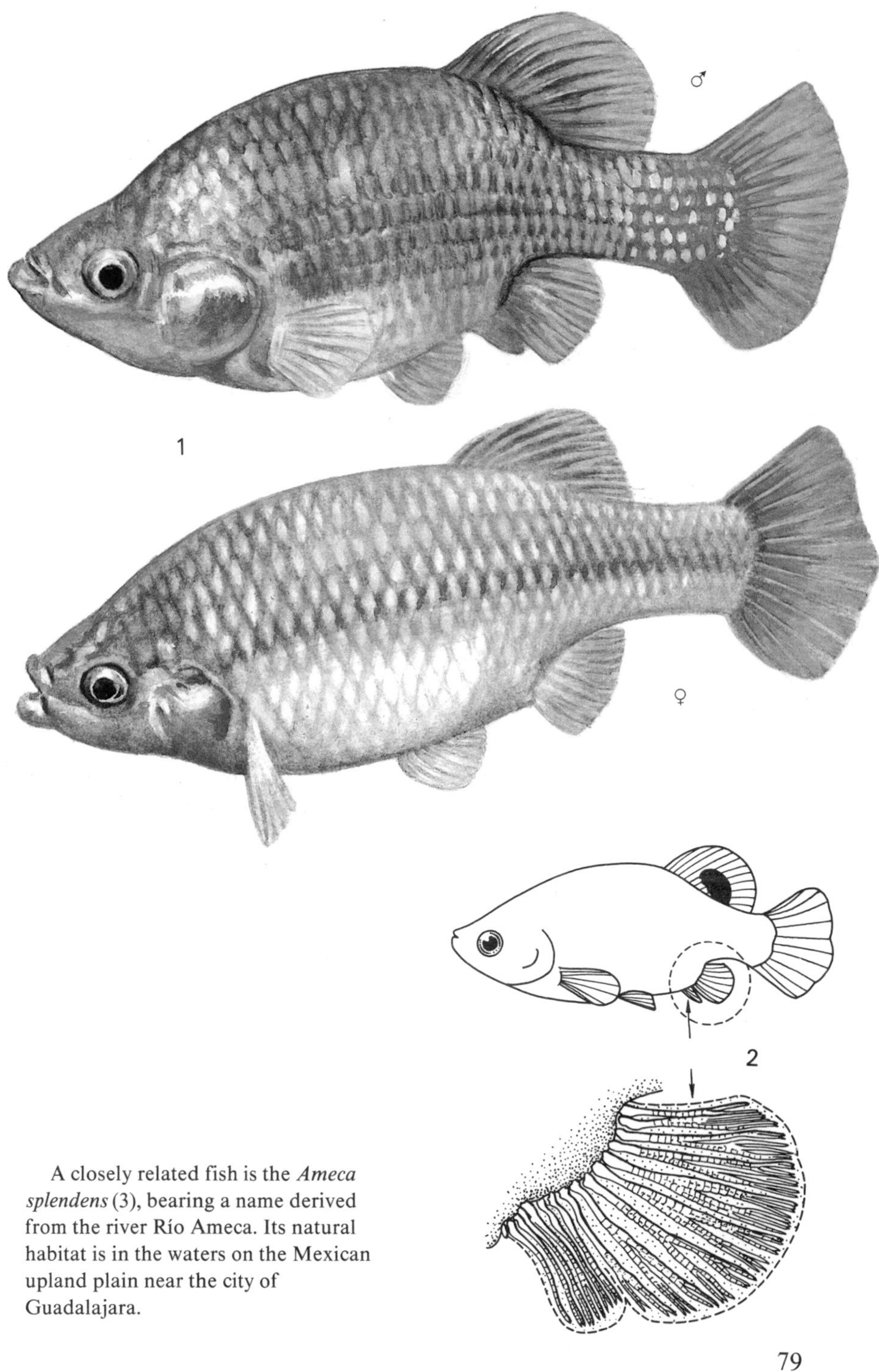

A closely related fish is the *Ameca splendens* (3), bearing a name derived from the river Río Ameca. Its natural habitat is in the waters on the Mexican upland plain near the city of Guadalajara.

Blue-eyed Live-bearer Poeciliidae
Priapella intermedia ALVAREZ, 1952

The live-bearer *Priapella intermedia* (1), unknown to science and to aquarists for a long time, is found in the running waters of the Tehuantepec Isthmus near Coatzacoalcos and in the river bearing the same name in southern Mexico. In Europe it probably appeared for the first time in the nineteen sixties and then only sporadically.

With the exception of the gonopodium in males, sex distinctions are almost absent in these fish. The length attained by the male is 5 cm and by the female 7 cm. In comparison with other live-bearers, the Blue-eyed Live-bearer is extremely sensitive, in particular as regards frequent changes of environment and low pH values. It is a good idea to add sea or kitchen salt to the water—one spoonful per 10 l.

In the females of the Blue-eyed Live-bearer, nothing appears to indicate their fertilization; the shape of the ventral region remains almost the same before and after giving birth to the young. The pregnancy mark is absent. It is therefore extremely difficult to determine the time of parturition. Young females, 3—4 cm long, bear a very small number of young—only about 10—15. The intervals between single deliveries are relatively long, more than five weeks; some authors suggest 30—32 days. The young fish are about 8 mm long, possess characteristic blue eyes, and grow rather slowly. To breed a large number of young, one should put the breeding group, consisting of more females than males, into a 50—100 l aquarium densely overgrown with plants especially near the surface. From time to time the fry should be transferred into a separate tank where they continue to grow in various age groups.

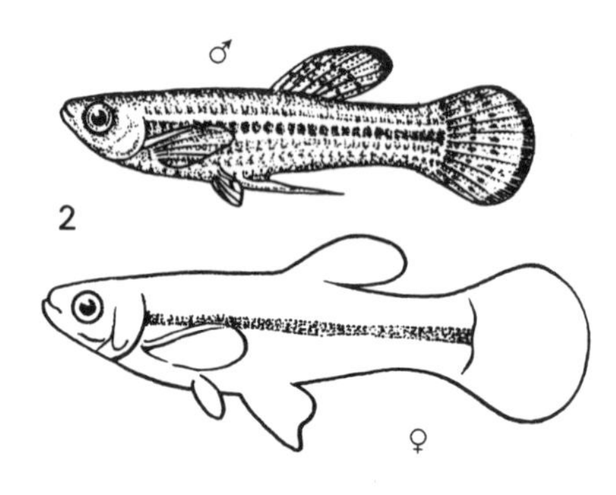

The full beauty of the Blue-eyed Live-bearer comes to the fore in large tanks with crystalline pure water at 23—25° C. Such an aquarium is best planted with fine-leaved plants.

Owing to the delicacy of this species, to the emphasis it lays on water purity and also its remarkable subtle beauty, the presence of other fish is bound to have a disturbing effect.

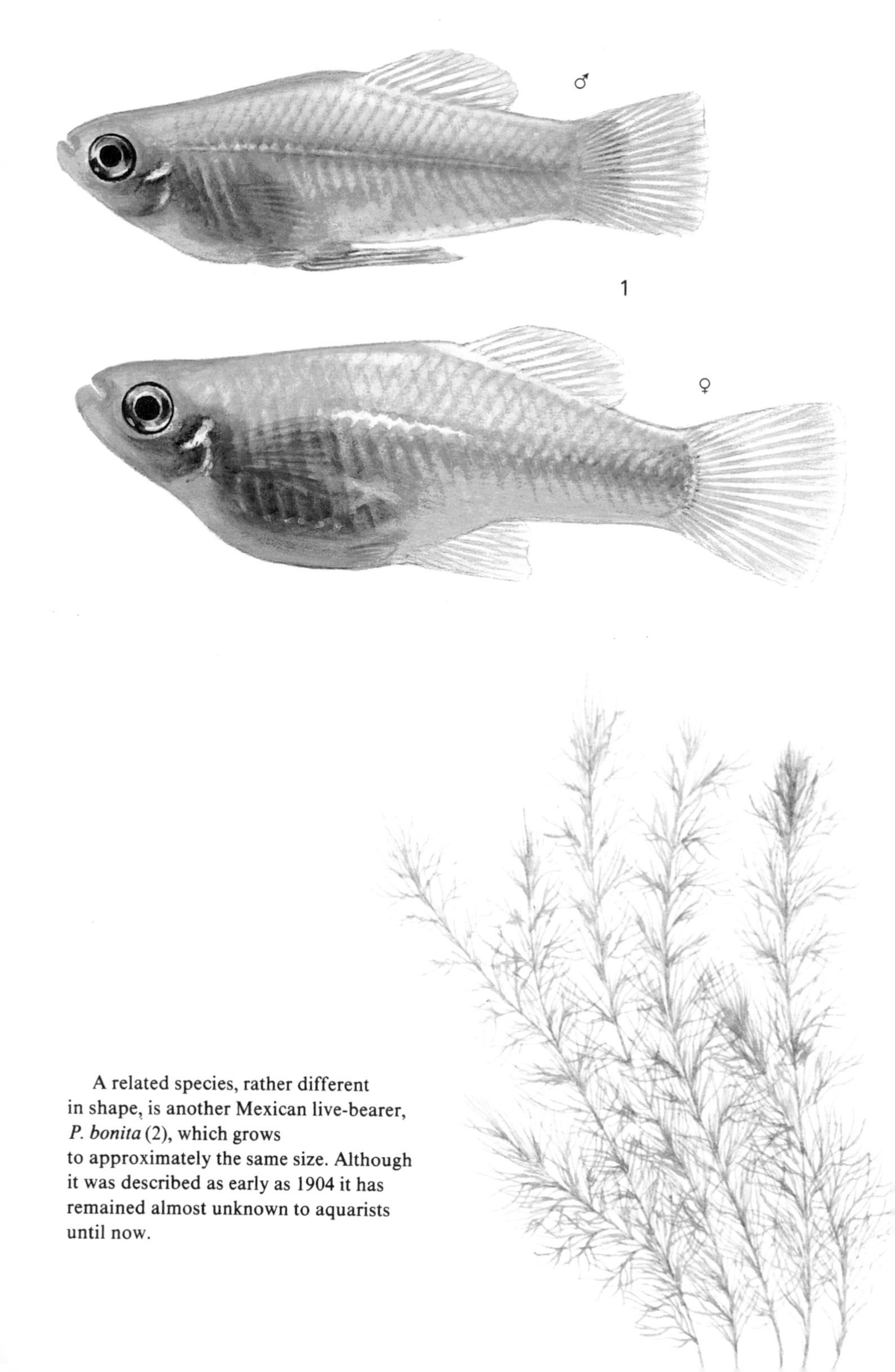

A related species, rather different in shape, is another Mexican live-bearer, *P. bonita* (2), which grows to approximately the same size. Although it was described as early as 1904 it has remained almost unknown to aquarists until now.

Mosquito Fish or **Dwarf Top Minnow**

Heterandria formosa AGASSIZ, 1853

Poeciliidae

This live-bearer is one of the smallest fish, the male measuring 2 cm, the female 3.5 cm. The range of this little fish extends over North Carolina and Florida. At present the geographic distribution of live-bearers is rather unclear as a consequence of the fact that a number of species has been artificially introduced into the wild, even in territories situated within the temperate zone, where they live in thermal springs.

Characteristic of live-bearers is their sexual dimorphism and their manner of reproduction. The asexual young become male or female during growth through the action of hormones. In a large number of species the third, fourth and fifth rays of the male's anal fin are transformed into a specialized mating organ—the gonopodium. The remaining rays are reduced. During union clusters of sperms travel along the groove of the gonopodium through the female's sexual opening into the ovaries where they fertilize the ripe eggs. The sperms partly remain in the folds of the ovaries and, for a certain period of time, fertilize the gradually ripening eggs. Thanks to this the females of live-bearers are capable of producing several broods in the absence of the male.

The Mosquito Fish was imported to Europe in 1912. It is a hardy fish capable of tolerating a temporary drop in water temperature to 15° C (the preferred temperature being 20—24° C). The females expel their young in twos or threes; as a rule the whole birth process lasts 6—10 days. The maximum number of young may be about 50. The interval between the separate births is 4—5 weeks. Adult fish do not prey on their young.

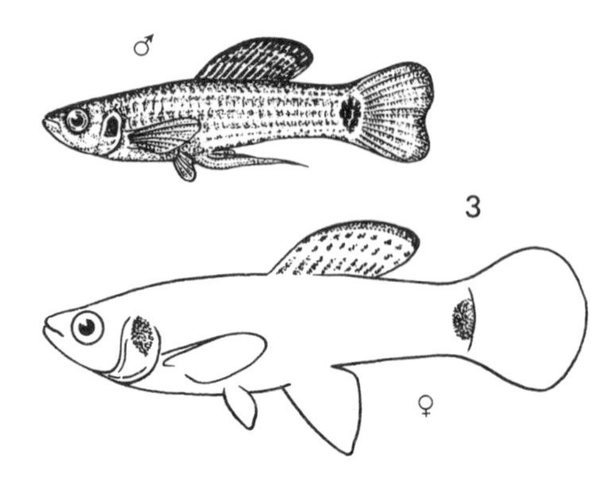

The Mosquito Fish (1) is well suited even to small and shallow aquariums. Plant food should never be omitted from its diet. Because of its minute size it is reared separately. Perhaps the Cuban live-bearer *Quintana atrizona* (2) may be considered an adequate companion, though it is more thermophilic (23—28° C). Just like all live-bearers also the species referred to here love aquariums plentifully supplied with plants and occasionally exposed to sunlight. Harder water with neutral to slightly alkaline reactions is suitable. The addition of kitchen salt to the water improves the well-being of the fish.

The pugnacious and predatory *Heterandria bimaculata* (3) is a related species and inhabits the brackish waters of southern Mexico, Guatemala and Honduras. It is substantially larger in size; the male measures 5 cm, the female 9 cm.

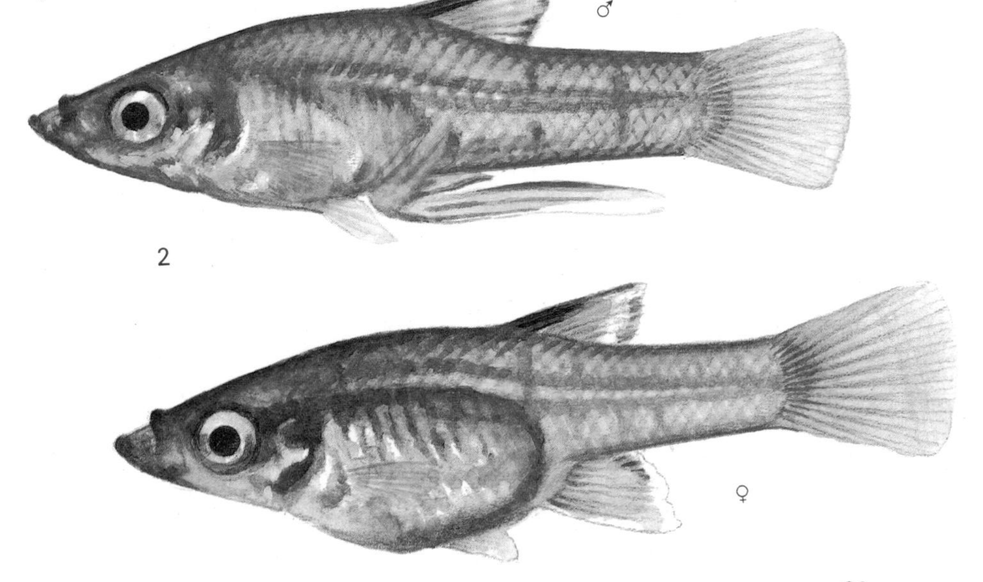

Sailfin Molly
Poecilia latipinna (LESUEUR, 1821)

The *Poecilia latipinna* (1) and the closely related *P. velifera* (2) resemble each other and produce a number of hybrids. To determine the generic connections of these fish is often extremely difficult. To all appearances both the species were imported to Europe for the first time in 1913. The males' anal fin has developed into a fertilizing organ—the gonopodium. In *P. latipinna* the male measures 10 cm, the female 12 cm. Its range extends over the eastern states of the USA from Carolina to Yucatan in Mexico. The dorsal fin is rectangular, its base length exceeding its height; the caudal fin is very large. In the lyrate strains (characterized by a lyrate elongation of the upper and lower rays of the caudal fin) the base of the dorsal fin is twice as long as its height. Besides the naturally found form there are the generally known speckled, albino, red (Starburst Molly) (3) and black (Black Molly) mutations having either a normal or a lyre-shaped caudal fin.

In *P.velifera* the male reaches 15 cm in length, the female 18 cm. It comes from Mexico, mainly from the Yucatan peninsula. Its dorsal fin is square-shaped, but in the lyrate mutations the base of the dorsal fin is substantially shorter than its height. In addition to the wild form there are albino, xanthoric, variously spotted or completely black strains with either a normal or a lyrate caudal fin. A short-bodied form was bred in Singapore and is known under the name of Balloon Molla (4).

In the diet of both *P. latipinna* and *P. velifera,* plant food plays an important role. Both the species are thermophilic (20—24° C). Since they are also found in the brackish waters of river estuaries, the addition of kitchen salt or, better still, of sea salt to the water (one spoonful to 10 l of water) does them good.
Many cultivated strains are rather delicate and difficult to rear in captivity.

The currently used breeding tanks are not particularly suited for breeding these fish: they remain stunted and their most beautiful feature, the prominent dorsal fin, fails to reach the required length. Ideal fish are obtained by breeding in heated hot-house basins, or wherever climatic conditions allow them to be kept in the open air.

Guppy

Poecilia reticulata PETERS, 1859

The wild form (1) of this fish was brought to Europe as early as the last century and became widespread among aquarists, being known by several successive names. In 1913 it was given the name *Lebistes reticulatus* and, after a revision in 1963, it was classified under the genus *Poecilia.* Owing to its capacity for producing abundant young, it soon ceased to be imported from nature. On the other hand, as a 'million fish' it was used in the struggle against mosquitoes transmitting malaria and was introduced by man to the infested areas. This has made its original habitat questionable; it comes quite definitely from Trinidad, the French island Martinique and the American island St Thomas. The island fish populations inhabit both brackish and sea water and are said to be extraordinarily colourful and large.

The length attained by the females can be as much as 6 cm, the variously coloured males are smaller. In the process of maturing, the males' anal fin becomes a fertilizing organ—the gonopodium (2). The interval between the delivery of each brood is four weeks. Pregnant females are segregated in breeding cages (3). During growth the males are separated from the females. Roomy tanks or pools containing pure, slightly alkaline water at 24° C provide the most suitable environment for the development of the fish; adding kitchen or sea salt to the water (one spoonful to 10 l of water) is beneficial to their health.

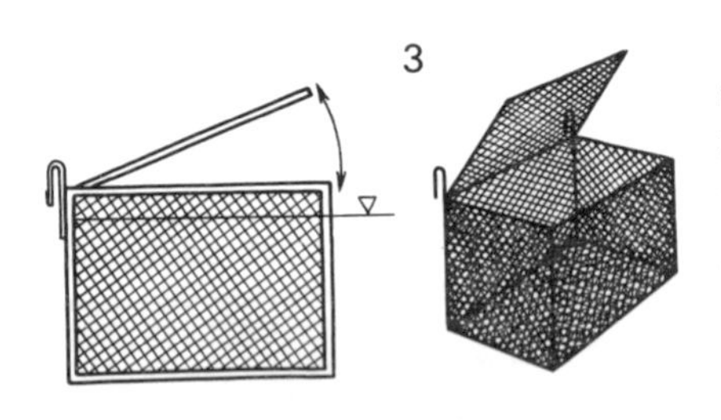

Adult fish should be given sufficient space and a mixed diet that includes plant food (algae, spinach purée, plant flake feeds).

Although the Guppy is recommended to beginners as a non-problematic fish, it is at the same time continuously being improved by top breeders.

One of the most prominent of these is the famous American breeder of German origin, the 'King of Guppies', Paul Hähnel. Today the greatest suppliers of cultivated Guppy strains (4) are breeders in the USA, Singapore and Hong Kong. The greatest customers and suppliers for Europe are wholesalers in the GFR.

This fish has been awarded the greatest number of medals and diplomas and has suffered most hardship in the small aquariums of beginners. It is also most commonly used in laboratory research, particularly in connection with testing the toxicity of waste waters.

Sphenops

Poecilia sphenops CUVIER ET VALENCIENNES, 1846

The Sphenops (1) ranges over a vast area of the American territory, from Texas, through Mexico and as far as Colombia and Venezuela. Owing to its great variability, this species has developed a large number of local populations more or less unknown to aquarists. The fish vary even in size, and the alleged length of 7 cm in males and 10 cm in females evidently relates to animals kept under the best conditions in reservoirs at some farms.

The Sphenops was brought to Europe for the first time in 1899, yet these imported fish must have perished. Another, probably again unsuccessful import dates back to 1908. However, there is a report from 1910 stating that in the breeding establishment at Konradshöhe in Magdeburg (Germany) the Sphenops was being reproduced successfully. The popular black strain 'Black Molla' came into existence in the late twenties in New Orleans, USA. In 1930 it was imported from the USA to Europe by the German firm Eimecke in Hamburg. The strain called 'Lyre Molla' (2) originated long after the Second World War in Singapore, where it was discovered and further improved by the Chinese breeder Cheah Yam Menga. The rearing of these fish is similar to that of other live-bearing species. Pregnant females are transferred into sufficiently spacious breeding cages. The growth of the young fish depends not only on enough food but also on sufficient room, environmental hygiene and a frequent supply of warm, fresh water.

The best environments for the Sphenops are roomy aquariums of 200 l or more, richly stocked with plants and exposed to sunlight for several hours a day. The sun contributes to the development of algae, both filamentous (genus *Cladophora*—3a) and unicellular (genera *Scenedesmus*—3b, *Synedra*—3c,

Navicula—3d, *Asterionella*—3e), which form a significant part of the food of these fish. The water should be relatively hard, enriched with kitchen or sea salt, with a pH value of 7.0—8.0 and temperature of 23° C or, for deep-black strains, 24—28° C. They may share community tanks with fish requiring a similar water composition and preferably with live-bearers.

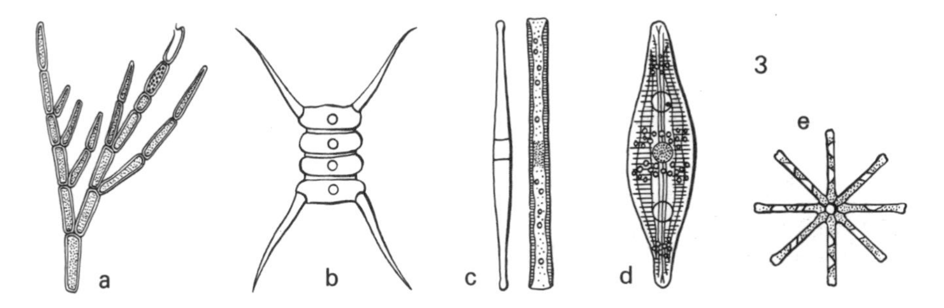

Swordtail or **Tuxedo Swordtail** Poeciliidae

Xiphophorus helleri (HECKEL, 1848)

One of the most successful live-bearers, the Swordtail, was brought to Europe in 1907. It occurs naturally on the Atlantic slopes of southern Mexico and Guatemala. Its original range was considerably expanded by artificial introduction. The basic colour of the wild form is green (1) but there are many different shapes and colours. The males grow to a length of 8—10 cm (excluding the 'sword') and the females to a length of 12 cm. The males' typical sexual features include the gonopodium and a sword-shaped extension on the lower edge of the caudal fin. In this species, a sexual transformation of fertile females into fertile males comes about from time to time. No reverse transformation has been known to occur.

The water should be fresh, with a neutral to slightly alkaline reaction, and have a temperature of 20—24° C. The addition of kitchen salt to the water contributes to the well-being of the fish. Before parturition mature females can be recognized by the increased size of their belly and a conspicuous, dark pregnancy spot. They are transferred into breeding cages suspended in smaller tanks, or into a common spacious cage accommodating more females which is placed in a large tank. This makes it possible for the young to escape out of the females' reach. Young fish of the same age are transferred together from smaller tanks to large ones, where they reach maturity in six months. Fully developed females may produce as many as 200 young in one brood. The interval between each delivery is five weeks. From May till September the young fish may be kept in garden pools where they grow very well.

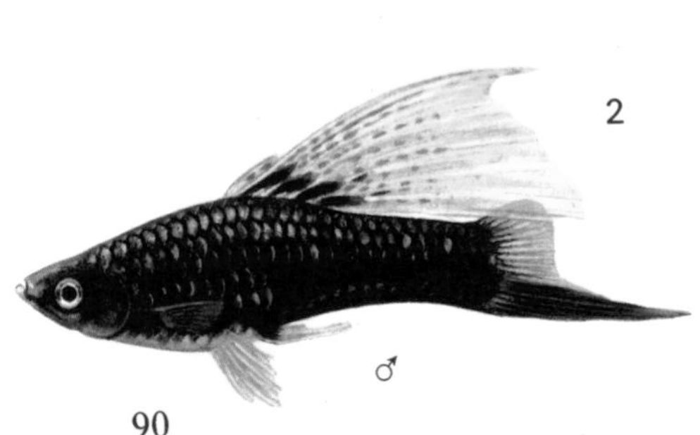

Swordtails thrive in large, densely planted tanks. They are hardy (with the exception of some artificially bred strains) and capable of tolerating transient falls in temperature to 10° C. In every case, fewer males and more females should be kept together. Weaker males are harassed and oppressed by the stronger ones, often to complete exhaustion.

Through selective breeding and further improvements, a great number of stable strains have been produced successively, differing at first in colour and colour combinations and later in length and fin shape—for example, the strain 'Simpson' (2) and the lyre strain, both bred in the USA. Red, black, Wagtail, Viennese, Berlin, Tuxedo and other strains are available nowadays to aquarists. Also a great many hybrids with the species *X. maculatus* have been produced as well as various interesting mutations (3).

Platy
Xiphophorus maculatus (GÜNTHER, 1866)

The generally used name 'Platy' is derived from the original designation of the genus *Platypoecilus,* applied today as a synonym only. The Platy is related and similar to the Swordtail but is smaller in size. The males grow to 3 cm in length, the females to 5 cm. The males' caudal fin has no sword, although hybrids with the Swordtail have a short one. A marked sexual characteristic of the males is the gonopodium. The colour variability of the species is seen already in the wild strains of fish in their natural surroundings. The original range of the species extends over the territories of southern Mexico and Guatemala. The fish were imported to Europe for the first time in 1907.

Intentional or natural hybridization in captivity has given rise to a great number of hybrids between the Platy and the following species: *Heterandria formosa, Poecilia nigrofasciata, P. reticulata, P. sphenops, P. velifera, Xiphophorus variatus,* etc. The principles of breeding and rearing are identical to those applied in the species *X. helleri.* One of the first stabilized strains is the red and black Wagtail Platy which has been genetically fixed with so much success that the black colour can be considered a dominant feature. This is due to the work of the American geneticist Myron Gordon (1900—1959) who carried out large-scale experiments on live-bearers and published numerous works answering a great number of questions about selection and heredity in these fish.

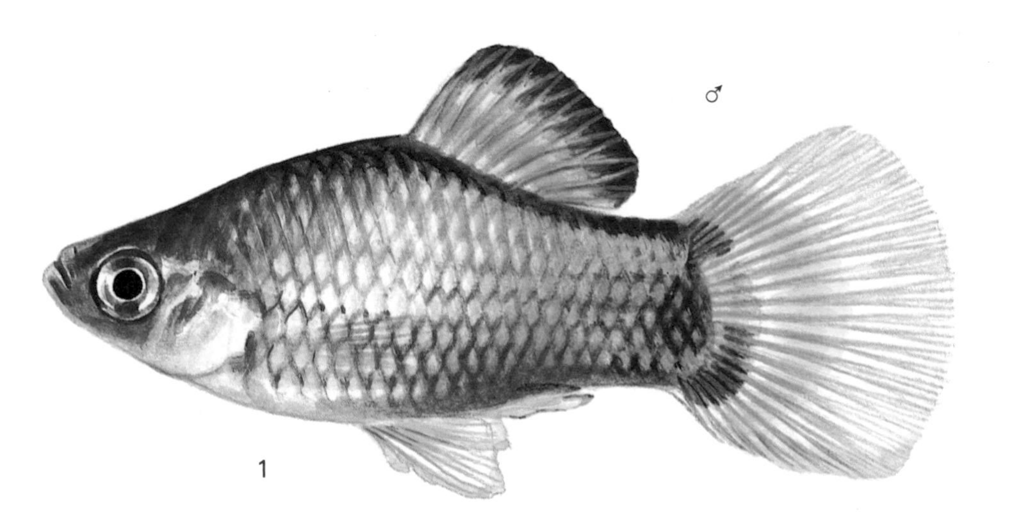

The Platy is kept in roomy, richly vegetated tanks. It is a peaceful fish well suited to community aquariums. It takes foods of all kind, plant food being an important component. Fish strains of extraordinary colours bearing a veil-shaped dorsal fin are known under the name of Papagai Platy. These arose through an intentional hybridization between *X. maculatus* and *X. variatus*. *X. maculatus* presents many colour deviations from yellow, red, blue (1) and spotty, to black, including various colour combinations (2, 3). In recent years variously coloured fish with the caudal fin tapering to a point or a brush and known under the name of Spitz Platy (4) have been produced.

Reitzig's Dwarf Cichlid or **Yellow Dwarf Cichlid** Cichlidae

Apistogramma reitzigi AHL, 1939

This fish was imported to Europe in 1936 and was described three years later. Reitzig's Dwarf Cichlid is a small fish coming from the central parts of the Río Paraguay basin. It attains a length of 7 cm, the females being smaller in size. Males have more prominent dorsal, caudal and anal fins. The dominant basic colour of these fish is yellow; several dark transverse streaks and longitudinal bands distinctly appear whenever the fish succumb to a state of excitement, and vary according to the situation involved—for instance, in a state of rest (1), in spawning (2), in assuming a warning attitude, in impressing, or in guarding the fry (3). These fish love an environment full of sheltered places with no disturbing influences from the surrounding world, and soft, crystalline water containing a peat extract (pH 6.5—7.0, up to 10° dGH and less than 1° dCH). Such an environment is also favourable for the development of eggs. It is a thermophilic species, so the temperature in the aquarium should not fall below 24° C. For rearing purposes aquariums should have a capacity of approximately 50 l and be abundantly stocked with plants. In the corners there should be bottomless flowerpots, where the pairs like to spawn. The inner sides are spread with oval, cherry-coloured eggs, which are relatively large and limited in number—approximately one hundred. When spawning is over, the female drives the male away and takes over the care of at first the eggs and later the brood. The young fry emerge in five days and take another six days to learn to swim freely. Brine shrimps serve as the most adequate nourishment at this stage. Even if carefully and well fed, the fry grow rather slowly.

The Dwarf Cichlids, just like large-sized species belonging to this family, are territorial fish and, in spite of their small size, they require large

aquariums. They prefer live food and usually make greater demands on their living environment. Containers with a rocky background and plenty of little caves and overhangs make a very decorative show. If the container is big enough, several species of small cichlids can be kept there together. The pairs occupy their territories within which they live and spawn. Even if broods reared in such an aquarium are minimal, they give a true picture of part of a South American pool or stream with its diverse fish community.

Ram, Ramirez' Dwarf Cichlid or **Butterfly Cichlid** Cichlidae
Papiliochromis ramirezi (MYERS ET HARRY, 1948)

In April 1947, the American H. Blass together with the hunter and breeder M. V. Ramirez from Venezuela caught a small cichlid in the river Apuré basin which, until that time, had been unknown to science. H. Blass took one hundred of these fish to Miami in Florida where they soon reproduced. In 1948 it was described and given the name *Apistogramma ramirezi.* In the same year it was imported to Europe. Later on it was reclassified under the separate genus *Microgeophagus.* Numerous changes in the piscine systematics and nomenclature are still under way, and the last valid designation of the genus is *Papiliochromis.* The Ram was also found in Colombia and Bolivia. The length it attains is 5 cm. Females have fuller and more vividly red ventral parts; the second ray of their dorsal fin is only slightly elongated.

The Ram is monogamous and the care of eggs and offspring is shared by both partners. The best environment for the development of eggs is water at 24—26° C, with a pH between 6.0 and 7.0 and carbonate hardness no more than 1° dCH. The female lays 200—400 yellowish-grey eggs, about 1 mm across, on a firm substrate; these are gradually fertilized by the male in the course of spawning. The larvae emerge in four days, and need eight more days to become free-swimmers. The eggs can be transferred into breeding tanks and the presence of the parent pair dispensed with. Brine shrimps and copepods serve as the first food, while coarser live food is offered later on. Even with good and plentiful feeding the fry's growth rate is relatively low.

The Ram is also bred in a xanthoric (yellow) strain (1). Characteristic of the xanthoric strain is the absence of pigment cells in the skin, with the exception of yellow and orange ones; the eyes are black.

Just like other small cichlids, these fish take predominantly live foods, e.g. copepods (Copepoda) (2).

They feel comfortable in large, densely vegetated aquariums, with sufficient cavities and other hiding-places, where the light is dimmed by plant growth.

Golden Dwarf Acara or Golden-eyed Dwarf Cichlid

Nannacara anomala REGAN, 1905

The Golden Dwarf Acara, a native of western Guyana, has been kept in European aquariums since 1934. Males grow to a length of 8 cm, females are smaller. The male's dorsal and anal fins are larger and terminate in a flap-like protrusion. Single pairs are set up separately in 50 l tanks. Floating plants are situated on the surface, while several flat pebbles and a perforated flowerpot, providing a welcome hiding-place, are placed on the bottom. Boiled tapwater (pH 6.5—7.0, 8—10° dGH and less than 2° dCH) at a temperature of 24—26° C is used. The female lays her eggs inside the flowerpot, but also in the corner of the aquarium or on stones, and the male fertilizes them successively. As soon as spawning comes to an end, the male is removed, for it sometimes happens that an aggressive female kills the male. The incubation of eggs goes on for three days, and the newly hatched fry are then transferred by the female into sand pits or into some tank corner. Five to seven days after spawning, the fry learn to swim freely and pursue even coarser copepod and brine-shrimp nauplii. Later they are given food in larger morsels, including chopped tubifex. In cases where spawning takes place in a community tank, the substrate strewn with eggs can be transferred into the breeding tank, or else the eggs can be sucked up and brought there by means of a small hose pipe. The female's presence is not necessary. Another method consists of waiting until the fry hatch. The fry are subsequently sucked up and transferred, together with the female, into a separate tank. In the majority of cases the female does not stop taking care of the young fry.

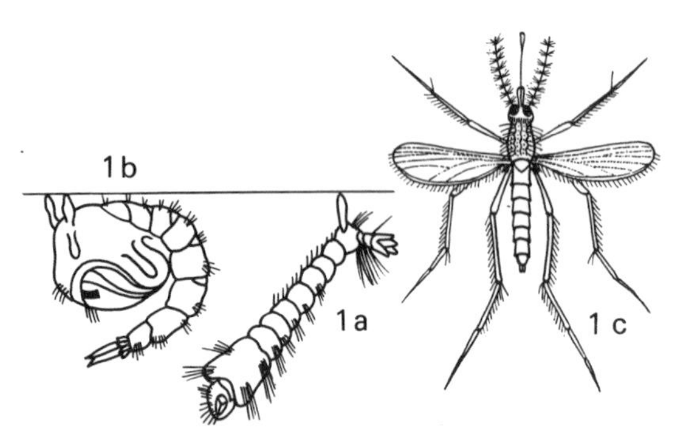

The Golden Dwarf Acara is relatively shy and peaceful, except at spawning time. It aptly complements mixed aquarium communities. The fish are provided with spacious and richly planted tanks abounding in hiding places. In large tanks with enough room for the individual pairs to set up territories of their own and to find sufficient space for escape, these fish can be reared in polyculture with other small-cichlid species. Placing flowerpots

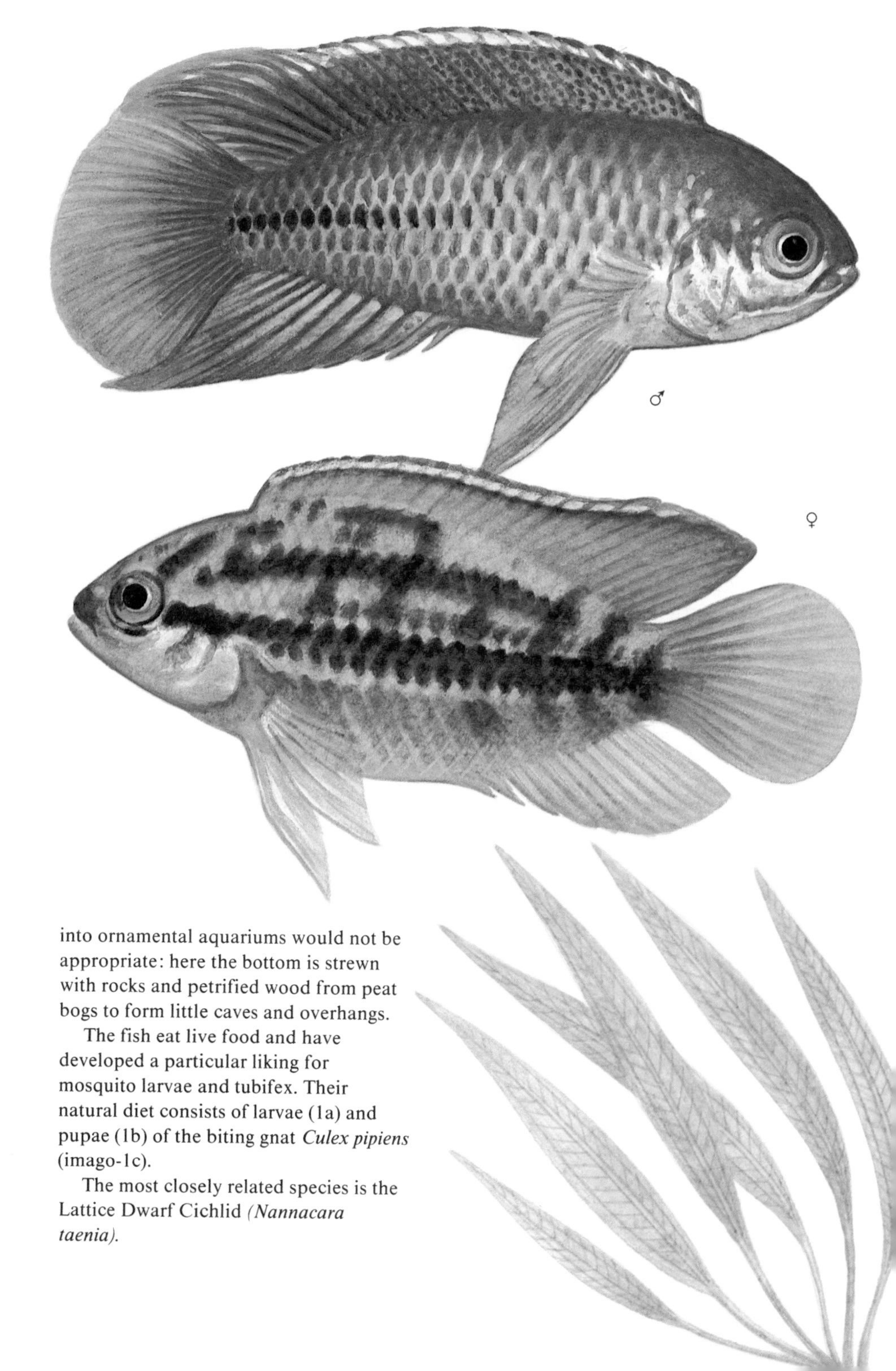

into ornamental aquariums would not be appropriate: here the bottom is strewn with rocks and petrified wood from peat bogs to form little caves and overhangs.

The fish eat live food and have developed a particular liking for mosquito larvae and tubifex. Their natural diet consists of larvae (1a) and pupae (1b) of the biting gnat *Culex pipiens* (imago-1c).

The most closely related species is the Lattice Dwarf Cichlid *(Nannacara taenia).*

Firemouth or **Firemouth Cichlid** Cichlidae

Cichlasoma meeki (BRIND, 1918)

A stately cichlid attaining a total length of 15 cm in nature and under optimal conditions also in captivity. It inhabits the waters of Guatemala and Yucatan. It was imported for the first time to Germany in 1939. Males are more robust; their dorsal and anal fins taper to a tip; their ventral region is vivid purple.

Adult fish are monogamous (living in pairs) and territorial, ferociously defending their territory often against substantially larger and predatory fish. They are lithophillic, i.e. they seek a firm substrate at the bottom for spawning, usually flat stones, to which the female attaches her eggs. Led by their strongly developed instinct, both partners look after their eggs and fry together. The Firemouth is a prolific fish. The optimal water temperature for breeding and for the development of eggs is 24° C; the pH should not drop below 6.0; hardness 10° dGH, 2° dCH. Acid water reactions below pH 6.0 and an increased nitrite content dangerously affect the health of the fish, and they perish without obvious reasons. The fry are fed first on brine shrimps or copepods and later with coarser feeds such as chopped tubifex, zooplankton, mosquito and midge larvae, or minced beef and heart. The fish consume large quantities of food. The intensive feeding of young fish entails the necessity to clean the tanks regularly. In breeding tanks that are overstocked with fish, the filters must be permanently kept clean and, once or twice a week, two thirds of the old water should be replaced by fresh water.

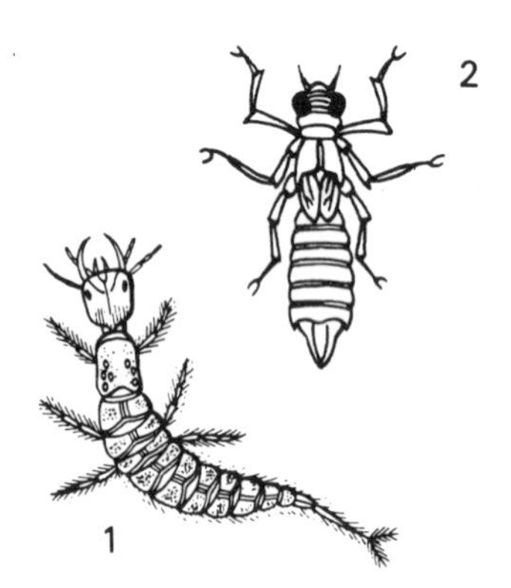

The mature fish are hardy: a temperature of 20° C has proved to be sufficient for them, they will even tolerate a temporary drop to 15° C. As regards nutrition, they prefer larger pieces in the form of earthworms, small fish and bits of beef; they like also to catch bigger larvae of water insects, e.g. diving-beetles *(Dytiscus marginalis)* (1) or dragonfly naiads (genus *Aeschna)* (2).

To observe the life cycle of these fish

to the full, it is necessary to obtain an aquarium of at least 100 l for a single pair. Under the confined conditions of small tanks, skirmishes and discord may come about even among mated pairs. At spawning time the Firemouth becomes quarrelsome and belligerent. Since the fish tend to alter the setting of the tank bottom and tear out plants, rocks should be used.

Oscar Peacock Cichlid or **Velvet Cichlid**

Astronotus ocellatus (CUVIER, 1829)

The Oscar Peacock Cichlid is one of the biggest aquarium fish: it may grow to a length of 35 cm. This large cichlid lives in the Amazon basin, and also in the Paraná, Paraguay and Río Negro basins. It has been bred in Europe since 1934.

Conditions necessary for successful rearing are spacious 300—500 l aquariums, an abundance of suitable food, fresh water and warmth. Sexual dimorphism is indistinct. Having attained the length of 12 cm, the fish start maturing and pairing off. The future couples join in cleaning stones and driving away other fish. It is essential to keep each pair separately. Water: temperature 24—28° C, pH 6.5—7.0, up to 2° dCH. The pairs are copiously fed, their diet consisting of living fish, fresh dead fish—either whole or chopped into pieces—slugs, earthworms, pieces of beef, etc. Barrel-shaped, dirty-white eggs are deposited side by side on a stone that has been carefully cleaned in advance. The eggs are 2 × 1,5 mm in size. They may number 300 or more. The spawning site is vigorously defended by the pair. The incubation time is three days. The freshly hatched larvae are insufficiently developed and have a large yolk sac. This serves as their source of nourishment for five days, when the young fry start accepting food. Brood-care is well developed in some pairs; others, on the other hand, prey on their own eggs and fry. This makes it advisable to transfer the stone with the eggs into another tank. If this is out of the question, a little hose pipe may be used to suck up the eggs. Eggs are treated with methylene blue, and the dead ones are removed during incubation. The fry have an attractive juvenile colouring (1).

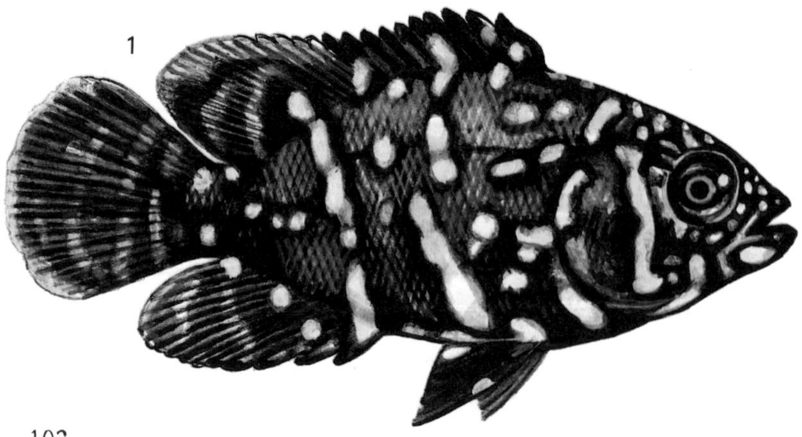

The Oscar Peacock Cichlid (2), also called 'Oscar', 'Peacock Eye' or 'Water Buffalo', has become a real pet in the aquarium. It is extremely tractable, takes food out of one's hand, tolerates caressing, but it can also bite, and its sharp, tiny teeth leave bloody scars on the hand. It is very popular in Thailand where it is kept in private homes, offices and even in temples. Almost every large fish-breeding establishment in the world includes these fish among its assortment. This popularity is apparently due to the fact that a red strain has been bred known under the name 'Red Oscar' (3).

Angelfish or **Scalare** Cichlidae
Pterophyllum scalare (LICHTENSTEIN, 1823)

Pterophyllum scalare (syn. *P. eimekei*) (1) is a 26 cm high and 15 cm long fish. Its habitats are in the rivers Amazon, Tapajos and their tributaries.

Sexual dimorphism in these fish is indistinct, only older males have a more powerful head bearing a small fatty protuberance. A large school of young fish kept together until the time of sexual maturity spontaneously breaks up into pairs. It is considered ideal to rear individual pairs together in containers able to hold at least 100 l of water. Water requirements are 26—28° C, pH 6.5—7.0, 10° dGH and up to 2° dCH. The fish spawn on the vertical surfaces of objects, glass panes or leaves of aquatic plants. Although the parents look after the eggs and tend them, they take care of the hatched fry only exceptionally. The eggs, having been wiped off the substrate with a goose quill, are taken into separate tanks either with the whole substrate or in a small-mesh net. The transferred eggs are treated with methylene blue, a constant temperature (26° C) is maintained, and the water is amply aerated. The incubation time is 48 hours, and clutches of newly hatched larvae are attached to the substrate by filaments. In a week's time the fry start swimming freely and grow quickly. They are given live food only.

In 1909 very similar fish belonging to the species *P. altum* (2) were imported to Europe from the Orinoco and its tributaries. This species, however, has vanished from the aquarists' tanks and is at present seldom reared.

The Angelfish has been produced in numerous colour mutations. It is possible to purchase both short-finned and veil-finned strains whose colouring ranges from the natural original colours to smoky grey, marble or rainbow coloured, blotchy, two-toned, or completely black or golden (3).

The elegance of these fish becomes particularly noticeable if more specimens are kept together in properly and tastefully arranged tanks capable of holding 500—1,000 l. With the exception of during the spawning period they are peaceful and can be reared with other placid fish. They eat all the usual sorts of live food. As they also greedily devour small fish fry, a group of prolific live-bearers *(Xiphophorus helleri* or *Poecilia reticulata)* can be kept in their company for feeding purposes.

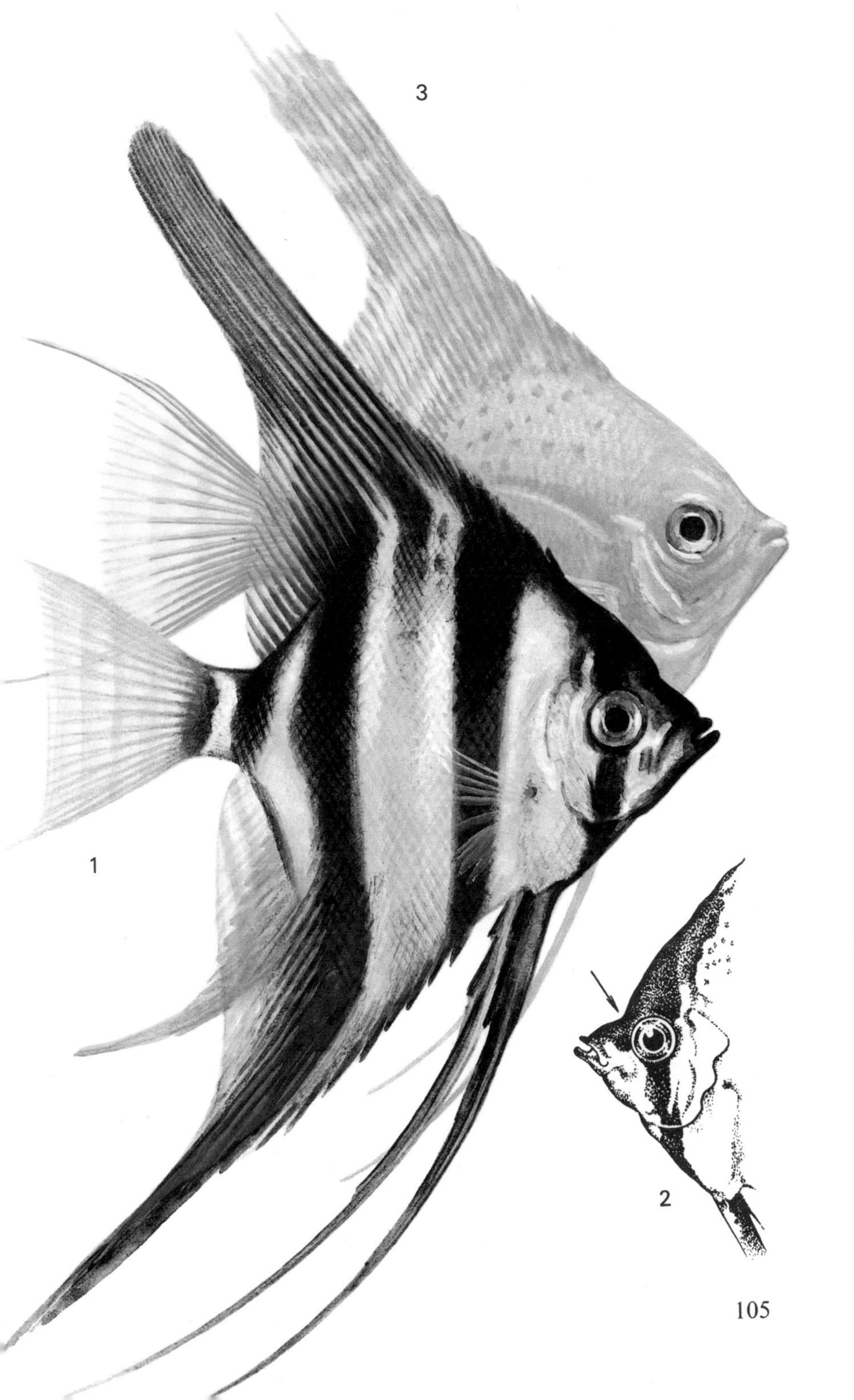
3
1
2

Brown Discus or **Yellow-brown Discus** Cichlidae

Symphysodon aequifasciatus axelrodi L. D. SCHULTZ, 1960

Already prior to World War II, aquarists were endeavouring in vain to breed fish of the genus *Symphysodon.* Although in their original home, in Brazil, these fish may be found in all kinds of waters, ranging from dirty, white waters saturated with urban waste with a pH value equal to 7.0 to black waters with a pH of 5.0, in captivity they are evidently more sensitive to the quality of water. In recent years, however, they have been bred with success, mainly in regions endowed with sufficient natural sources of suitable soft water with a carbonate hardness of 0° dCH. Cases of successful breeding have been reported even under less favourable conditions.

Large specimens may attain a length of 15 cm. The sexual dimorphism being indiscernible, sex may be safely determined only at spawning time. Single pairs that have separated from the group of young fish are kept in large 200 l tanks at a temperature of 28—30° C. The fish spawn on the back or glass sides of the tank or on a smooth, hollow brick. The incubation of eggs takes 48—50 hours; the hatched larvae are suspended on short filaments. After a further 60 hours, when the fry have learned to swim, they cling to their parents' flanks. The skin of the parents exudes a secretion serving the fry as their first food. In a few days the fry start actively chasing brine shrimps, and they grow rapidly. Breeding difficulties arise particularly in connection with the parents' cannibalism or in their failure to produce the fore-mentioned secretion.

Besides the Brown Discus, *Symphysodon aequifasciatus axelrodi* (1), other species currently reared are the Green Discus, *S. aequifasciatus aequifasciatus,* the Blue Discus, *S. aequifasciatus haraldi,* and the red, so-called True Discus, *S. discus* (2). Picture 3 shows the hybrid of the male *S. aequifasciatus haraldi* x hybrid female *S. a. haraldi* x *S. discus.*

Mature fish live happily in fresh tapwater. They require a higher temperature and sufficient food (the usual live food, scraps of beef and heart and also spinach purée).

Blackbanded Sunfish Centrarchidae

Enneacanthus chaetodon (BAIRD, 1854)

This perch comes from the northeastern regions of the USA (New York, Maryland and New Jersey) where it grows to a length of 10 cm. From here it was imported to Europe in 1897, and was first made to reproduce as late as 1902 by Vogt in Hannover and several aquarists in Dresden.

The Blackbanded Sunfish is a eurythermal fish—i.e. it lives in environments characterized by considerable temperature variations throughout the year. This is why the fish overwintering at temperatures only slightly above zero fall into a lethargic torpor and refuse to take food. Yet the first March sunshine brings such aquariums to life. The plants start to grow profusely and assimilate oxygen. Strings of fine bubbles rise from the leaves to the water surface, and the mating season of the Blackbanded Sunfish begins. As soon as the thermometer climbs up to 14° C, the males start digging shallow pits in the sand and the females' dark pattern becomes more conspicuous. A temperature of 18° C already brings the onset of spawning, and eggs are laid in the prepared sand pits. The eggs are transparent and covered with little grains of sand: this makes them difficult to see. The brood care is taken over by the males; it is better to remove the females. Strong and healthy fish are extremely fecund. As soon as the fry learn to swim freely about the tank, the males, too, are removed and the fry are offered powdered food in the form of copepods and brine shrimps; the fry grow very quickly. The more advanced young fish can be accommodated in a garden pool over the summer.

The Blackbanded Sunfish, if kept in warm water throughout the year, also produces offspring; yet these lack the beauty the fish display in their proper environment: a cool-water aquarium.

The Blackbanded Sunfish (1) takes only live food.

Enneacanthus obesus (2) and *E. gloriosus* (3) are related species.

Dwarf Sunfish or **Pygmy Sunfish** Centrarchidae

Elassoma evergladei JORDAN, 1884

The Dwarf Sunfish, a small perch measuring usually 3.5 cm, can grow to a greater size under optimal conditions in captivity. It is native to the swampy regions along the eastern coast of North America, from North Carolina down to southern Florida where the Everglades National Park is situated. It was imported to Europe in 1925.

These undemanding, hardy fish are kept separately in well-planted tanks where in winter time the temperature may fall to 8°C. In summer, on the other hand, they tolerate temperatures of about 30°C. During mating games the lustrous sheen of the males' dark wedding attire is striking. The inconspicuously coloured female lays about 60 eggs, scattering them usually among plants. The adult fish take no notice of either eggs or fry and, as a rule, several generations of young fish grow up in their parents' presence. A precondition of economic breeding is good knowledge of the state and numbers of eggs and fry; this may be attained by setting up either one or several pairs of fish in a series of about 10 l tanks each of which is supplied with running tapwater, an aerator, and a cluster of plants. Every week the breeders are transferred into further tanks in the series. The fry hatch in 2—3 days, according to water temperature. Free-swimming is reached in about one week after spawning. Though very tiny indeed, the fry are endowed with a large mouth enabling them to swallow newly hatched brine-shrimp nauplii with no difficulty at all.

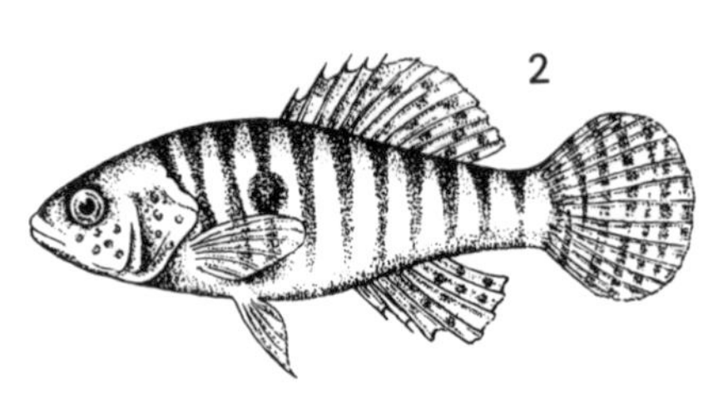

The Dwarf Sunfish eats only live food in the form of minute insect larvae and zooplankton. The latter consists in part of a cladoceran species, *Moina macrocopa* (1), characterized by winter and summer females. The Dwarf Sunfish, being resistant to temperature fluctuations, is an ideal fish for aquariums placed in winter gardens or in glass verandas. Also aquarium plants usually thrive in such an environment.

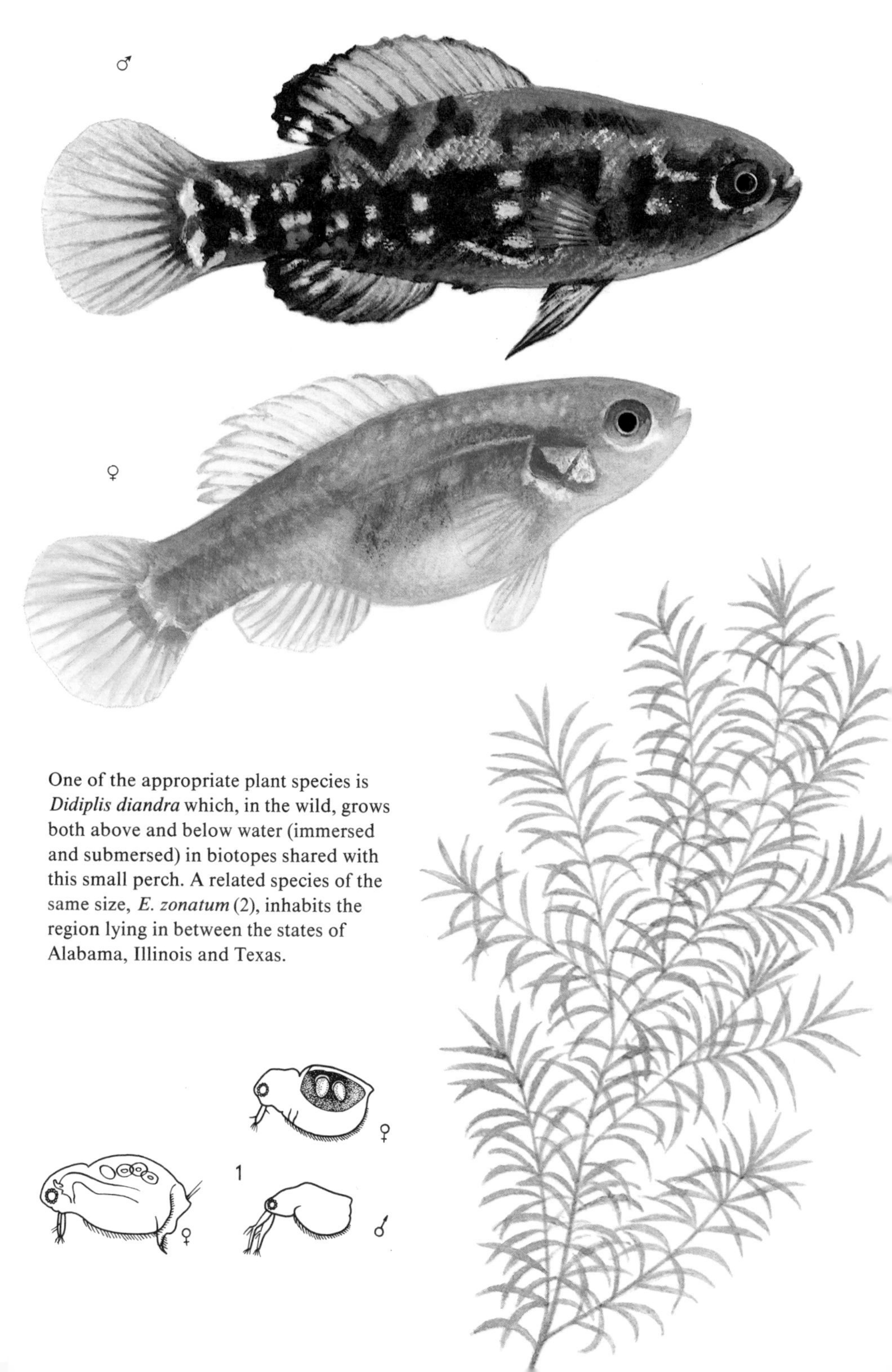

One of the appropriate plant species is *Didiplis diandra* which, in the wild, grows both above and below water (immersed and submersed) in biotopes shared with this small perch. A related species of the same size, *E. zonatum* (2), inhabits the region lying in between the states of Alabama, Illinois and Texas.

Congo Tetra
Characidae

Phenacogrammus interruptus (BOULENGER, 1899)

The largest African river, the Congo, flows into the Stanley Pool covering an area of 450 km². Its brownish, warm waters are rich in fish. Among these are large shoals of characins of the species *Phenacogrammus interruptus* (syn. *Micralestes interruptus*). Males grow to 8 cm in length, females are somewhat smaller and less conspicuously coloured. One of the characteristic features of these fish is their big eyes, and a flag-like extension of the caudal fin in males. The Congo Tetra was brought from the wild in 1949 and, without much acclimatization, was made to reproduce in Neustadt as early as 1951.

Large aquariums and an abundance of soft water are prerequisites for successful breeding. A group of fish with more males than females is placed in a 100—200 l tank supplied with a protective grid. Water with a pH of 6.5, up to 1° dCH, and a temperature of 26° C is best for the development of eggs. If sufficient soft water to fill up the breeding tank is not available, the eggs must be sucked out immediately after spawning and transferred into a smaller tank containing water of the given values. The non-sticky eggs, 1.8 mm in diameter, fall to the bottom. They are spherical and transparent. In six days the fry emerge from the eggs; shortly afterwards they learn to swim freely and take food. In the first days they are offered only the finest sort of brine shrimps, copepod nauplii and Rotatoria. The diet may be complemented by high-grade artificial fry foods.

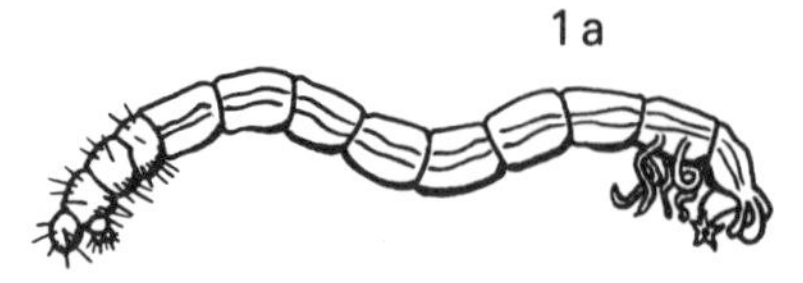

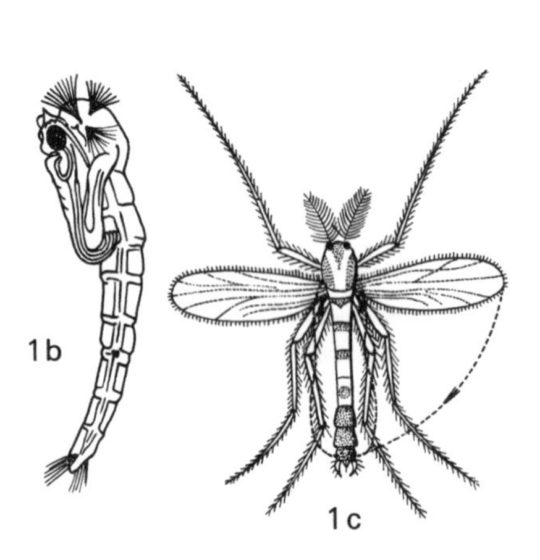

Large, well-planted aquariums with sufficient free space for these exceedingly mobile fish are a marvellous sight. The Congo Tetra is a gregarious, sun-loving fish. It is always reared in larger shoals.

It takes live and artificial food of all kinds. Besides insects from the surface, it has a special liking for larvae (1a) and pupae (1b), eventually even for imagos (1c) of a midge belonging to the genus *Chironomus*.

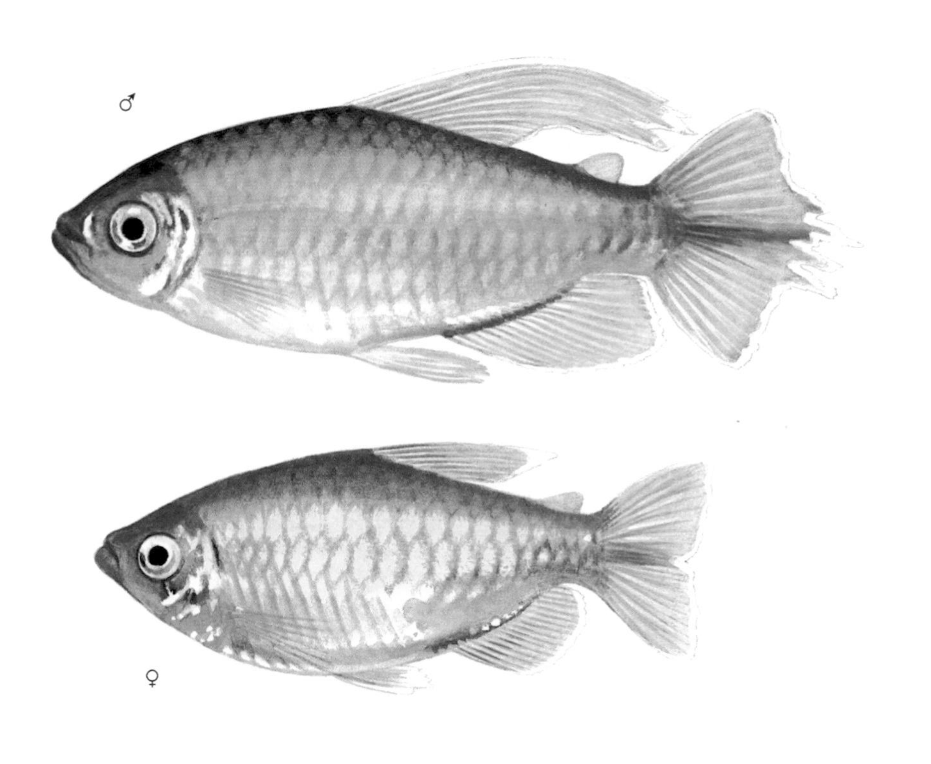

In spite of the numerous existing species of African carp fish, it is only rarely that they may be seen living in aquariums. This is probably attributable to the fact that a number of species either are too large in size or possess an unattractive colouring.

Barbodes ablabes grows to a length of 10 cm. Males are somewhat smaller and slimmer than females; their fins are of a more vivid orange. The fish are ready to spawn in pairs or in whole groups at a temperature of 25° C. They are extremely prolific, the rearing of 1,000 young produced by a single pair being no exception. In deference to the size of the fish and to the great number of eggs, it is expedient to use larger tanks, e.g. ones with base dimensions of 50 × 50 cm. Eggs are protected against their parents' voracity by a spawning grid placed at the bottom. Spawning is vigorous and, during the act, pairs seek support among the plant clusters. After spawning, the breeders are removed and the eggs are treated with methylene blue to avert the spreading of mildew. Eggs develop well in water with a pH of 6.5—7.0, a hardness of 10° dGH and up to 2° dCH. No difficulties arise in rearing the fry on brine shrimps or copepods. With intensive feeding the fry grow quickly up to three weeks of age when they attain a length of 1 cm.

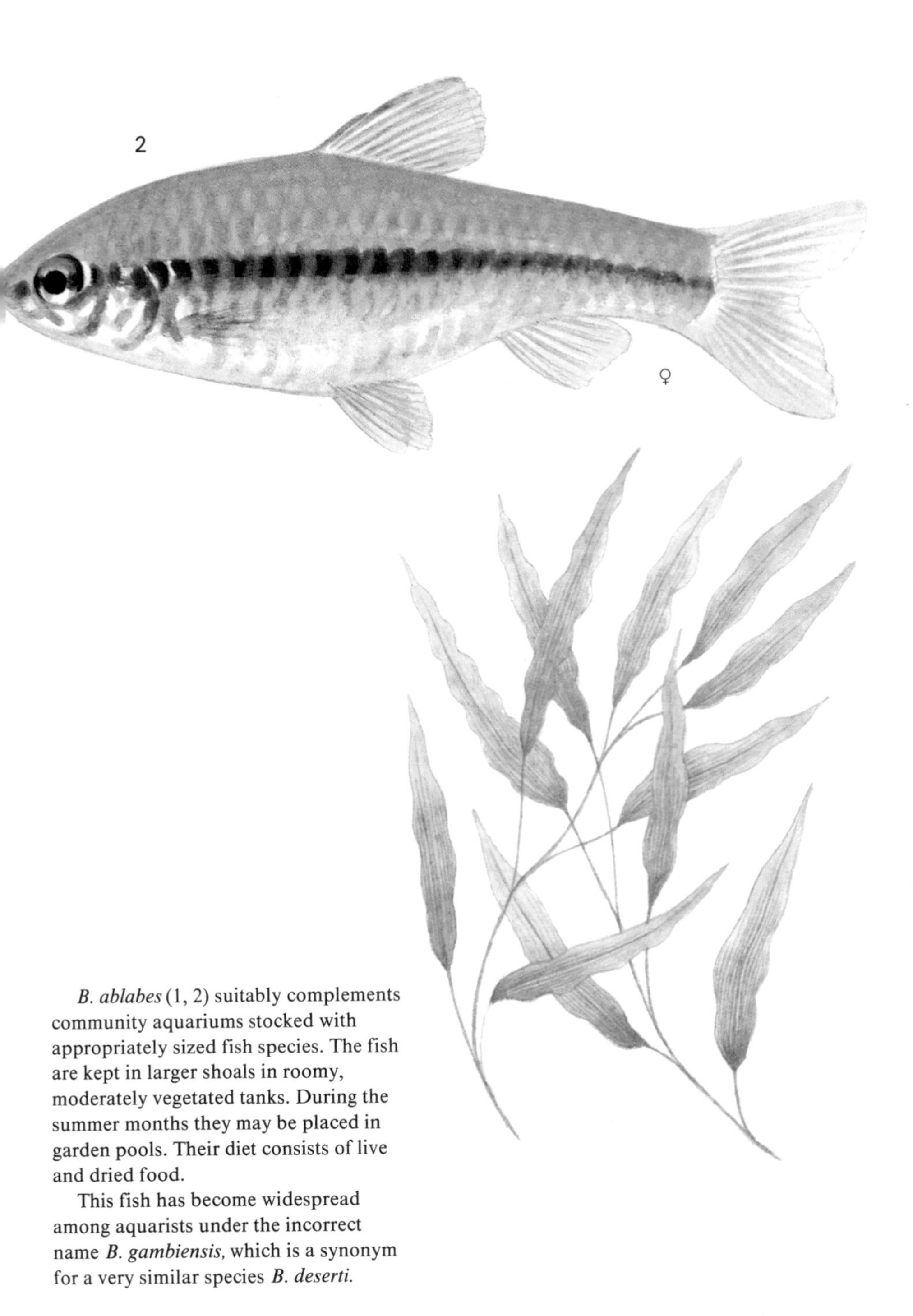

B. ablabes (1, 2) suitably complements community aquariums stocked with appropriately sized fish species. The fish are kept in larger shoals in roomy, moderately vegetated tanks. During the summer months they may be placed in garden pools. Their diet consists of live and dried food.

This fish has become widespread among aquarists under the incorrect name *B. gambiensis,* which is a synonym for a very similar species *B. deserti.*

Upside-down Catfish or **Congo Backswimmer** Mochocidae
Synodontis nigriventris DAVID, 1936

This catfish was imported in 1950 from the Congo estuary to Amsterdam. Since then it has been caught occasionally for wholesale trade and offered in special shops in many European countries. Information on its life both in the wild and in captivity is rather sketchy. The Upside-down Catfish becomes active at dusk and at night. It spends the day under cover, showing a special predilection for cavities. Fish kept in captivity live to be 9—10 years old, while a still longer life span is not unknown. Some females create the impression of being ready to spawn but, when dissected, are found to have no ripe ovaries but only considerable fat layers in the ventral cavity. The length reached by females is 8—9.5 cm and by males about 6 cm. It is assumed that sexual maturity is attained in the second or third year of life. The fish are kept in smaller schools at temperatures between 24 and 26° C. The desirable subdued lighting may be effected by floating plants. Draining pipes or bottomless flowerpots are placed at the bottom of the tank. If one is lucky enough, the fish will spawn in the twilight or during the night in some suitable cavity. The fry are fed on brine shrimps.

Fish of the genus *Synodontis* have developed the habit occasionally to swim on their back. In the Upside-down Catfish (1) this habit has become a rule and is one of the curiosities of the fish kingdom. It also necessitated a change in the protective colouring, which is inverse

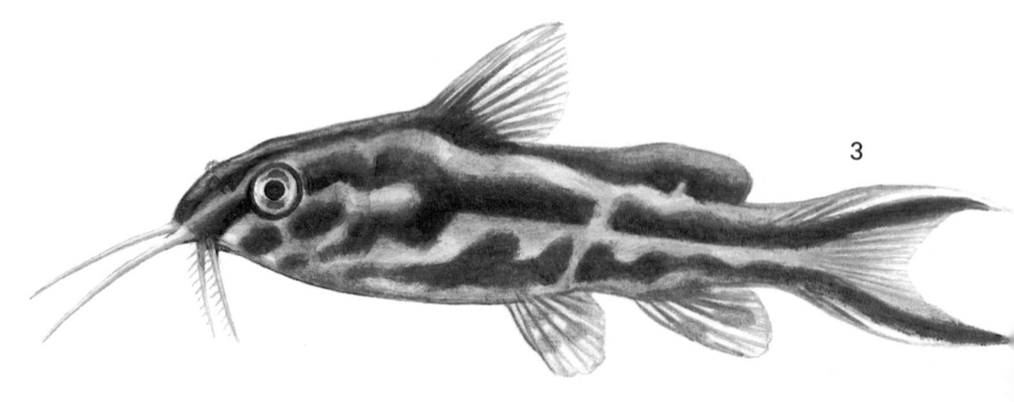

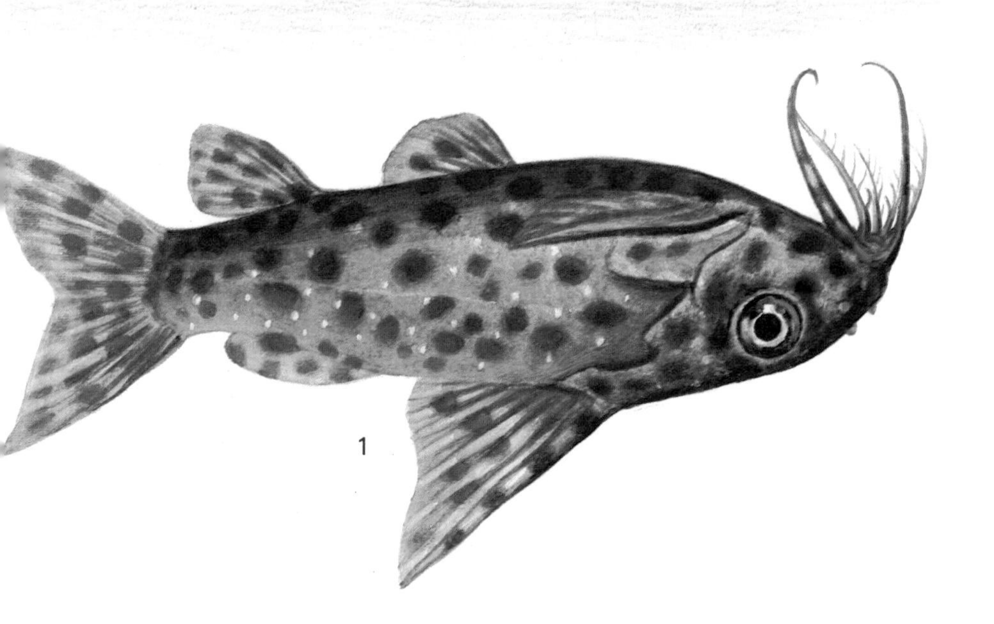

here: the dorsal parts are paler and the ventral parts are dark to black. When picking up food at the bottom, the catfish swim in a normal position. They eat both artificial and live food. Their search for food is facilitated by three pairs of tactile whiskers, but evidently also by sight, because in comparison with other catfish species their eyes are remarkably large. A further characteristic is a large adipose fin. In order to study their life in greater detail, it is better to breed them separately.

Among the large number of related species are the *S. angelicus* (2) and *S. flavitaeniatus* (3).

Butterfly Fish

Pantodontidae

Pantodon buchholzi PETERS, 1876

The Butterfly Fish is native to tropical west Africa (Niger, Cameroun, the Congo basin, the upper-Zambezi region). It lives close to the surface in calm stretches of water. With the arrival of twilight and night, the life activity of these fish grows more intense. They catch insects that fall onto the surface and small fish. Butterfly-like pectoral fins enable them to make a long leap, and thus get hold of prey flying above the surface. According to a written communication, this species was imported for the first time in 1905. The first spawning was recorded in 1912 by the Berlin breeder Lahmann. The first instance of successful breeding was achieved in the same year in Prague by the Czech breeder Siegel.

The male's anal fin is characterized by a deeply notched black edge (1), while in the female the black edge of this fin is straight (2). Rearing is difficult. The breeding fish are put into roomy tanks with a large surface area, where open water alternates with floating plants. Water should be soft, at a temperature of 26—30° C. Long courting games are followed by actual spawning which may continue for several days. Relatively large, dark brown eggs with a high oil content float on the surface. These are collected and transferred into the breeding tank. The larvae hatch in three days and fall to the bottom. After absorbing the yolk sac, the fry return to the surface. They do not hunt food actively but lie waiting for what the water brings. They are also fed on brine shrimps, and later they are offered small springtails, aphides and fruit flies.

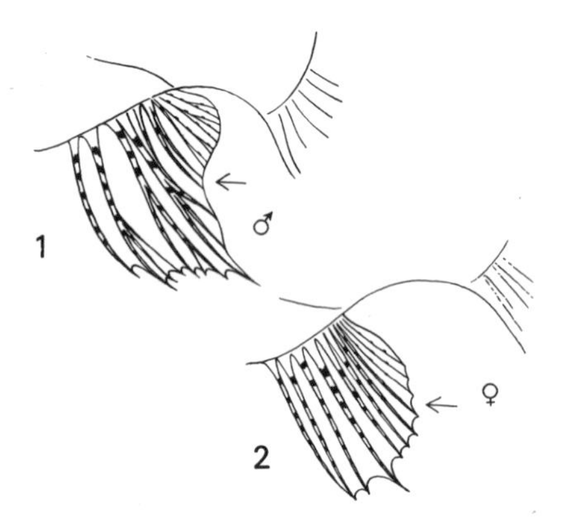

The Butterfly Fish feels safe in a sligtly shaded, large aquarium among clusters of floating plants. Some free surface must be available which it can regard as its territory to be defended against other members of the species. The species is kept separately in small numbers. It is a thermophilic fish. As regards nutrition, it prefers large morsels, leaving the small ones untouched. Spiders, caterpillars, big moths, locusts, cockroaches and small fish are sought-after delicacies. If need be, it is possible to provide additional

food in the form of coarse zooplankton, water-insect larvae, and small pieces of meat offered at the surface. The Butterfly Fish is a species requiring individual care from the egg to adulthood.

Lyretailed Panchax, Cape Lopez Lyretail or **Aphyosemion**

Cyprinodontidae

Aphyosemion australe (RACHOW, 1921)

The Lyretailed Panchax, inhabiting the muddy coastal waters from the Congo as far as the Gabun, has been reared in Europe since 1913. In comparison with the inconspicuous female, the male is varicoloured and larger (6 cm).

Prior to spawning, the females are separated from the males for a week and given an abundant supply of food. 10—15 l aquariums with a protective grid at the bottom are filled with water at 24° C, with pH values 6.5—7.0 and carbonate hardness 2° dCH. The fish are set up in the ratio of 1 male to 3—4 females. These fish often embark the act of spawning within several minutes. It is recommended to let them spawn for one week only, never longer, otherwise hatching might be unnecessarily protracted and disproportionate differences in size might arise among variously aged fry. The incubation of eggs continues for a fortnight, under a full depth of water. The protective grids are left in the tanks until the hatching of the last fry. This is because only a small number of the eggs falls through the grids to the bottom. Most eggs get stuck in the meshes, as well as between the glass panes and the frame of the grid. After making sure that no egg is going to be wasted, the frames are removed. The fry feed on brine shrimps at first and on chopped tubifex later on. As soon as the fry grow to be 2 cm long, they are transferred into a spacious tank where the temperature may gradually be lowered to 20° C. The fry attain sexual maturity in three months.

The Lyretailed Panchax (1) makes an attractive showpiece in tanks stocked with fine-leaved plants, with a dark background, and in the absence of other fish species. In rearing mixed communities consisting of various species included in the genus *Aphyosemion*, it is necessary to bear in mind that the females of a great many species resemble each other and can be distinguished only with difficulty.

The natural nourishment of the Lyretailed Panchax is mosquito larvae and pupae. In captivity the fish readily consume all kinds of live food and high-grade dry food as well.

The German breeder Gerhard Hjerresen from Flensburg discovered and stabilized by careful selective breeding a mutant which H. Meinken called *Aphyosemion australe hjerreseni* (2). The Lyretailed Panchax willingly crossbreeds with the species *A. gardneri*. The ensuing hybrids have bizarrely shaped fins and are infertile.

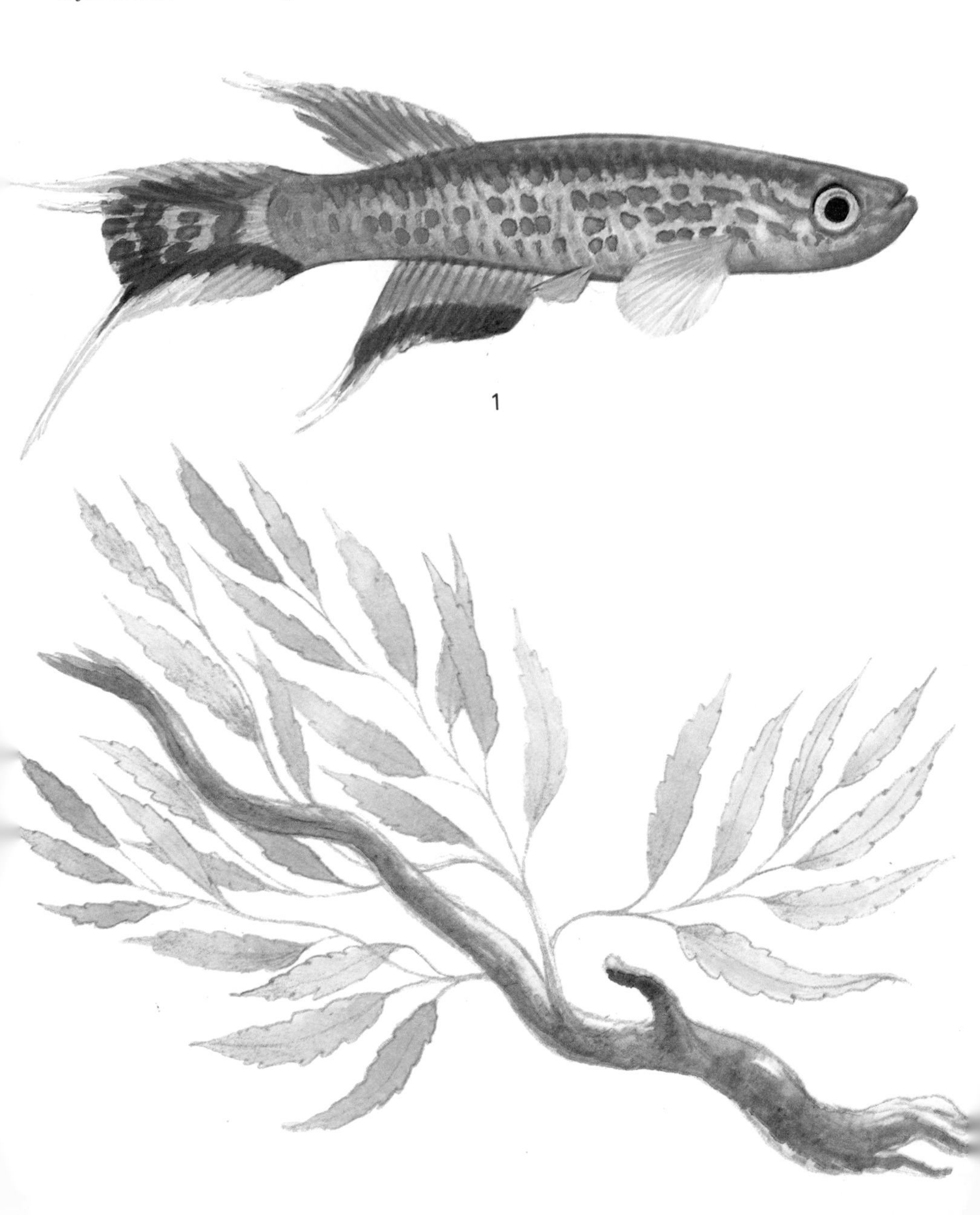

Nothobranchius rachovi was imported to Europe in 1925 from the waters of east African savannas. Characteristic of these areas is the periodical partial or complete lack of water. The range of this species lies in the vicinity of the city of Beira in Mozambique, and in the territory of the Kruger National Park in South Africa. The temperature in these areas is high, and there are great differences between periods of rains and drought. The fish inhabiting these parts are called periodic-water fish. It was as late as post World War II that specialists (Foersch, Scheel, Peters and Wourms initially) threw light on the biology of these fish.

N. rachovi spawns in pairs and also in groups (1 male to 3—4 females). Eggs are laid in the surface layer of peat, boiled for 5—10 minutes and rinsed in advance. The fish are left to spawn for four weeks. Then the peat is sifted, squeezed gently to remove the water and deposited in polyvinyl sacs with attached labels indicating the time of spawning, the expected time of hatching and the name of the species. After six weeks soft water at 25° C is poured over the peat. In a short time the fry begin to hatch. They are fed on live food, grow incredibly quickly and, in 3—4 weeks, reach sexual maturity. The males are gaily coloured and 7 cm long; the females are greyish brown and smaller.

N. rachovi (1) is kept in tanks well stocked with plants not rooted in the bottom, with a soft bottom (peat layer), and in company with related species only. The females of the separate species closely resemble each other, and it is consequently difficult to distinguish them. The recommended water temperature is 25° C.

The fish are fed on live food. A very good and natural diet consists of mosquito and midge larvae.

N. rachovi is sometimes infested with a ciliate of the genus *Amyloodinium.* Treatment is difficult because of the sensitiveness of the fish to medicaments based on $CuSO_4$.

Among the other most frequently reared species are *N. orthonotus, N. palmquisty* (2), *N. furzeri* (3), *N. korthausae, N. guentheri* and *N. kirki.*

Clown Killie

Epiplatys annulatus (BOULENGER, 1915)

Cyprinodontidae

The Clown Killie is a native of western Africa—Guinea, Sierra Leone and Liberia. Within this territory it has formed several ecotypes. Differently coloured or striped fish can be found even among individuals belonging to the same group. The length reached by the Clown Killie is 3—4 cm. The males have coloured fins; the caudal fin extends into a flap-like appendage. The females' fins are transparent and more rounded. In their habitats the water temperature exceeds 25° C, the pH value is 6.7° and the hardness 5° dGH. Nevertheless, eggs will develop even in harder water with 10° dGH and up to 2° dCH. Twenty fish (fewer males than females) are introduced into a 50 l tank. The water should be clean and fresh and the surface dotted with floating plants. The fish spawn in turns, the females depositing minute eggs provided with a short filament among plants and their roots. If the breeding fish are supplied with an abundance of suitable live food, the fry start appearing in a fortnight at the latest. They are most frequently found at the point where the surface touches the glass, in the bend of the water film. They give themselves away by a metallicaly glistening speckle on the top of their head. The fry are regularly collected by a little glass bell. They are very small indeed but their mouth is relatively large. Immediately after starting to swim freely the fry readily accept newly hatched brine-shrimp nauplii, and their growth is quick.

The Clown Killie is a small and placid fish unsuitable for community aquariums. The fish prefer to live among themselves, and it is also only then that their colourful beauty comes fully to the fore. The fish content themselves also with small, well-planted aquariums where sunrays penetrate from time to time.

The Clown Killie's structure is characteristic of the genus *Epiplatys* (1). The fish are given live food only. Though well able to cope with relatively large mouthfuls, they prefer smaller prey, including various wheel worms (2).

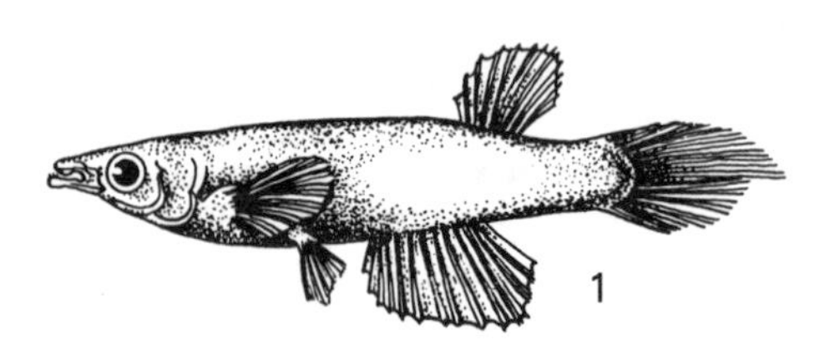

♂
♀
2

Arnold's Killie

Cyprinodontidae

Epiplatys dageti monroviae DAGET ET ARNOULT, 1964

The natural habitat of the *Epiplatys dageti monroviae* (syn. *E. chaperi*) is in the coastal savanna to the north of the city of Monrovia in Liberia. Here there are shallow, calm waters of larger puddles, ditches and pools richly overgrown with plants, mostly with water-lilies and bladderwort (genus *Utricularia*). The water is often muddy, considerably acid and soft.

The history of the import of this fish is veiled in vague conjectures. An oral version states that, in 1908, the species discussed here was for the first time included in one of the shipments of aquarium fish. Having obtained these fish, J. P. Arnold probably induced them to reproduce, and it is maintained that all the fish reared until 1963 were descendants of the original pair he selected.

The males grow to a length of 6 cm; the less conspicuous females are somewhat smaller. Rearing in captivity requires no particular efforts; the fish are so adaptable that the development of eggs proceeds favourably even in tapwater with pH values of 6.5—7.0, 10° dGH, up to 2° dCH and at temperatures between 24 and 26° C. In the breeding group, the ratio of 1 male to 3—4 females should be maintained. The spawning period lasts for several weeks, and the females gradually deposit their eggs in the plant growth. The fry emerge in ten days and are 1.5 mm long. They keep close to the surface whence they can be easily collected with a glass trapping bell. Another rearing method consists of inserting plant tufts into the breeding tank and replacing them with new ones every week. The egg-strewn plants are taken to a separate aquarium. The fry are fed on small live food (brine shrimps or copepods).

1

2

Arnold's Killies feel content in the green shade of aquatic plants, but also need sufficient open and calm surface below which they spend the major part of their life. They are kept either separately or together with species of similar properties and requirements. They are aggressive to equal-sized or smaller fish. Besides other live food, the small fry of live-bearers are a welcome prey.

The linedrawing shows the differences in design characterizing the following related species: *E. dageti monroviae* (1), *E. chaperi sheljuzhkoi* (2) and *E. dageti dageti* (3).

Playfair's Panchax

Cyprinodontidae

Pachypanchax playfairi (GÜNTHER, 1866)

According to the information gained from the noted Czech ichthyologist Professor O. V. Hykeš, Playfair's Panchax was brought to Hamburg in 1924 from Zanzibar, where it was caught in rather neglected pools in a park. The fish of this first import spawned, and thus the species became an inhabitant of aquarists' tanks. Today its range is known to extend over the territory of east Africa, the Seychelles and Madagascar.

Playfair's Panchax attains a length of 10 cm. It is reared only occasionally and sometimes vanishes from the aquarists' tanks for long spells, only to appear there again for a short time. Inexplicable trends have shifted this species into the background of attention in spite of the fact that Playfair's Panchax is a beautifully coloured and undemanding fish. Males are multicoloured, with slightly protruding scales; females have a characteristic black blotch on their dorsal fin. Playfair's Panchax has no special requirements as regards water composition. The optimal water conditions seem to be pH values of 6.5—7.0, up to 10° dGH, up to 1° dCH and a temperature of 22—26° C. A group of breeding fish including more females than males is introduced into a 50 l tank supplied with plant clusters. These are weekly replaced by new ones. The original plants are taken to a smaller all-glass tank where the fry start hatching in 12 days. If supplied with an abundance of small live food, they grow fast. When they are over two months old, the fish spawn regularly until their death. They develop to their full beauty when one year old.

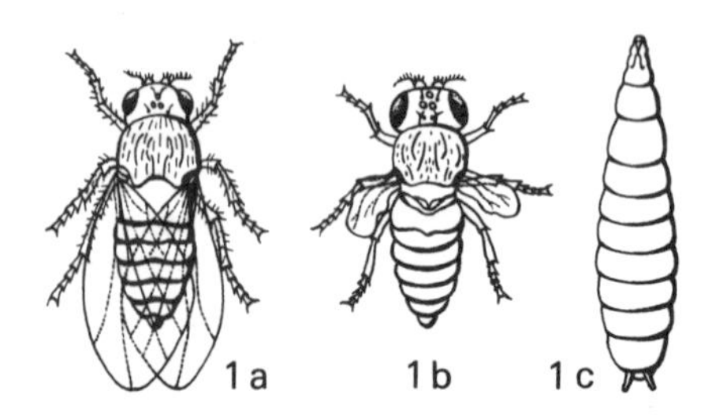

Playfair's Panchax has one unpleasant characteristic: almost without exception it attacks fish of other species, biting off their caudal fins up to the base. This makes it unacceptable as a member of aquarium communities. Among themselves, however, these fish live in perfect harmony.

Though preferring live food, they will also eat good artificial food. With zest they devour both winged (1a) and wingless fruit flies (1b), their larvae and pupae (1c). For these purposes, wingless forms of fruit flies are reared to add variety to the diet of these and other fish.

Kribensis or **Red Dwarf Cichlid** Cichlidae
Pelvicachromis pulcher (BOULENGER, 1901)

Tropical central and western Africa is the home of multicoloured cichlids; of these, the species *Pelvicachromis pulcher* (syn. *Pelmatochromis kribensis*) (1), imported to Europe in 1951, enjoys the greatest popularity among aquarists. The adult fish are 10 cm long. One of the characteristic features of females is their ruby-coloured flanks. Females are also smaller and plumper than males.

The rearing of the Kribensis presents no problems. The best water conditions are a temperature of 24—26° C, pH 7.0, 10° dGH and 2° dCH (tapwater). The fish form stable pairs. They spawn in 50—100 l tanks. Several base-less flowerpots are situated on the floor of the tank. The female lays brownish red eggs, 2 mm in diameter, on the top or on the vertical walls of the cavities. The fry emerge on the third day and learn to swim freely in ten days. The parents take care of the young for three weeks. Sometimes it is the female alone who takes over the brood care. Exceptionally, some pairs are cannibalistic. In such cases the eggs must be taken away and hatched separately. The fry are offered brine shrimps as their first food.

The Kribensis is a representative fish in each ornamental aquarium. Outside the spawning period the fish are placid and may be kept therefore in communities with fish of approximately the same size. However, their interesting life cycles and their real beauty come fully to the fore only when they do not have to share the tank with any other species. Since they often head shoals of their fry, the aquarium is sufficiently crowded with one pair only.

The fish are fed on live food and also on valuable flake food.

Besides the Kribensis the species *P. taeniatus* (2) and *P. roloffi* (3) are frequently reared by aquarists.

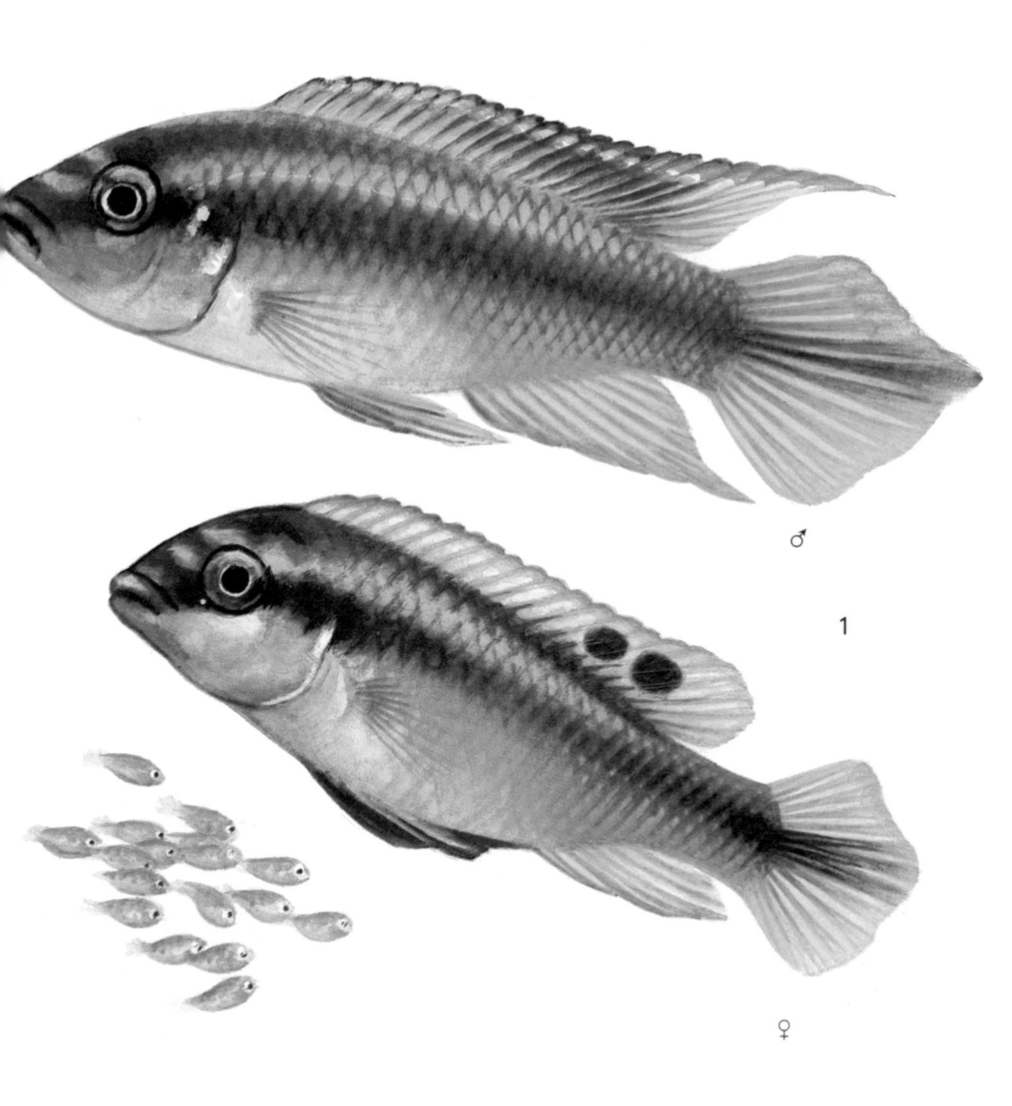
♂
1
♀

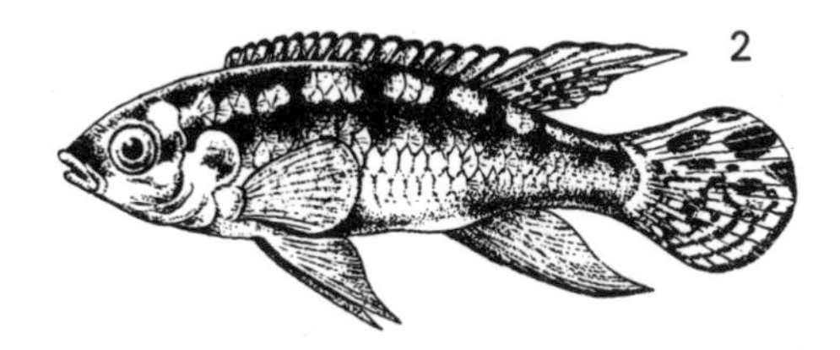
2

Jewel Cichlid, Jewelfish or **Red Cichlid** Cichlidae

Hemichromis bimaculatus GILL, 1862

After the import explosion of African endemic cichlids in the seventies, the Jewel Cichlid continues to be considered one of the most beautiful of them. However, a large number of novelties has definitely pushed this species into the background. The Jewel Cichlid is abundant in the river systems of the Niger, Nile and Congo. It was imported to Europe as early as 1907. The length attained by this fish is 15 cm. At spawning time the females are bright red; the males are larger and less colourful.

The reproduction of Jewel Cichlids is very easy indeed. The breeding pair is put into a spacious, at least 100 l tank containing water at 22—28° C. Several flat stones are placed on the bottom. Being lithophilic, these fish deposit eggs on stones that they have cleaned carefully in advance. Intensive care of eggs and progeny is characteristic of both partners. With prudent feeding, the fry grow very quickly. If the breeding fish are about to spawn again, or if the fry have surpassed 1 cm in length, the latter are transferred into a separate tank. Here they are fed with copepods, cladocerans, chopped tubifex, and even perhaps scraps of beef. In six months the young fish grow to be 7 cm long and reach sexual maturity. The Jewel Cichlid is an extremely prolific fish.

The Jewel Cichlid is a territorial, pugnacious and intolerant fish. For these reasons the single pairs are kept separately. A tank provided with stones has been found most suitable. It should be planted with larger and more resistant plant species with the roots protected by a surrounding layer of stones. The fish like to dig on the bottom, particularly at spawning time.

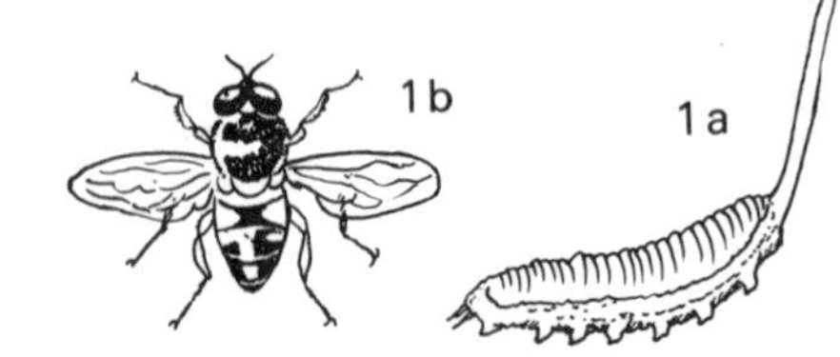

As far as food is concerned, they prefer large morsels, e.g. small fish and earthworms, insect larvae including *Eristalomyia tenax* larvae (1a, imago 1b) living in dung-water, in lavatory cesspools and other dirty waters. Characteristic of the larva is a long breathing tube at the end of its body.

A further representative of the genus, *Hemichromis fasciatus* (2), a predator habitually feeding on fish, is reared only rarely.

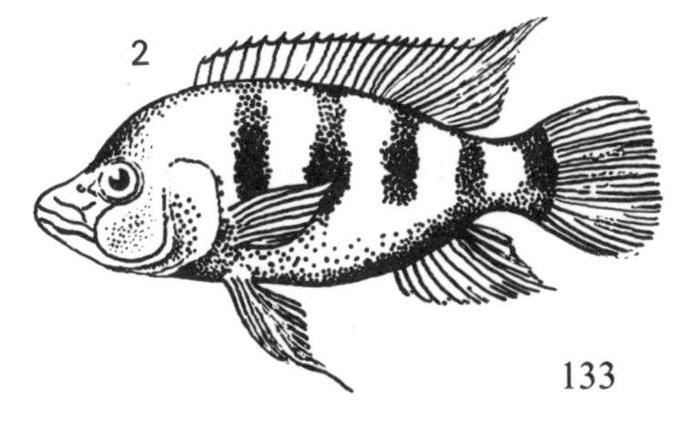

Dwarf Egyptian Mouthbreeder

Pseudocrenilabrus multicolor (HILGENDORF, 1903)

The Dwarf Egyptian Mouthbreeder is well distributed in the waters of east Africa and in the Nile basin. It was probably bred and reared prior to World War I. In the course of years it has been subjected to considerable changes in taxonomy, and in literature it has been, and still is, classified under different names: *Paratilapia multicolor, Haplochromis multicolor, Hemihaplochromis multicolor.* It attains a length of 8 cm.

The breeding group is introduced into a 50—100 l tank. Fresh tap-water with a neutral reaction pH 7.0, at 26° C, is used. Large tanks with abundant shelters can accommodate fewer males in proportion to the number of females (1 male to 3—4 females). The males dig shallow pits in the sand where spawning is to take place later on. Where no sand is available, they will put up with a firm substrate or a pipe (1). The eggs are orange-coloured and the female's throat sac is so broad that it is capable of taking in as many as 100 eggs at once. After spawning is over, the female takes cover in some hiding-place, or she can be put in a separate tank—even small 6—10 l aquariums may serve this purpose. The female must be transferred with caution, together with the pipe (2). The eggs need 10—12 days to develop. Then the fully developed, 6 mm long fry leave their mother's mouth, but for several subsequent days continue to find refuge there in case of danger or at night time. The female may be removed after several days. The fry are fed on live food; rearing is simple.

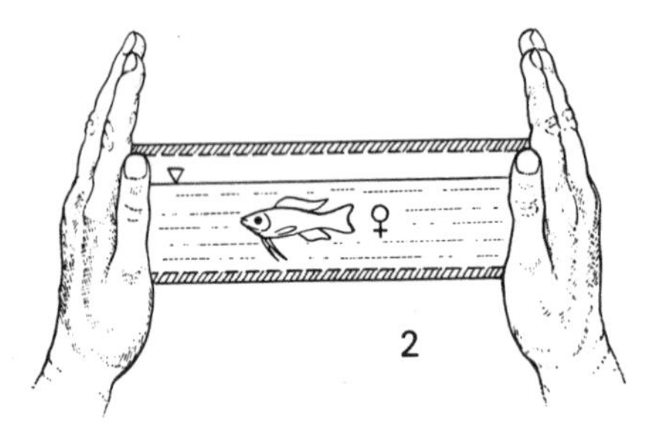

The Dwarf Egyptian Mouthbreeder is a peaceful species well suited to community aquariums. With the exception of the spawning period it is content with a temperature of 20° C. The fish are given live food.

Owing to its vast distribution range, this species forms several ecotypes differing both in colour and in size. The

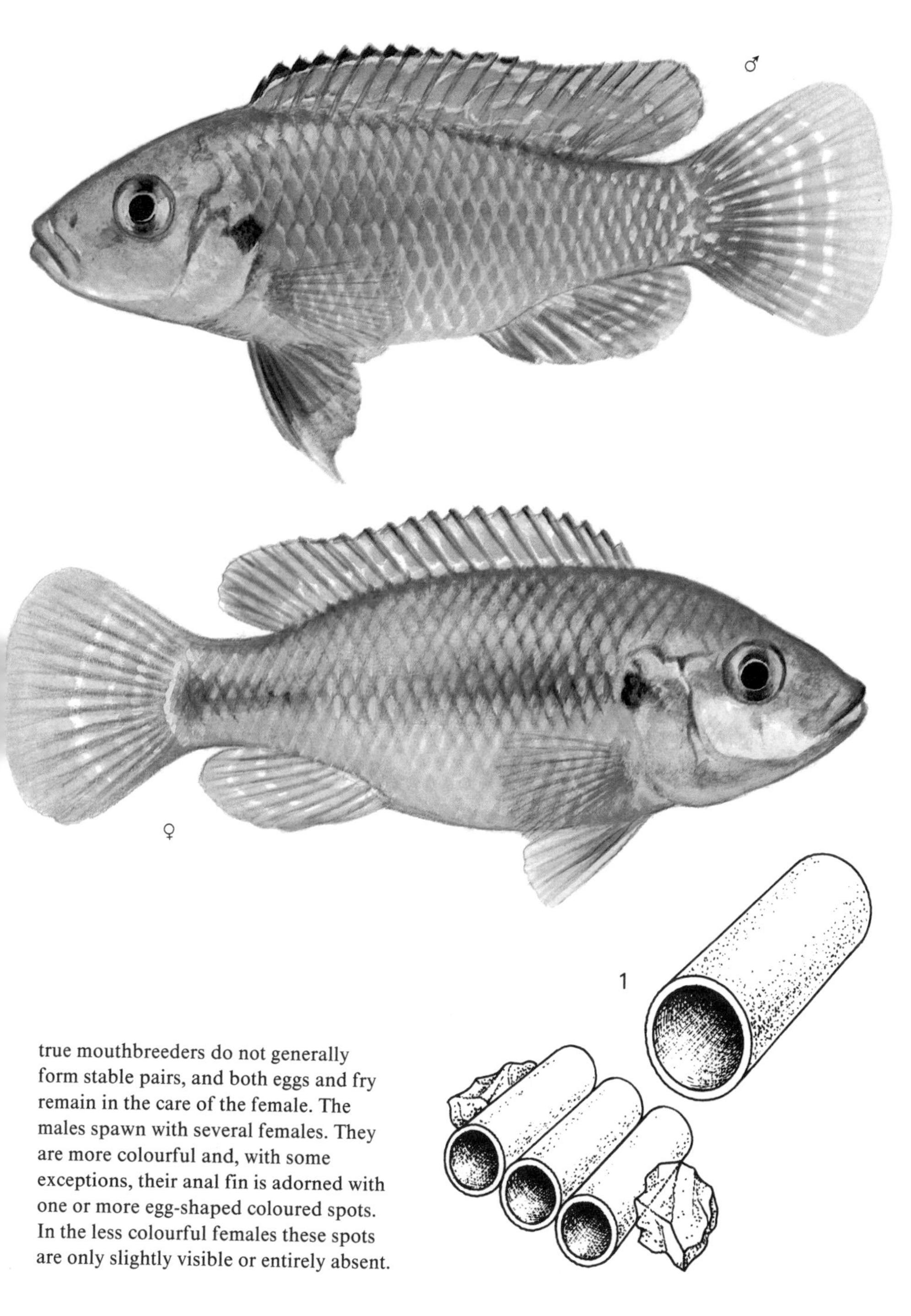

true mouthbreeders do not generally form stable pairs, and both eggs and fry remain in the care of the female. The males spawn with several females. They are more colourful and, with some exceptions, their anal fin is adorned with one or more egg-shaped coloured spots. In the less colourful females these spots are only slightly visible or entirely absent.

South African Mouthbreeder

Pseudocrenilabrus philander dispersus (TREWAVAS, 1936)

Beginning in 1911, when it was probably brought to Europe, this mouthbreeder can be found in professional literature under the scientific name *Haplochromis moffati,* and later under *Hemihaplochromis philander dispersus.* It inhabits African rivers and lakes to the south of Angola. As a result of its numerous and widely differing habitats, a number of strains of various sizes and colours have developed. The peculiar colouring of these fish gave rise to their German name Kupfermaulbrüter (Copper Mouthbreeder). In comparison with the females, the males are variegated and somewhat larger, and their anal fin is decorated with a characteristic bright red spot. The average length attained by these fish is 8 cm.

A 50 l aquarium is suitable for spawning. The breeding group consists of one male and 3—4 females. A flat stone, the future spawning site, is placed at the bottom, where draining pipes also are appropriately arranged. Half the water is replaced every fortnight. Harder water at 22—26°C suits the purpose. Spawning assumes the form of a 'merry-go-round', as is the case in other mouthbreeder species. The eggs are yellow, 2 mm across. A fully developed female can produce and take into her throat sac as many as 150 eggs. After spawning she retires into seclusion provided by the draining-pipe hollows. From here she is transferred, together with the draining pipe, into the breeding tank. The incubation time is 12 days during which the female refuses to take food and grows thin. Immediately on leaving the female's mouth, the 7 mm long fry are fully self-sustaining. For several days to come they continue to seek refuge in the female's mouth in case of danger or during night hours. Rearing is easy. In contrast to other mouthbreeder species, however, the fry grow relatively slowly.

The South African Mouthbreeder is also unlike other mouthbreeder species in that it is a relatively peace-loving fish.

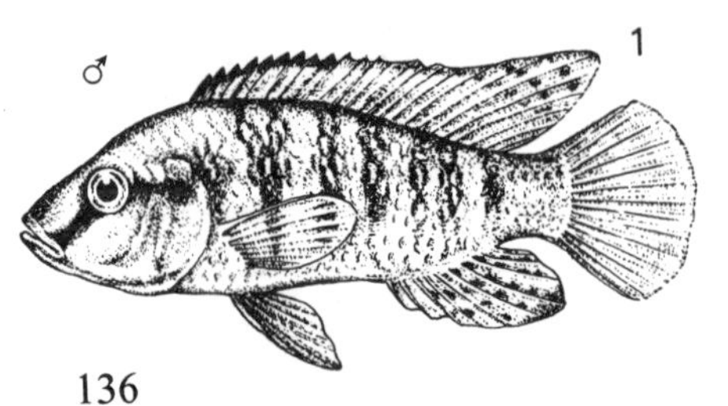

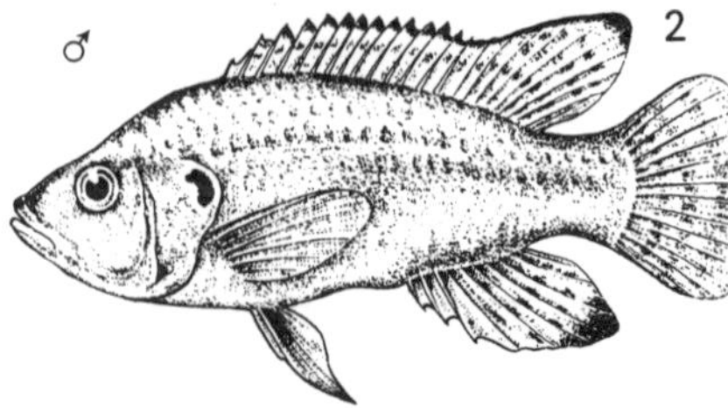

It is capable of tolerating considerable differences in the chemistry of the water, as well as short-term falls or rises in temperature (16—28° C). A temperature of 22° C seems to be best.

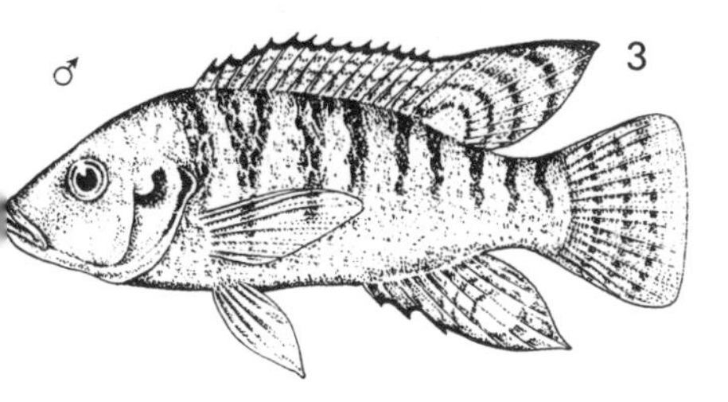

A suitable diet for these fish is composed of tubifex, coarser cladocerans, mosquito and midge larvae, small fish fry and pieces of earthworms or beef. *Pseudocrenilabrus philander dispersus* (1) resembles the species *P. multicolor* (2), from which it differs by having a red spot in the anal fin. A further similar species is the *Haplochromis pectoralis* (3). The differences in the design of these otherwise very similar species are shown in the line drawing.

Julie, Banded or **Yellow Julie**
Julidochromis ornatus BOULENGER, 1898

Lake Tanganyika is fed by an extensive water system. In the north a number of torrents rush down into the lake, and a river comes flowing from Lake Kivu. The fauna and flora of Lake Tanganyika are remarkably rich to a depth of 100 m. The temperature of the surface water ranges between 27 and 29° C. The water is hard, with pH values 8.5—9.2.

The 8 cm long Julie loves to hide among rocks, so the tanks should be furnished appropriately. Hollow bricks, broken flowerpots, coconut shells and suitably arranged rocks will serve this purpose. An aquarium holding 50 l will suffice for one pair. Well oxidized, fresh water at 26—27° C, with a pH of 7.0 or more, relatively hard and devoid of nitrites, is necessary for successful breeding. Adult fish are territorial and form stable pairs. There is no apparent sexual dimorphism. Males, as a rule, are more aggressive. In females, a peculiar behaviour suggestive of subordination has been observed; they ward off the male's attack by wriggling and exposing their ventral parts. The fish spawn in hollows. The female, with her belly upturned, lays greenish eggs on the ceiling of any cavity and the male assumes a similar position in order to fertilize them. The spawning site and the eggs are protected chiefly by the male. The number of eggs ranges from 20 to 30; the pair spawns every 3—4 weeks. Breeding productivity is raised by removing the eggs to separate tanks. The 4 mm long fry emerge in 2—3 days, and learn to swim freely by the eighth day. They are fed on brine shrimps and later on small copepods. The fish grow relatively slowly.

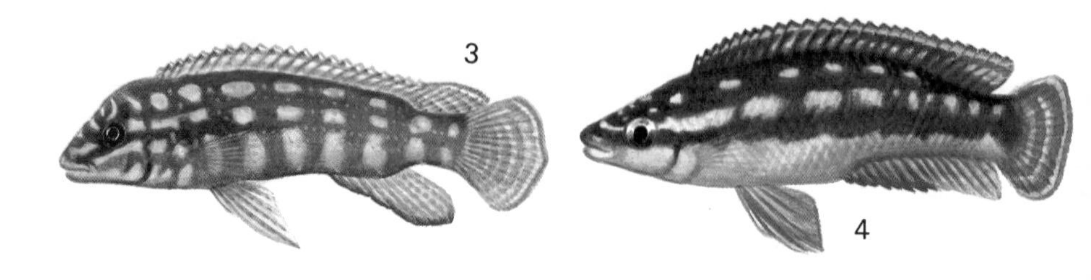

The fish are kept separately. In large aquariums of a rocky character, the following related species with a similar behaviour may be kept together: *Julidochromis ornatus* (1) (8 cm), *J. regani* (2) (10 cm), *J. dickfeldi* (10 cm), *J. marlieri* (3) (10 cm) and *J. transcriptus* (4) (10 cm).

Because of the uniqueness of Lake Tanganyika's ichthyofauna and also because the lake itself represents a large natural laboratory, it was decided to keep fishing for commercial purposes within bounds. The use of strong poisons and of dynamite were outlawed. Thus export is controlled by law, and it has become mostly a matter for the aquarists themselves to preserve fish of the genus *Julidochromis* in captivity for the future.

Lyretail Lamprologus

Lamprologus brichardi POLL, 1974

Cichlidae

This attractive fish comes from Lake Tanganyika where it lives in rocky localities down to a depth of 10 cm. The largest fish of this species caught there measured 8.9 cm. This fish was described for the first time in 1952 as *Lamprologus savoryi elongatus*. However, this scientific designation was a compound of the names of two species, *Lamprologus elongatus* and *Lamprologus savoryi*. In order to avert a possible confusion in nomenclature, the Belgian ichthyologist Professor Poll undertook a revision in 1974 and listed this fish as a separate species, *Lamprologus brichardi*.

The Lyretail Lamprologus is a territorial fish living in stable pairs. Within the bounds of its territory, it is capable of killing superfluous fish of its own species, as well as substantially larger, predatory fish endangering its young. To do this, the fish make good use of their jaws, which are well endowed with sharp teeth. There is no apparent sexual dimorphism; only older males sometimes bear a small fatty protuberance on their head.

For rearing it is advisable to choose tanks 100 l in volume. A mechanical filter with packing partly consisting of limestone to stabilize the pH values is placed on the tank bottom. The bottom should further be furnished with base-less flowerpots or flat stones arranged so as to form sufficiently spacious hollows. A single pair is always set up. The water should be 26° C, pH 7.0, 15° dGH and 4° dCH. The female produces about 200 dark red eggs, 1 mm across, sticking them onto the ceiling of the hollows. The fry emerge on the third day and start swimming freely after a further nine days. Intensive care of the fry of as many as three generations at a time is shared by both parents, who exhibit no cannibalistic tendencies.

3

An ideal environment for the Lyretail Lamprologus (1) is a rocky bottom abounding in caves and hollows. Stones must be arranged around the plants to prevent their excavation. The water temperature should

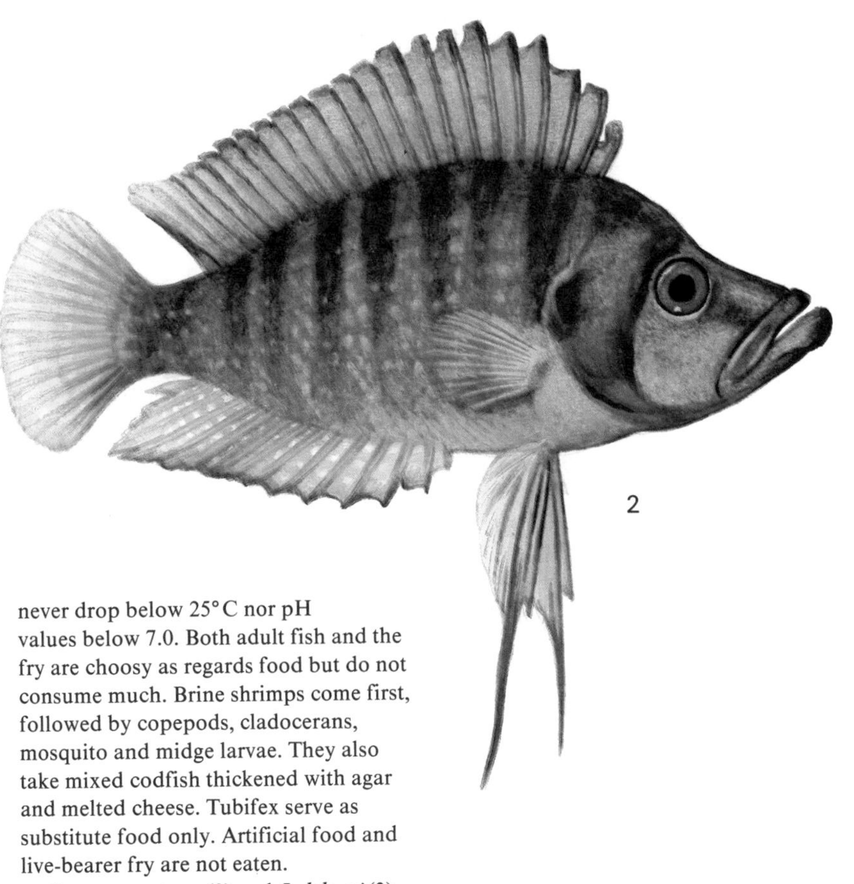

never drop below 25° C nor pH values below 7.0. Both adult fish and the fry are choosy as regards food but do not consume much. Brine shrimps come first, followed by copepods, cladocerans, mosquito and midge larvae. They also take mixed codfish thickened with agar and melted cheese. Tubifex serve as substitute food only. Artificial food and live-bearer fry are not eaten.

L. compressiceps (2) and *L. leleupi* (3) illustrate the diversification of this species.

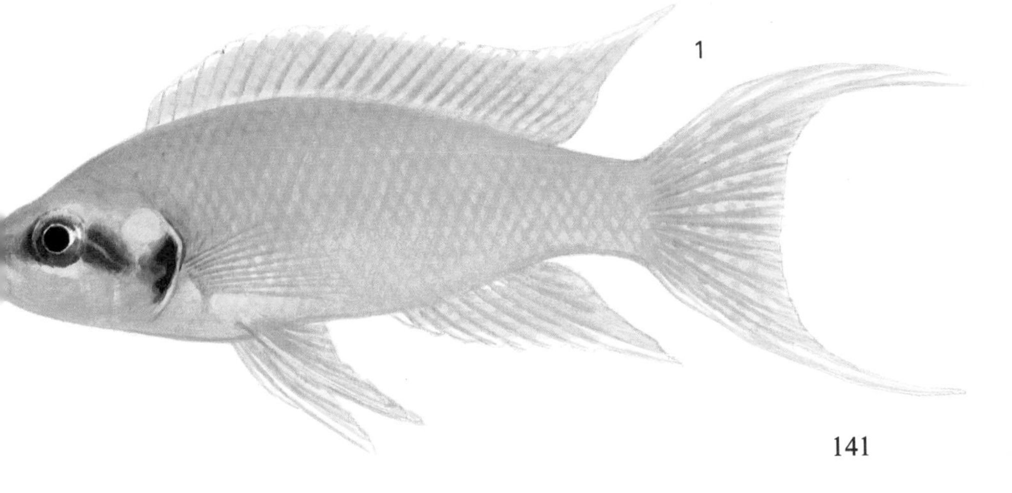

Blunt-headed Cichlid

Tropheus moorei BOULENGER, 1898

Bolder screes, towering rock walls with many cracks, a flickering play of light and shade—this is the scenery of the littoral zone of Lake Tanganyika. The large group of endemic mouthbreeders is represented here by the species of Blunt-headed Cichlids. They grow to a length of 10—12 cm.

The primary precondition for successful breeding is a roomy aquarium with a capacity of 200 l or more. The water must be pure, free of nitrites, rather hard, with an alkaline reaction (pH 7.5—8.0) and a temperature of 26—28°C. Draining pipes are placed at the bottom. The breeding group consists of one male and 3—4 females. In this species there is no discernible sexual dimorphism. During the act of spawning, the female lays 7—17 eggs, 7 mm in diameter; these she picks up in her mouth. After spawning is over, she retires to a secluded place. She may be transferred, together with the draining pipe, into a separate tank where she hides. According to various authorities, the incubation period in the female's mouth is 30—46 days. At this time the female takes food, an exceptional phenomenon in mouthbreeders. The fry, with a characteristic dark striped juvenile colouring, leave the female's mouth when 12—14 mm long, and are quite capable of looking after themselves. Between the ages of five and eight months they lose their juvenile colouring, and in a year's time they attain sexual maturity. Their manner of spawning is remarkable: the fish clean stones and dig little holes for which they will have no use at all as they spawn in open water where the females pick up the eggs in their mouths. In some authors' opinion this digging phenomenon represents an unfinished evolutionary process involving the residual behaviour of ancestors spawning on a firm substrate.

These fish thrive in large, rocky, diversified aquariums. The Blunt-headed Cichlid (1) is a territorial, aggressive and extremely voracious fish. Besides plant food it eats little pieces of meat, mosquito larvae, cladocerans and tubifex, nor will it refuse granulated or flake food. In the lake it forms local ecotypes in delimited and segregated populations. These differ primarily in colouring, from black, bluish

black, olive green to variously striped, orange, yellowish red, yellow (2), rainbow-hued, etc.

The species *Tropheus duboisi* (3) inhabits the northwestern and eastern parts of the lake. The occurrence of local ecotypes and closely related species illustrates the evolution taking place in the African inland lakes.

Burton's Nigerian Mouthbreeder Cichlidae
Haplochromis burtoni (GÜNTHER, 1893)

Lakes and rivers situated in the vast stretches of eastern and central Africa are inhabited by 12 cm long, Burton's Nigerian Mouthbreeders. The variegated males lure the less conspicuous females into their territory, displaying their anal fin adorned with 5—7 egg-like orange spots rimmed with black. In their effort to take the dummy eggs into their mouth, the females suck in the milt instead. Subsequently they deposit eggs on a firm substrate and collect them without delay into their throat sac where they are fertilized. This is repeated several times, while the spawning pair goes on spinning round each other sometimes for as long as $1^1/_2$ hours. Having deposited all the eggs the female leaves the spawning site and seeks a hiding place. Now she can be removed carefully into another tank. The incubation time is 15—20 days at a temperature of 25—27°C. The eggs develop without any difficulties in aged tapwater of the following values: pH 7.0, 10° dGH and 2° dCH; however, small deviations from these values do not affect the development of eggs. Entirely self-sustaining young fish leave their mother's mouth, to which they continue for several days to take recourse in danger or in the night. Rearing in captivity is easy; the fry feed on brine shrimps, small copepods, chopped tubifex, and, as the fish grow, they are gradually given bigger morsels. The young fish consume a large amount of food and grow quickly.

Burton's Nigerian Mouthbreeders, particularly the males, are intolerant and pugnacious fish. Their preference is an aquarium of a capacity for 200 l where only one male and three to four females are kept. The bottom should abound in hiding places. In large tanks, Burton's Nigerian Mouthbreeder may be kept together with fish of the same size possessing the same features. The species *H. desfontainesi* is very similar though having more spots on the anal fin.

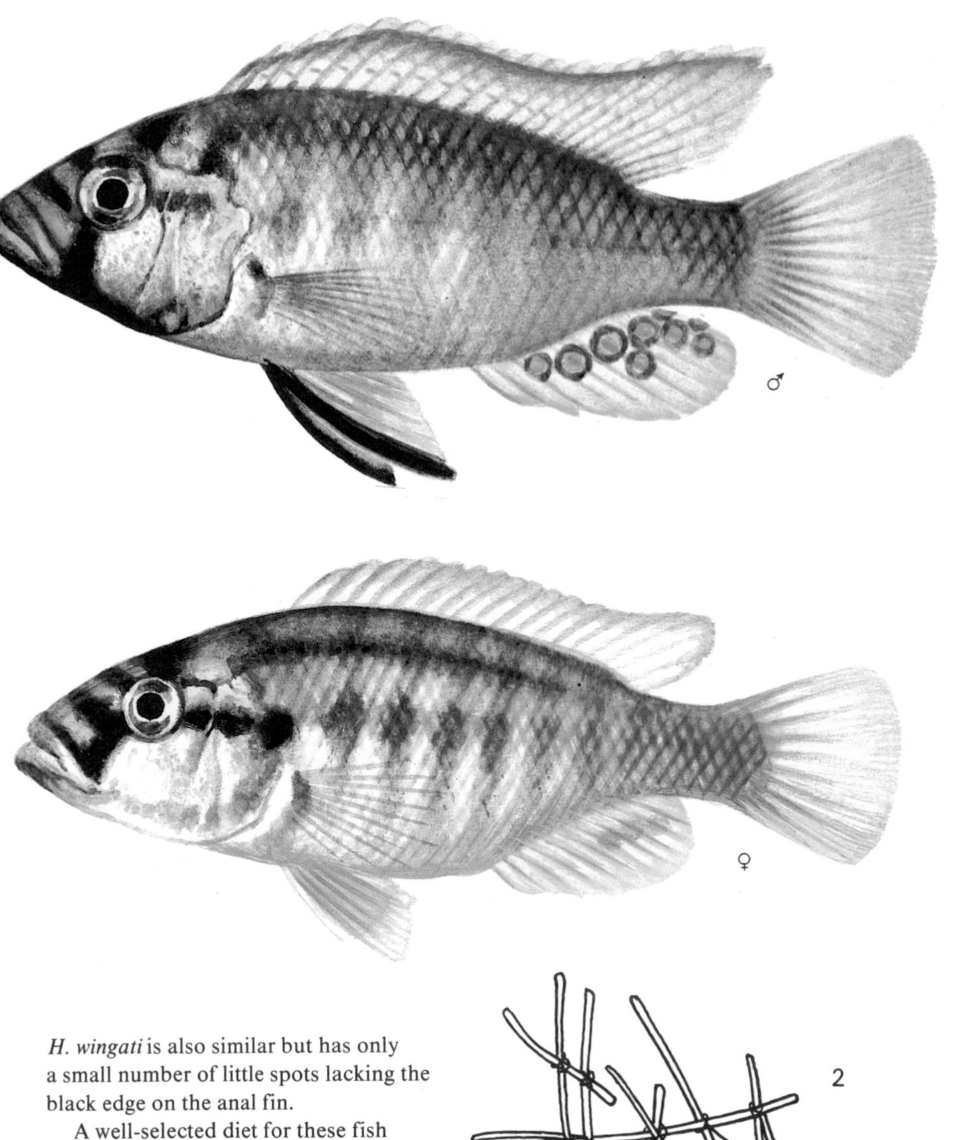

H. wingati is also similar but has only a small number of little spots lacking the black edge on the anal fin.

A well-selected diet for these fish includes tubifex, earthworms, insect larvae, pieces of beef and small fish.

In recent years the African fish populations have been jeopardized by barbarous hunting with the aid of cyanides and plant poisons. These have replaced the former, primitive indigenous traps (1, 2).

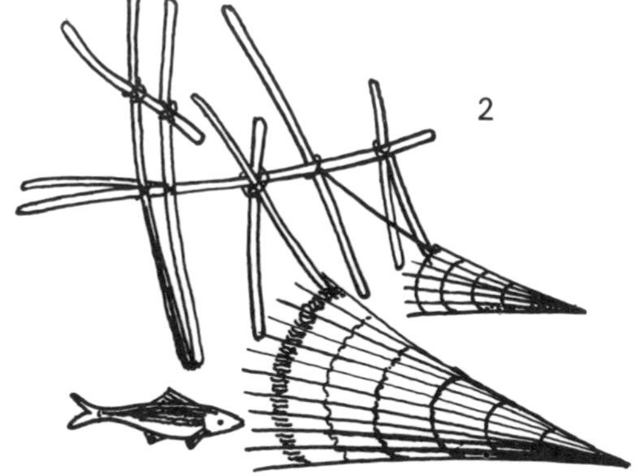

The African upland plain, scarred with a huge ravine called the Great Rift Valley, provides a fantastic natural scenery dominated by vast lakes. One of these is Lake Malawi, the home of the mouthbreeder *Haplochromis livingstonii* (1) which grows to a length of 20 cm.

The breeding aquarium should hold no less than 200 l. The ideal breeding group consists of one male and two or three females. The young fish (2) and females are yellowish white with irregular brown spots all over the body. The dominating male is dark brown with a bluish hue, especially around the head. The males possess prominent dorsal and anal fins tapering to a thread-like extension. In the wild they let only spawn-ripe females willing to mate enter their territory. Their behaviour to other members of their own species as well as to other fish is aggressive. Thus in smaller aquariums they quite frequently kill not only weaker males but also adult females. This can be avoided by inserting an upright partition of transparent glass into the tank leaving a gap of about 10 mm under it at the bottom (3). The male remains in one compartment, the female in the other. Later, spawning takes place at the gap. As soon as the female has finished spawning, the partition is dropped right to the bottom to prevent the free-swimming fry from getting through to the male. Usually there are about 50 yellowish white, pear-shaped eggs, 3 × 4 mm in size. The incubation time within the female's mouth is 25 days. Then the fry leave their mother's mouth but continue to return to it for several days. The fry are 1 cm long, entirely self-sufficient and colourful.

The assets of these fish come to the fore only in large aquariums containing 500 l or more. In polyculture *H. livingstonii* is reared together with African lake cichlids of the same size, e.g. with the species *H. venustus* and *H. polystigma*. The fish thrive in pure, harder and slightly alkaline water at 24—26° C.

The fish are fed on small fish, earthworms or pieces of beef, chicken or fish. Zooplankton and tubifex are to be considered as emergency food only. Young fish develop well on granulated or flake food.

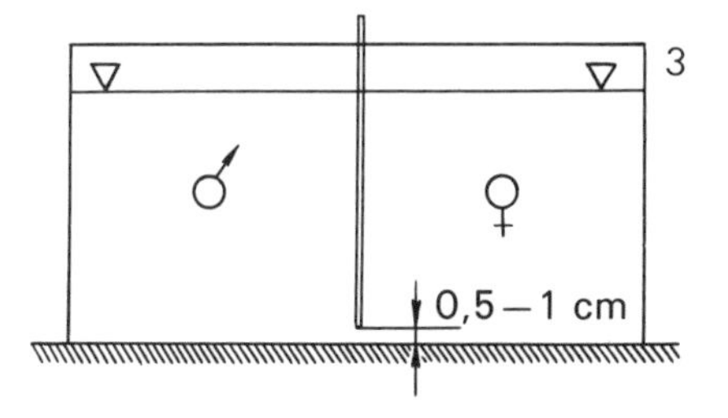

Fuelleborn's Cichlid

Labeotropheus fuelleborni AHL, 1927

African endemic cichlids include fish of varied colouring (1, 2) and also a great number of species that are strikingly similar (specific swarms). Many species are narrowly confined to their biotopes. The Fuelleborn's Cichlid grows to be 12 cm long. The females are less highly coloured than males. Just like all other mouthbreeders they shelter the eggs in their mouth. In this species, the incubation time is 19—20 days. During the long development of the eggs the females do not take any food, live in privation and become thin, so breeders have tried to discover a method of rearing eggs outside the mother's mouth. As soon as the female has finished spawning (which becomes apparent from the characteristic sac that forms in the lower part of her mouth) she is carefully picked up, considerately but firmly placed in a wet handkerchief, dipped into a prepared small container filled with water of the same values, and turned upside down. A pointed, blunt instrument is used to hold her mouth open for as long as she needs to spit out all her eggs. The expulsion of eggs or embryos (3) may be carried out at any time during the incubation period. The eggs and the embryos are put into clean Erlenmayer's flasks that are sufficiently aerated to cause the heavy eggs at the bottom to roll about slightly. The water in the flasks must be absolutely pure, at a temperature of 25—28° C, with a pH of 7.2—7.5 and 10—15° dGH. The flasks are deposited in a dimly lit place and the eggs are treated with a weak solution of methylene blue. This artificial incubation method decreases the number of fry lost, and the females take food immediately after the withdrawal of the eggs; so they need not suffer privation and can spawn more frequently.

These mouthbreeders are kept only in the largest possible aquariums with a rocky substrate. Although the fish are hardy and undemanding, water with a pH lower than 7.0 and a higher nitrite content may do them harm. On the other hand, the addition of kitchen salt to the water (one spoonful per 10 l of water) is to their benefit. Because of the voracity of these fish it is necessary to attend to the

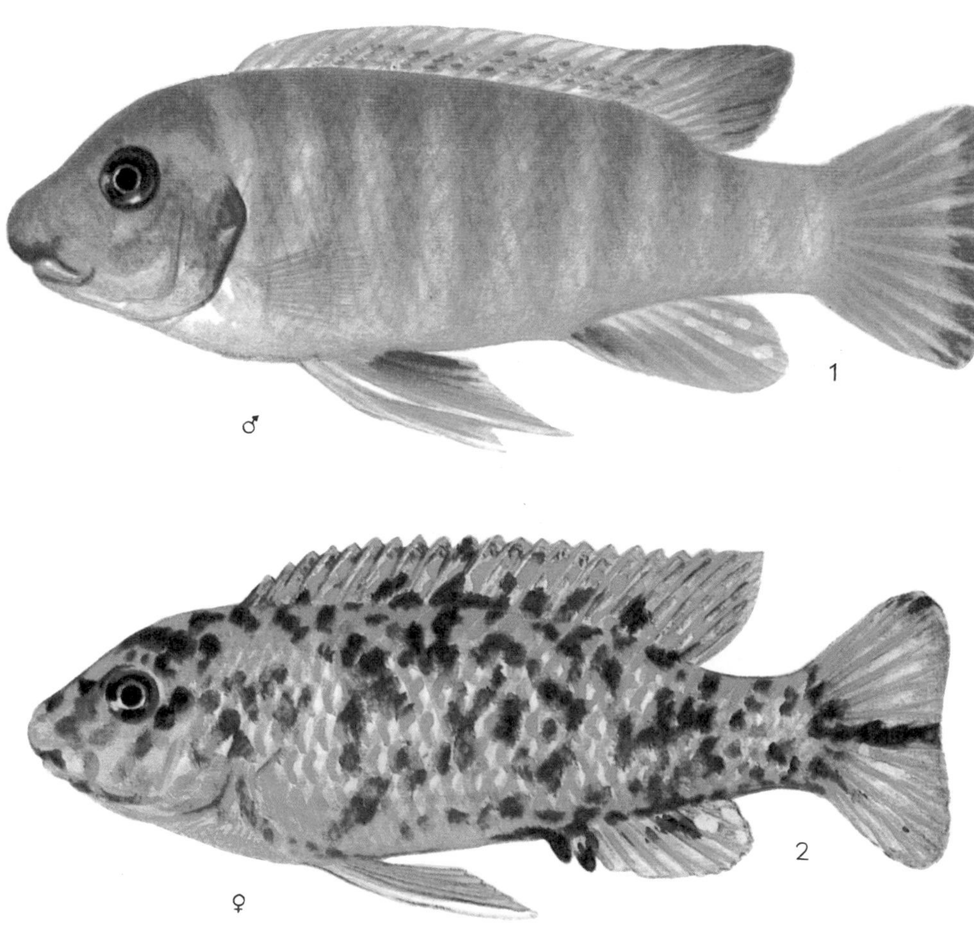

tank more frequently and to replace half of the water once a fortnight. Limestone which increases both water hardness and the pH may be included in the filtration substrate.

The fish are fed on beef, chicken or fish chopped in small pieces, earthworms, larvae and nymphs of water insects, cladocerans, and occasionally also with scalded spinach or lettuce leaves.

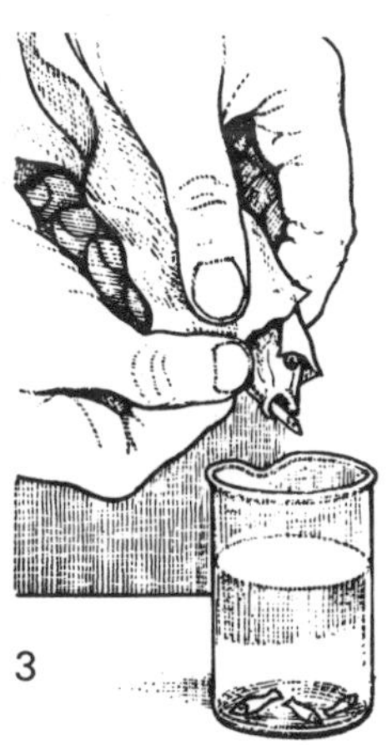

Red-top Cichlid
Labeotropheus trewavasae FRYER, 1956

The rocky, waterside zones of Lake Malawi are the home of an endemic mouthbreeder, the Red-top Cichlid (1). Morphometric studies have revealed its close relationship to the species *L. fuelleborni.* Both the species share common habitats, while the *L. trewavasae* occurs more rarely. This mouthbreeder grows to a length of approximately 10 cm. Males are blue, with 8—12 dark transverse bands along the flanks and a rusty-coloured dorsal fin. Females are somewhat smaller, greyish or yellowish brown, spotted with black and orange. The Red-top Cichlid is confined to a stony bottom and does not travel over areas of a different character (sandy, muddy); this leads to an isolation of individual populations. Consequently, because of the great variability of the species, numerous colour varieties (2) have come into existence. The waters of Lake Malawi are alkaline (pH 7.6—8.5), clear, devoid of organic substances and rich in carbonates (3.5° dCH). The extreme composition of the water is one of the probable reasons for the profusion of endemics in the lake.

Large aquariums containing water at 26° C, with draining pipes laid at the bottom (3) in such a way as to allow the cavities to be controlled by sight, are recommended for rearing purposes. The development of eggs in the female's mouth lasts 20 days. The young are fully developed by then and do not find it difficult to eat small copepods and brine shrimps. As the young fish are growing, their diet is gradually enriched with plant food.

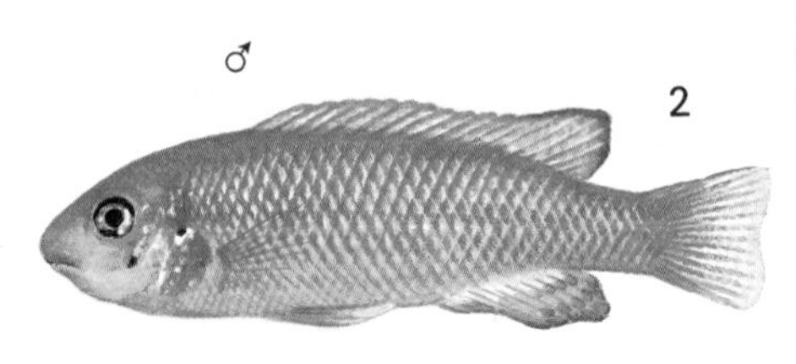

The fish prefer large aquariums able to hold 300 l or more and containing broken stones. The Malawi-Lake cichlids, bound to a stony substrate, are often called *Mbuna.* This is a part of the native name 'mbuna kumwa', i.e. fish striking against rocks. The name stems from the movement of the fish scraping off algae growths from rock walls.

In aquariums the Red-top Cichlid feeds on live and dry food, small pieces of meat and fresh dead fish. This diet is regularly supplemented with plant food.

Nyasa Golden Cichlid

Cichlidae

Melanochromis auratus (BOULENGER, 1897)

In Latin the word *auratus* means gilded, and this is in fact a true description of these endemic mouthbreeders, which inhabit the rocky areas of Lake Malawi. Their shining, yellow colouring is marked with black stripes. Adult males reach a length of 11 cm, and the lower part of their body is velvet-black. It seems that the first imports to Europe were in 1958.

The Nyasa Golden Cichlid is willing to reproduce in captivity, but it must be given enough space. The recommended volume of aquariums is no less than 200 l, and there should be plenty of hiding places. In rational breeding, suitably arranged draining pipes are used. Water must be crystalline pure, free of nitrates, hard, slightly alkaline and have a temperature of 26° C. Males of this species are strictly territorial and vigorously defend their spawning places. In colouring they resemble the species *Julidochromis ornatus,* which, however, does not belong to the mouthbreeders. In the females the end of spawning is marked by the swollen throat sac in the lower part of their mouth. Each of them is then carefully transferred, together with the draining pipe of course, into a separate, smaller-sized tank. Any inconsiderate handling might provoke the female into swallowing the eggs. The incubation of eggs in the female's mouth takes 22—26 days. After this, entirely self-sustaining and coloured young fry, 1 cm in length, leave their mother's mouth. As a rule, the number of young fish is not great, and their rearing is easy because of their size.

As has already been pointed out, the fish thrive in large aquariums; in smaller ones they are apt to kill each other. In each tank there should never be more than one male and several females. The presence of other appropriately sized African mouthbreeder species, which thwarts the aggressiveness of these fish, is consequently desirable.

The diet consists of beef or dead sea-fish, small earthworms, coarser cladocerans or water-insect larvae. Ephemera nymphs (1) are offered only as an occasional delicacy; however, at the time of the ephemera, a large number of imagos (2) may be obtained with the aid of a light source. Dried ephemera imagos are a suitable nourishment for all piscine species. The Nyasa Golden Cichlid does not spurn high-grade granulated or flake food.

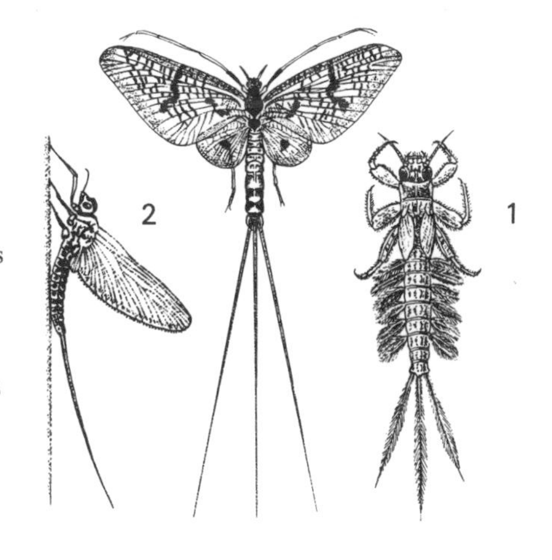

In the distant past, geological catastrophies in eras of intense tectonic or volcanic activity gave rise to deep and now ancient lakes concentrated into lake areas. These include also tropical lakes with high surface temperatures showing negligible seasonal differences. The water layers of deep lakes mix only partially and therefore the depths, where the environment is very extreme and toxic, are usually lifeless. To put it more simply: the lake can be divided into two zones (1): A) the littoral (coastal) zone and B) the pelagic zone (open waters above the depths). The littoral zone is composed of various localities (sandy, muddy, rocky) accommodating various, never mixing communities. It is especially here that algae, plankton, plants and fish are concentrated. On the other hand, the pelagic zone is affected by the intensity of solar radiation in relation to depth, and life may be found primarily in the upper layers of water.

In the littoral zone of Lake Malawi in Africa, the endemic mouthbreeder *Melanochromis brevis* has its home in rocky areas. It was not brought to Europe before the late sixties. It grows to a length of 12 cm. Breeding and rearing are identical to those of the species *M. auratus*. The incubation of eggs in the female's mouth lasts 17 days. The entirely self-sufficient fry, 8 mm in length, are brown and shy right from the start. Rearing is simple.

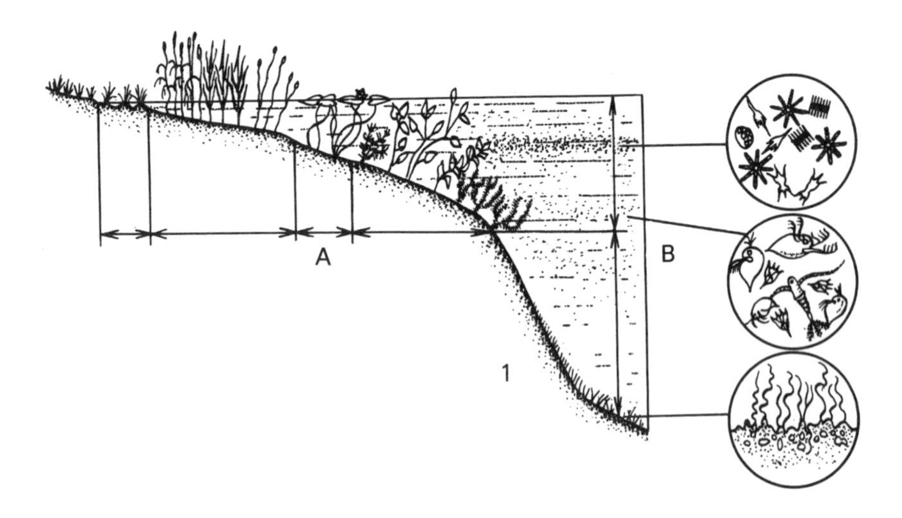

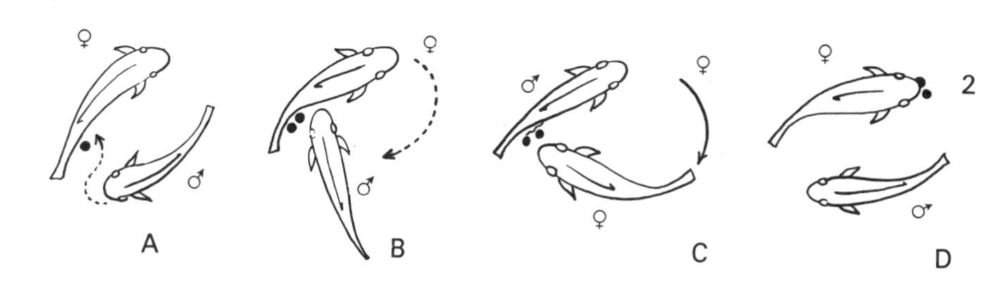

A number of ichthyologists and experts in pisciculture, who were given the opportunity not only to visit African lakes but also to dive in them with a camera, could see for themselves the world of littoral rock barriers. In arranging the tanks for these mouthbreeders, endeavours should be made to simulate the rocky character of the natural substrate in miniature. In such aquariums the *M. brevis* may live in company with various species of the African mouthbreeders in the same way as it does in the clear waters of Lake Malawi. Its diet is the same as that of the Nyasa Golden Cichlid. Fig. 2 shows the mouthbreeders' 'spawning merry-go-round'.

Nyasa Blue Cichlid
Pseudotropheus zebra (BOULENGER, 1899)

The waters along the rocky shores of Lake Malawi are the home of the superb Nyasa Blue Cichlid, a 12 cm long mouthbreeder of variable colour (1—4). European aquarists became acquainted with this species as late as 1964, at the beginning of the explosive import of African endemic and lake cichlids.

The Nyasa Blue Cichlid is an explicitly territorial and aggressive fish. This is why large aquariums of a capacity of at least 200 l are recommended for breeding. Several draining pipes with a large enough opening are placed at the bottom, in a position facilitating the checking of the hollows by sight. Then the breeding group is introduced into the tank in the ratio of one male to 2—3 females. The water must be free of protein substances, transparently pure, rich in oxygen, slightly alkaline and hard. The water temperature should range from 25 to 28° C. On the males' anal fin there are bright yellow spots rimmed with black. During the 'spawning merry-go-round' the female lays 20—35 eggs, 4 mm in diameter. After spawning, with her mouth full of eggs, she seeks shelter in the draining-pipe hollow. The female is put into a separate aquarium, together with the pipe. In 21 days the 1 cm long and self-sufficient fry leave their mother's mouth. The breeding method described above is practised also by other species of African mouthbreeders.

Ornamental aquariums holding 500—1,000 l, with a substrate abounding in various stone structures, give an impression of the littoral zone of African lakes. In such tanks several species of

African cichlids may join to form communities, yet there must never be more than one male of each species. A large community consisting of several species somewhat mitigates the inborn aggressiveness of the fish. It lessens its intensity because it is then not directed towards one object.

The fish are given coarser morsels of food: beef, chicken or fish, earthworms, insect larvae, etc. This diet is complemented with good flake food containing a plant component or with scalded spinach and lettuce leaves.

Madagascar Rainbow

Atherinidae

Bedotia geayi PELLEGRIN, 1907

The Madagascar Rainbow is one of the few species of the family Atherinidae inhabiting fresh waters. The marine origin of these fish is evident from their split dorsal fin and their demand for hard water rich in minerals. The Madagscar Rainbow was brought to Europe from Madagascar in 1953. The fish attain a length of 12 cm; the males are larger and more colourful. They are most willing to spawn in a shoal at 25—28° C. Single spawning periods may take up several days and are followed by short pauses; then the fish start spawning again. In most cases spawning takes place among plants, but it also occurs in free water. The pale yellow eggs, 1.4 mm across, have a bundle of filaments with which they are attached to the substrate. The incubation of eggs depends on water temperature and takes 6—8 days. After hatching, the fry swim in free water in a slanting position, head upwards, filling their gas bladder. After 24 hours they start actively hunting for food. The eggs develop in water with hardness values ranging between 8 and 30° dGH, up to 3° dCH and with pH values of 7.0—7.5. Large populations of young fish may be obtained by transferring the breeding fish into a different tank each week or by regularly withdrawing the plants covered in eggs and concentrating them in a separate aquarium. It is easy to rear the young fish on brine shrimps and also, where necessary, on good artificial fry food.

The sight of a shoal of fully grown, healthy fish is so impressive that it makes the presence of other fish superfluous. They require roomy aquariums where free water alternates with plant thickets. A dark background will enhance the pastel colours of these fish.

They eat all kinds of food, and insects that fall onto the surface and tiny fish are taken as delicacies.

Dwarf Australian Rainbow, Dwarf Rainbowfish or Black-lined Rainbowfish

Melanotaeniidae

Melanotaenia maccullochi (OGILBY, 1915)

Australia, a remarkable continent surrounded by vast seas and oceans, has become the home of an impressive animal and plant community. The fish travelled up inland waters from the sea. For example, numerous species of the family Atherinidae populated the flats of warm seas. In time, some of them moved instead to brackish and fresh water.

Another example of an originally sea fish is the Dwarf Australian Rainbow inhabiting the waters of northern Australia near the seaside town of Cairns. This 7 cm long school fish loves light and sun. The split dorsal fin is witness to its marine origin. It has been known to European aquarists since 1934. Rather hard water with a neutral to slightly alkaline reaction, at 23—25° C, is suitable for spawning. The expelled eggs are attached to plants by short filaments. Incubation lasts 7—10 days, and the dark larvae are suspended on the tank walls or on plants. In a few days the fry start swimming freely and move ceaselessly keeping close to the surface. Rearing the fry on brine shrimps is not difficult. A large number of young fish may be obtained by regularly transferring plant clusters into a separate tank. Of course, this method may be applied only in breeding tanks where plants are not set in the ground permanently.

2

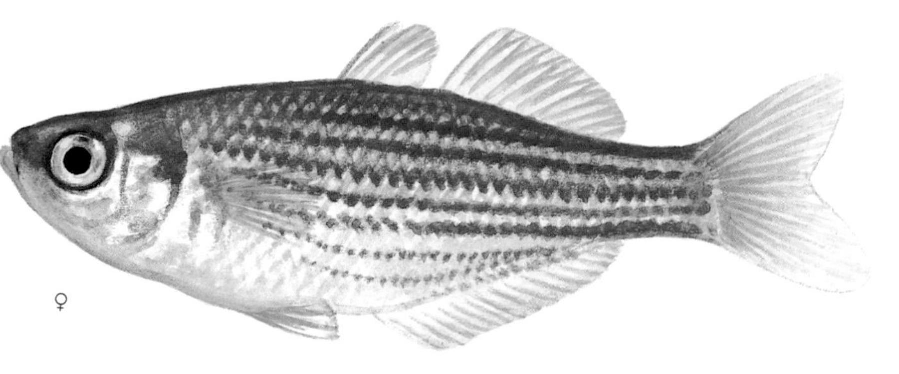

The Dwarf Australian Rainbow (1) is always reared with other specimens. Since motion is one of the substantial characteristics of the fish, they should be given sufficient space for swimming. Their diet is varied and consists of both live and artificial foods. The addition of kitchen or sea salt to the water enhances the well-being of the fish.

The following related Australian species are reared occasionally: *M. fluviatilis* (2), *M. nigrans*, *M. sexlineata*, *M. splendida*. The same applies to species from New Guinea: *M. maculata*, *Chilatherina lorentzi*, *Ch. axelrodi* and *Glossolepis incisus*.

Celebes Rainbowfish Atherinidae

Telmatherina ladigesi AHL, 1936

The 8 cm long, glittering, bluish green Celebes Rainbowfish is a typical example of a secondarily freshwater fish whose ancestors developed in the sea. It inhabits stony mountain streams that wind through the tropical vegetation of the Celebes Island. Here it was also caught and taken to Europe in 1935. Its origin suggests that, in captivity, it must be supplied with a quite specific environment: fresh, translucent, hard water. The fish successfully reproduce at a temperature of 24—26°C, with pH 8.5, 11°dGH and 2°dCH. The filtration of water over crushed limestone and the addition of kitchen salt (1 spoonful/10 l of water) help to maintain an appropriate environment. Males are characterized by a butterfly-like elongation of the rays of the second dorsal fin and of the anal fin (1). For spawning, a series of well-lit tanks, about 50 l in volume, is prepared. A small group of fish (in the ratio of three females to one male) is transferred every tenth day into the next tank in the series. Yellowish eggs are deposited in dense tangles of aquatic plants. Spawning continues unceasingly, with small pauses. The development of eggs takes ten days, and the free-swimming, highly mobile fry may be found close to the surface. The fry are regularly caught and concentrated in a separate larger tank, and the whole spawning cycle making use of the tank series starts again. The ideal fry food is brine-shrimp nauplii which stay alive for a long time in water containing salt. Even if well fed, the fry grow very slowly.

Spacious aquariums exposed to morning sunshine, with a dark bottom covering and sparse groups of plants, enhance the glittering and delicate beauty of this species. The fish are always reared in bigger shoals. The presence of other

piscine species produces a disturbing effect. In this respect a species of the same family from the waters of northern and eastern Queensland in Australia, *Pseudomugil signifer* (2), presents an exception. It is smaller, attaining no more than 4.5 cm in length, and prefers to live in schools.

Both these fish species readily consume small live food moving about in free water. Also fruit flies and other small insects are nimbly caught at the surface. The fish also take flakes of high-grade artificial food.

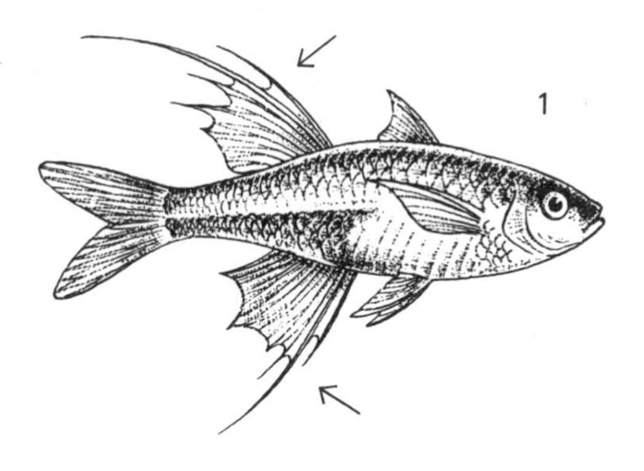

Badis or **Dwarf Chameleon Fish** Badidae
Badis badis (HAMILTON–BUCHANAN, 1822)

The fish was imported in 1905 from India to the German breeding establishments of Matte and Thum. In a short time it was reproduced there and distributed all over Germany. Soon it made its appearance also in other European countries. It inhabits stagnant waters and grows to be 8 cm long (males).

A 20 l aquarium containing a plant thicket and half of a small flowerpot or a pebble of about 10—15 cm across will suffice for breeding purposes. The light should be subdued. The fish are set up in pairs. The aquarium is filled with water taken from the tank of adult fish and having the following values: temperature 26° C, pH 6.5, 7° dGH, 1° dCH. Spawning takes place in or on the flowerpot or on concealed stones and the surrounding plants. Some males prepare the spawning site in the sand by making shallow pits. Males are territorial and aggressive to each other. The male glistens with a metallic sheen showing a whole range of rapid colour changes. His fins are more powerfully built; older males are slightly arched and their ventral region is concave. Females are smaller; their colours are duller and their ventral region is markedly convex. The male takes care of both eggs and fry, but his presence is not necessary. The female is removed after spawning. The eggs are transparent, sticky, and 0.8 mm in diameter. The larvae emerge in 48 hours. After seven days they may be given their first food: brine shrimps. The fry, being incapable of ready movement, remain at the bottom. With the exception of black dots on the head and in the caudal region, they are transparent and hence easily overlooked. Although the Badis is currently described as not being too prolific, 200 and more fish may be reared from a single spawning.

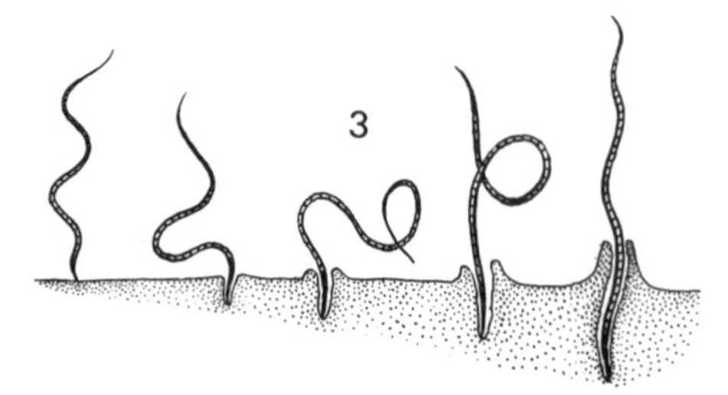

The Badis (1) is a representative of the ancient family Badidae which seems to be dying out. The fish live under cover, finding the company of other fish species disagreeable. For this reason they are kept separately in dimly illuminated tanks, rich in hiding places and plant growths.

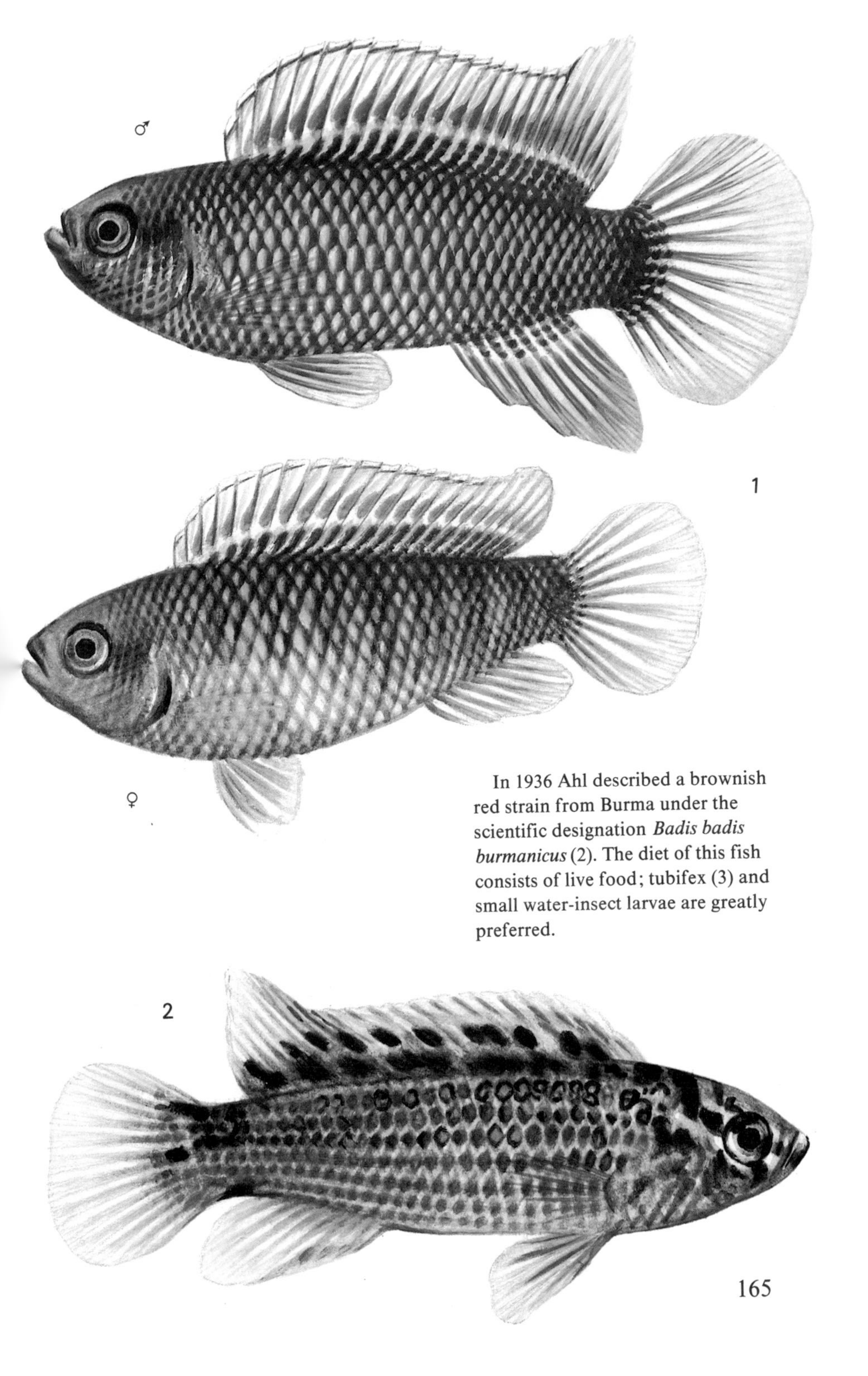

In 1936 Ahl described a brownish red strain from Burma under the scientific designation *Badis badis burmanicus* (2). The diet of this fish consists of live food; tubifex (3) and small water-insect larvae are greatly preferred.

Comb Tail or **Comb-tail Paradise Fish**

Belontis signata (GÜNTHER, 1861)

The Comb Tail (1) is a robust labyrinth fish which may grow to be 13 cm long. It lives in the mountain streams of Srí Lanka, Sumatra, Borneo and Java. Here the watersides are overgrown with the plant *Lagenadra ovata*. Under its large leaves which fuse on the surface, the males build up their bubble nests, just as they do in captivity. The data of the water of these streams are pH 6.7, 0.65° dGH and temperature 28° C. Although the water of their natural habitat is very soft, no problems arise in connection with spawning or the development of eggs in water of about 10° dGH, no more than 2° dCH and at a temperature of 24—26° C. There are no marked sexual differences, but the male is stouter, more vividly red and the rays of his caudal fin are somewhat longer than in the female and form a comb-like extension. The fish spawn in pairs that join in an unyielding defence of their spawning sites. The eggs, 1.2 mm in diameter, include an oil droplet which makes them rise to the surface in the course of spawning. Embryos with a markedly dark pigmentation leave the eggshell after 48 hours and in the following three days they learn to swim. They grow quickly if supplied with abundant live food. A characteristic feature of the juvenile colouring is a black spot in the base of the caudal fin (2). Sometimes the nest is looked after by both partners; usually, however, it is only the male. After the fry have learned to swim freely, the adult fish are removed.

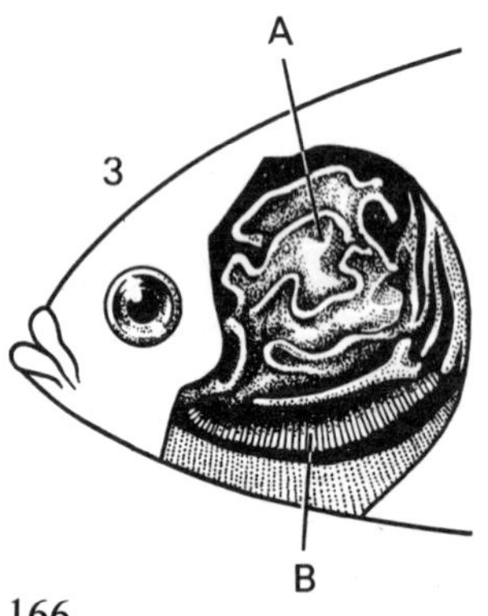

Since the Comb Tail is an intolerant, territorial and predatory fish, the only communities it should be allowed to join are those consisting of fish with similar characteristics. The aquariums should be spacious and richly supplied with aquatic plants. The preferred water temperature for adult fish is 24° C, but the fish are capable of tolerating transient drops in temperature to below 20° C.

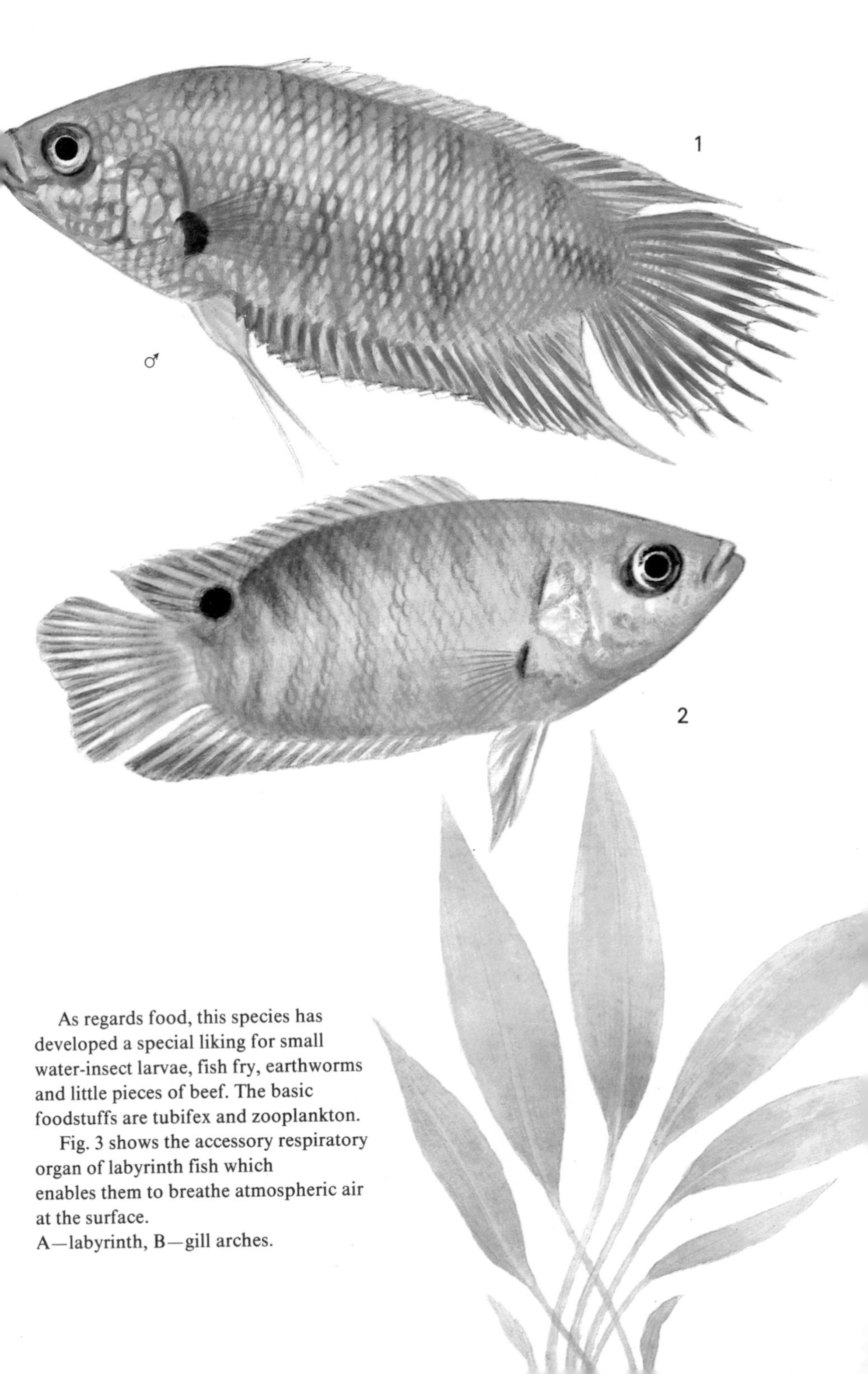

As regards food, this species has developed a special liking for small water-insect larvae, fish fry, earthworms and little pieces of beef. The basic foodstuffs are tubifex and zooplankton.

Fig. 3 shows the accessory respiratory organ of labyrinth fish which enables them to breathe atmospheric air at the surface.
A—labyrinth, B—gill arches.

Paradise Fish
Belontiidae

Macropodus opercularis (LINNAEUS, 1758)

Korea, China, South Vietnam and Taiwan are the home of this, the oldest of aquarium fish. It grows to a length of 9 cm. In 1869 the Paradise Fish was imported to Paris where it was successfully bred and reared by Carbonnier. Thus the foundation stone of modern pisciculture concerned with tropical fish was laid. The males are larger in size, with longer unpaired fins tapering into threadlike projections. The male builds a bubble nest where he spawns with one or, exceptionally, several females. When spawning has taken place in a large community tank, the whole nest containing the fry is transferred to a separate tank. When a spawning tank is used this should be larger, holding 20—50 l. Water from the community tank or boiled tapwater (pH 7.0, 10° dGH and up to 2° dCH) is suitable. A plant tuft is placed on the surface to provide the female with shelter and the male with a support for the nest. One pair is set up for spawning. The female is removed after spawning has been completed, and the male after the fry have become free-swimming. The fry are easy to rear.

At present it is mostly weak and poorly coloured fish that are offered for sale in shops. The Paradise Fish is an aquarium fish which is slowly but surely nearing its extinction. It seems that under the primitive conditions of breeders at the beginning of the present century the fish were getting along far better. This was primarily due to the fact that, in comparison with nowadays, the number of aquarium-fish species was very small indeed, and the fish were given far greater individual care.

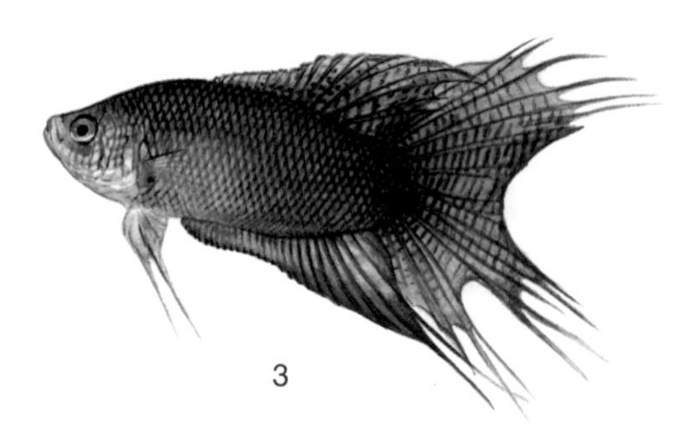

The Paradise Fish (1) is endowed with an inscrutable character—both placid and pugnacious individuals can be found. In the spawning period, however, all of them are aggressive. It is a hardy fish which may be kept in garden pools

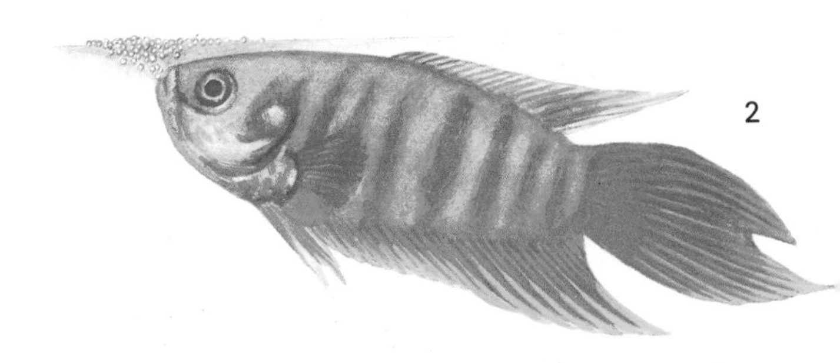

from June till the end of September. It prefers coarser live food, especially worms, larvae, fish fry, spawn, pieces of beef, etc. In the aquarium it checks the undesirable reproduction of slugs and flatworms.

The albino strain (Albino Macropodus) (2) was produced in captivity. No less beautiful is the strain *M. opercularis concolor,* the Black Paradise Fish (3), whose systematic classification has remained ambiguous until now.

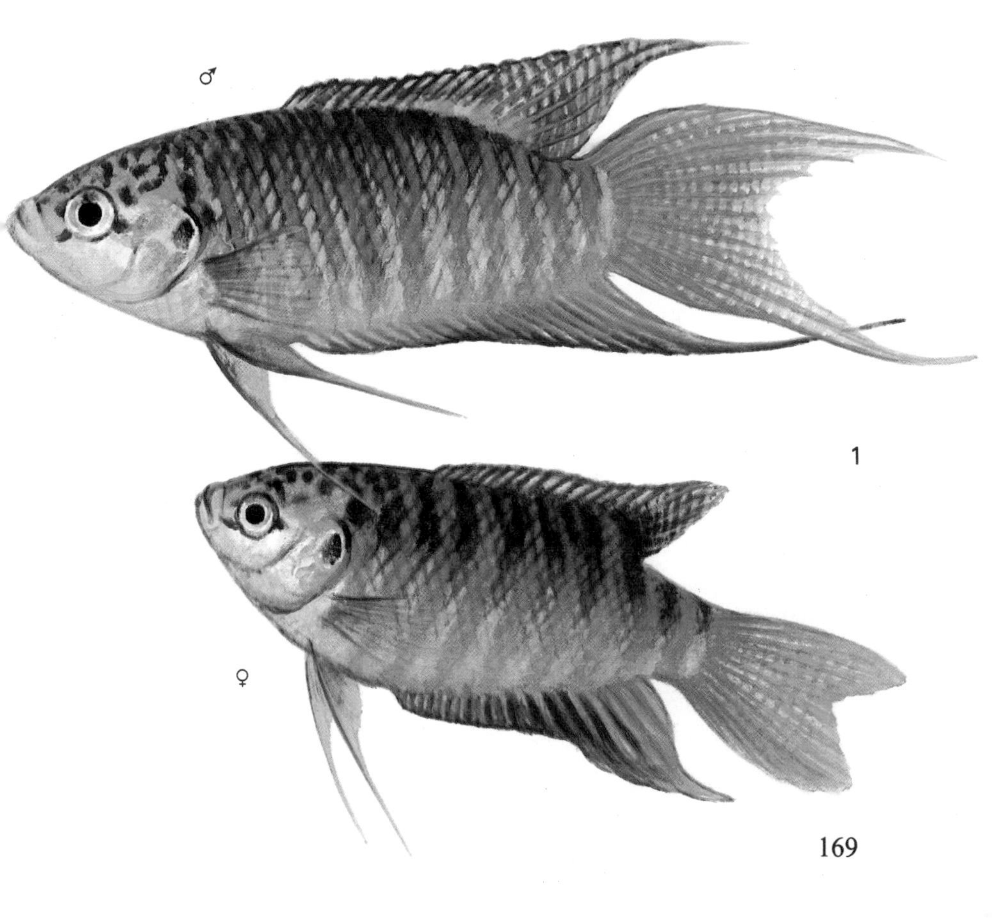

Betta or **Siamese Fighting Fish** Belontiidae

Betta splendens REGAN, 1909

The Betta (1) is a native of shallow, warm waters of the East Indies, Siam, Vietnam and the Malay Peninsula. In 1892 it was imported for the first time to Paris whence it was distributed further into Europe. Adult fish attain a length of 6 cm. In comparison with the females, the males' dorsal, caudal, anal and ventral fins are longer and may become extremely veil-shaped. After attaining sexual maturity, the males are separated into small flasks arranged side by side. They continuously try to impress each other with outstretched fins, and this promotes their growth.

The Betta spawns in pairs even in small aquariums holding no more than 3 l. During spawning there should be no aeration. Several plant tufts are placed on the surface; here the female may find shelter against the much too aggressive male. The male builds a foam nest on the surface, made of bubbles covered with saliva. In the course of spawning, both the male and the female collect the falling eggs and squeeze them into the nest. After spawning is over, the male drives the female away and she may then be removed. The development of eggs requires boiled tapwater with the following values: pH 7.0, 10° dGH and up to 2° dCH. The incubation time is 30 hours at a temperature of 26—28° C. As soon as the fry leave the nest, the male also is removed and the level of the water column is lowered to 5 cm. The first nourishment is brine shrimps and later, chopped tubifex. The intensive metabolism of these fish necessitates regular water replacement. The young fish grow very quickly.

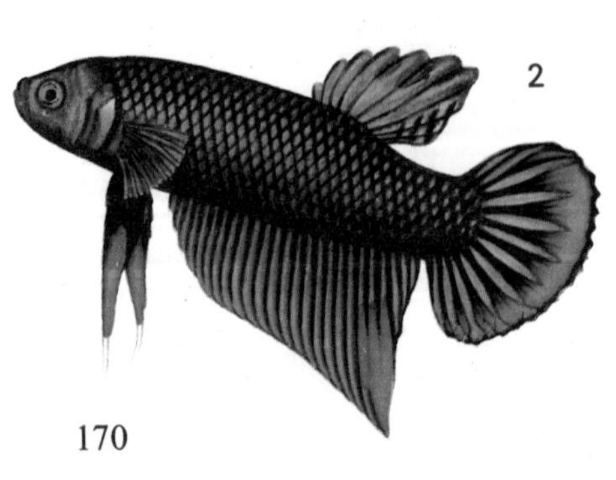

Adult males have life-and-death struggles for their territories. It is this characteristic that gave the species its name 'Fighting Fish'. Only pairs, or one male with several females, can be reared together. The fish thrive in richly planted, warm aquariums in the presence of other placid labyrinth fish. They crossbreed with the species *Betta imbellis* (2).

The favourite diet of these fish includes tubifex, boiled spawn of industrial fish, mosquito and midge larvae, minced beef or dead fish, nor do

they refuse zooplankton or granulated or flake foods. They hunt slugs and flatworms.

The Betta is variable in colour: white, orange, green, blue, crimson, and almost black fish are reared in aquariums.

Dwarf Gourami

Colisa lalia (HAMILTON—BUCHANAN, 1822)

The Dwarf Gourami (1) is a very nicely coloured, 5 cm long labyrinth fish. It lives in India, Bengal and Asam, where it inhabits shallow, warm waters. In 1874 the fish were imported to Paris for the well-known breeder and pioneer in aquaristics, P. Carbonnier. However, the first large-scale imports were organized by German firms as late as 1903. In price-lists the fish was introduced under the name *Trichogaster lalius.*

The colourful males build bubble nests interwoven with bits of plants near the surface; here spawning takes place later on. The females are very fertile. During spawning, small eggs with a high content of oil rise to the surface. There they are collected by the male and taken into the nest. The conditions required are a water temperature of 26—28° C, pH of 6.5—7.0, 10° dGH and up to 2° dCH. The fish are set up in pairs in tanks holding at least 6 l. The female is removed after she has finished spawning and the male after the fry have learned to swim. The free-swimming fry are very tiny at first. A laboratory monoculture of infusorians (genus *Paramecium*), Rotatoria, and the smallest nauplius stages of copepods have proved suitable as the first food. After ten days of life and with intensive feeding, the fry become capable of catching brine-shrimp nauplii. The young fish grow unevenly and rather slowly.

3

In 1979, males of an interesting colour mutation appeared in the glasshouses of West German stores under the commercial designation 'Red Lalius', and caused much sensation in the aquaristic world. Later the American professional press brought out a report about the origin of this mutant. *Colisa lalia,* 'the Sunset', (2), was cultivated in secret for a long time at a well-guarded fish farm in Singapore, together with further novelties. Information appeared in the Singapore newspapers that about 32,000 Sunset Laliuses had been stolen from this

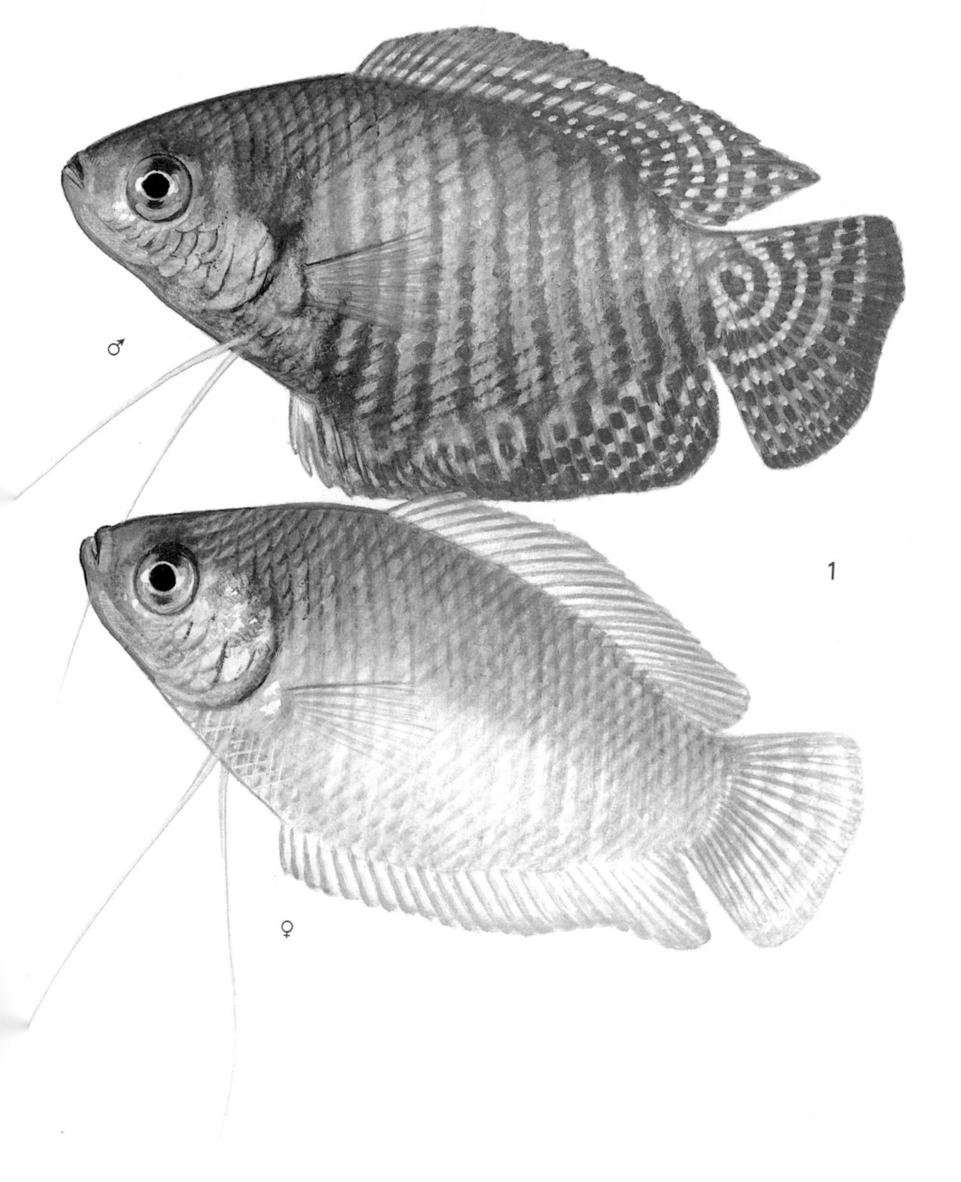

farm. The fish was then offered for sale under the name *Colisa 'gukengi'*, and also males of a smaller and similarly coloured species, *C. chuna* (3), were passed off as such.

The wild strain as well as the mutant referred to above thrive in shallow, warm and well-planted aquariums. They prefer live food.

Pearl Gourami, Mosaic Gourami or **Leeri**
Trichogaster leeri (BLEEKER, 1852)

The Pearl Gourami is a native of the Malay Peninsula, Thailand, Sumatra and Borneo. It is caught in great numbers in places where sewage from native villages flows directly into the water. It is a 11 cm long labyrinth fish, reared in Europe since 1933. The male's ventral region is blood red, his long dorsal fin tapers to a point, the anal fin is more prominent and its rays are extended into thread-like appendages.

In spawning the male clasps the female and turns her on her back so as to make her belly face the bubble nest. An outflow of eggs rich in oil droplets rises towards the surface. In the course of spawning, the male concentrates the eggs into a large bubble nest. Immediately after spawning is over, the female is removed. The male takes over the care of the eggs and, later, of the hatched larvae. When the fry start leaving the nest, the male also is removed. Although the Pearl Gourami is a large fish, the fry are very small and possess a minute mouth. The water column is lowered to 5 cm, and in the first 3—4 days the fry are fed infusorians, Rotatoria, or the finest copepod nauplii. After a further four days it is possible to change to brine-shrimp nauplii. These can also be used as the first food but must then be of the finest sort. The coarser the first food given to the fry, the more uneven is their growth. The fry grow relatively slowly. Only larger aquariums capable of holding 50 l and more are used for spawning and rearing. The water should be boiled tapwater of a temperature of 25—28° C, pH 7.0, 10° dGH and up to 2° dCH.

The Pearl Gourami is a warmth-loving, mild and easily startled fish. It likes warm, well-planted aquariums and the company of placid fish species.

Although it prefers live food, particularly tubifex and mosquito or midge larvae, it does not refuse good artificial food.

In dirty, overpopulated and badly maintained tanks the fish are infested by a ciliate of the genus *Amyloodinium,* or by an infectious skin bacteriosis manifesting itself in the form of small reddish ulcers and, ultimately, by extensive necroses of tissues and the death of the fish.

Blue Gourami

Belontiidae

Trichogaster trichopterus trichopterus (PALLAS, 1777)

The Blue Gourami is a hardy, larger-sized labyrinth fish notable for exterminating the much-feared polyps in aquariums. It grows to a length of 15 cm and its habitat includes the Malay Peninsula, Thailand, South Vietnam and the Greater Sunda Islands. It was first imported as early as 1896.

The male, with a big dorsal fin extending to a point, builds a rather disorderly and outspread bubble nest on the water surface. Here he spawns with one female. Boiled tapwater at 24—26° C and a roomy aquarium holding approximately 50 l will meet the requirements for breeding. The pair need an absolutely peaceful environment. The company of other fish, including members of their own species, has a disturbing effect and the fish become reluctant to spawn. In the course of spawning, eggs containing a relatively large amount of oil rise towards the nest. With the onset of spawning, the aerator must be put out of operation and not started again until the fry become free-swimming. As is the case with many other labyrinth fish, the nest of even this species remains in the care of the male, who is removed after the fry start swimming freely in the vicinity of the nest. The growth rate of the young fish is fairly uneven: the more quickly growing fish oppress their smaller siblings and turn into cannibals; their hasty growth tells its own tale. It is therefore necessary to sort the fry several times during their growth and separate the bigger fish from the smaller ones. The fry are fed 3—4 times a day with brine shrimps or copepods. The level of the water is lowered to 5 cm and raised again gradually during growth.

The Blue Gourami (1) is a suitable species for roomy, well-planted aquariums shared with larger, placid fish. The only natural deviation coming from the waters of Sumatra is the *Trichogaster trichopterus sumatranus,*

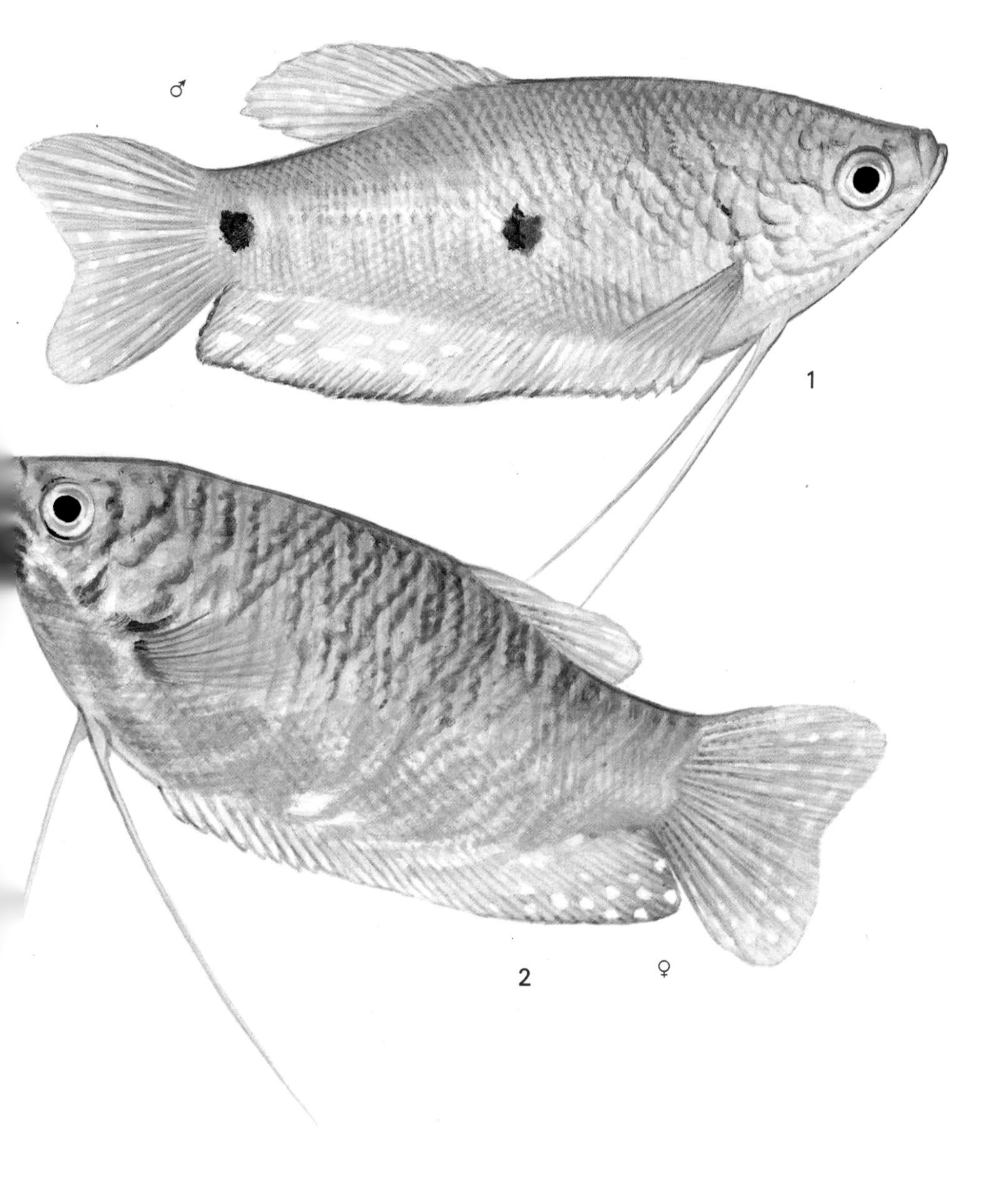

from which a new strain was developed by the American breeder Cosby—the *T. trichopterus* 'Cosby' (2). Relatively recently a golden (3) and a silver strain have been achieved. Today, however, the various strains have become so confused because of indiscriminate crossbreeding that there can be no expectation of their being thoroughbreds. This applies to both wild and cultivated strains.

Pygmy Gourami or **Dwarf Croaking Gourami** Belontiidae
Trichopsis pumilus (ARNOLD, 1936)

The Pygmy Gourami (1) is a small, 3.5 cm long labyrinth fish. It lives in South Vietnam, Thailand, and in the Greater Sunda Islands. Since 1913 it has been reared in European aquariums. The male has longer fins and his colouring is more variegated. The fish spawn in pairs. The male builds a small bubble nest in the middle layers of water, on the underside of aquatic-plant leaves. During courtship display and spawning the fish give off weak croaking sounds. How these sounds are produced has not yet been unambiguously proved but it is assumed that their source lies in the paired labyrinth cavities located above the gills (2). The impact of air caused by letting out bubbles from the left and the right cavity alternatively gives rise to the croaking sound.

The female lays 50—100 eggs, and is removed when spawning is over. Water of the following values is suitable for the development of eggs: temperature 25—28° C, pH 7.0, 10° dGH and up to 2° dCH. The incubation time is 36 hours; the larvae hang on threads which disappear in the course of development. The male also is removed after the larvae have emerged from the eggs. In their critical age the minute fry can be reared on infusorians, Rotatoria, or the finest sort of copepods. Later, the fry may be given coarser sorts of copepods or brine shrimps. In case of need, breeding is also possible by letting the pair spawn in a relatively large tank that has been used for a longer time. After the fry have learned to swim, the adult fish are removed, the water level is lowered to 5 cm, and the fry are left for several days to their fate. Within the large space a small number of alevins are sure to find subsistence in the form of microscopic organisms and grow to be large enough to swallow dust food.

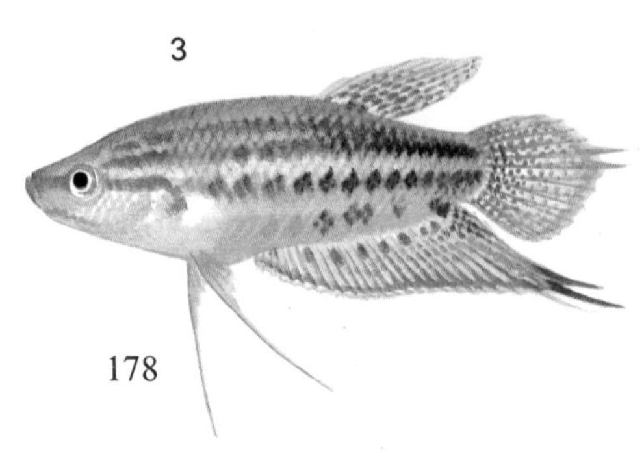

The fish thrive best in monoculture, or in the company of the related species *Trichopsis vittatus* (3) and *T. schalleri*. Single pairs will be content even in small 10 l tanks, as long as these are sufficiently heated and richly overgrown with plants. *T. vittatus* (syn. *Osphromenus striatus, Ctenops vittatus*)

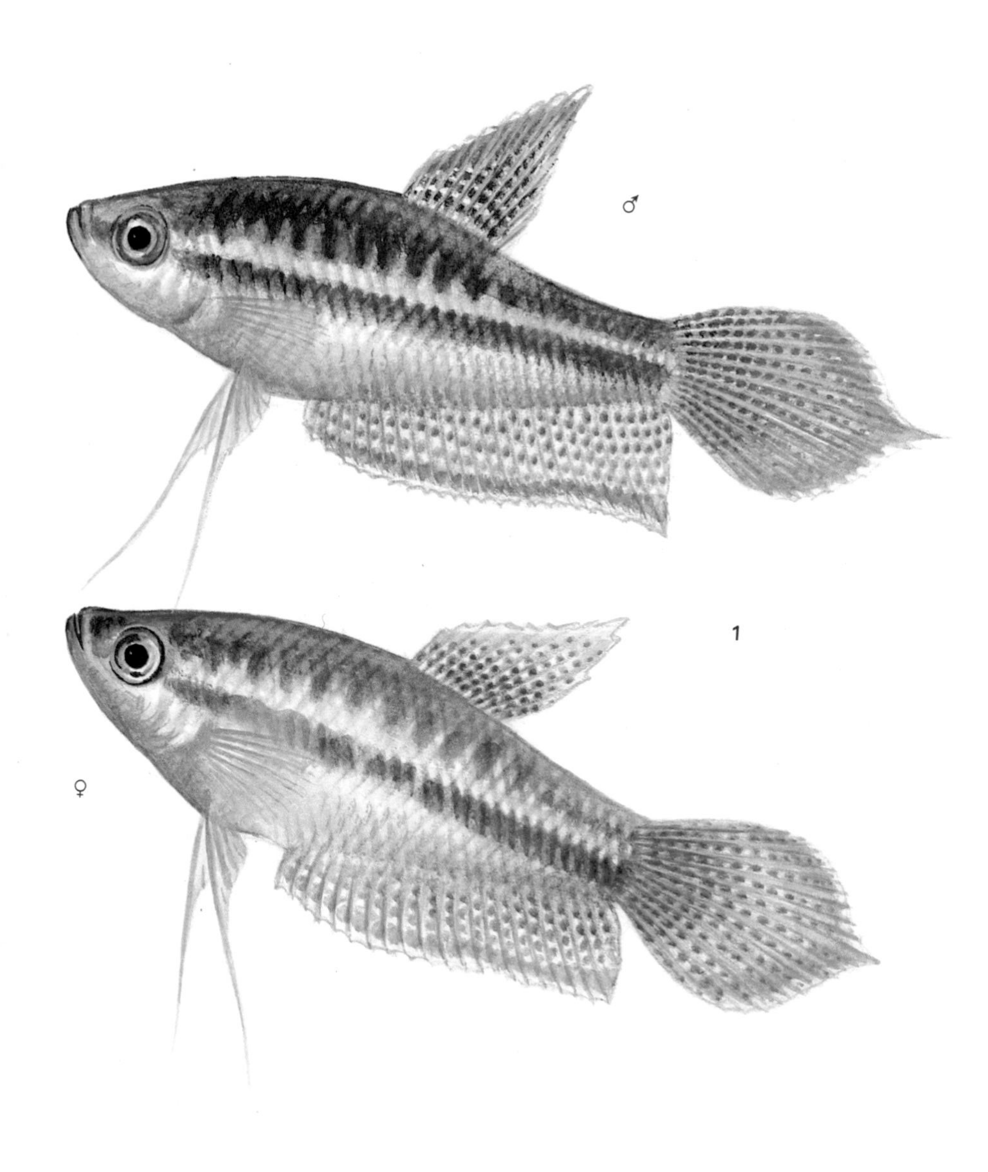

was imported to Europe for the first time as early as 1903. In 1960, the species *T. schalleri* was brought from Thailand. It closely resembles the species *T. pumilus,* but morphological studies have led some ichthyologists to assume that *T. schalleri* is not an independent species but is a subspecies of *T. vittatus.*

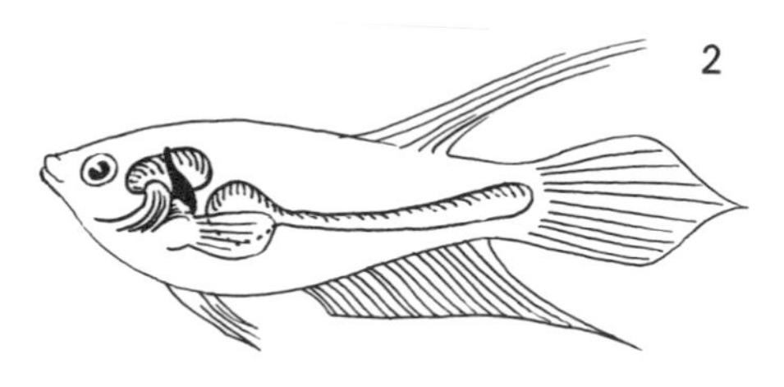

Several years ago, the small carp-like fish *Barbodes fasciatus* appeared for the first time in the European aquaristic market. It is a native of southeastern India, grows to be 7.5 cm long and has four barbels.

The males are very aggressive to the females whose fertility is low. This is why the fish must not be set up in small mating tanks: within a small space the male often beats the female to death without having spawned. The situation is entirely different if the breeders are set up in a small shoal in a roomy aquarium. Three pairs of fish may be set up in a tank of 40 × 50 × 50 cm that is provided with a protective grid and a plant cluster. In such an environment they are willing to spawn without further problems. The water should be kept at a temperature of 26° C, pH 6.5, up to 10° dGH and less than 1° dCH. The sticky eggs, 1.3 mm in diameter, take 31 hours to develop. The hatched larvae possess a large yolk sac. They need four days to become free-swimmers. The fry grow quickly when well fed on brine shrimps or copepods. After a fortnight it is advisable to add small quantities of normal tapwater, thus helping the young fish to get acclimatized to the new environment.

B. fasciatus is kept in larger shoals in spacious aquariums containing dense vegetation. In polyculture they are kept with mobile fish species of equal or larger size. They live on dry and live food of all kinds.

Scientists have been acquainted with this carp-like fish since as early as 1849 when it was described as *Cirrhinus fasciatus*. A number of other synonyms appeared later on. At present, in accordance with the law of priority and morphological features, the name *Barbodes fasciatus* is valid. This has given rise to an extraordinary situation—there exists simultaneously another fish

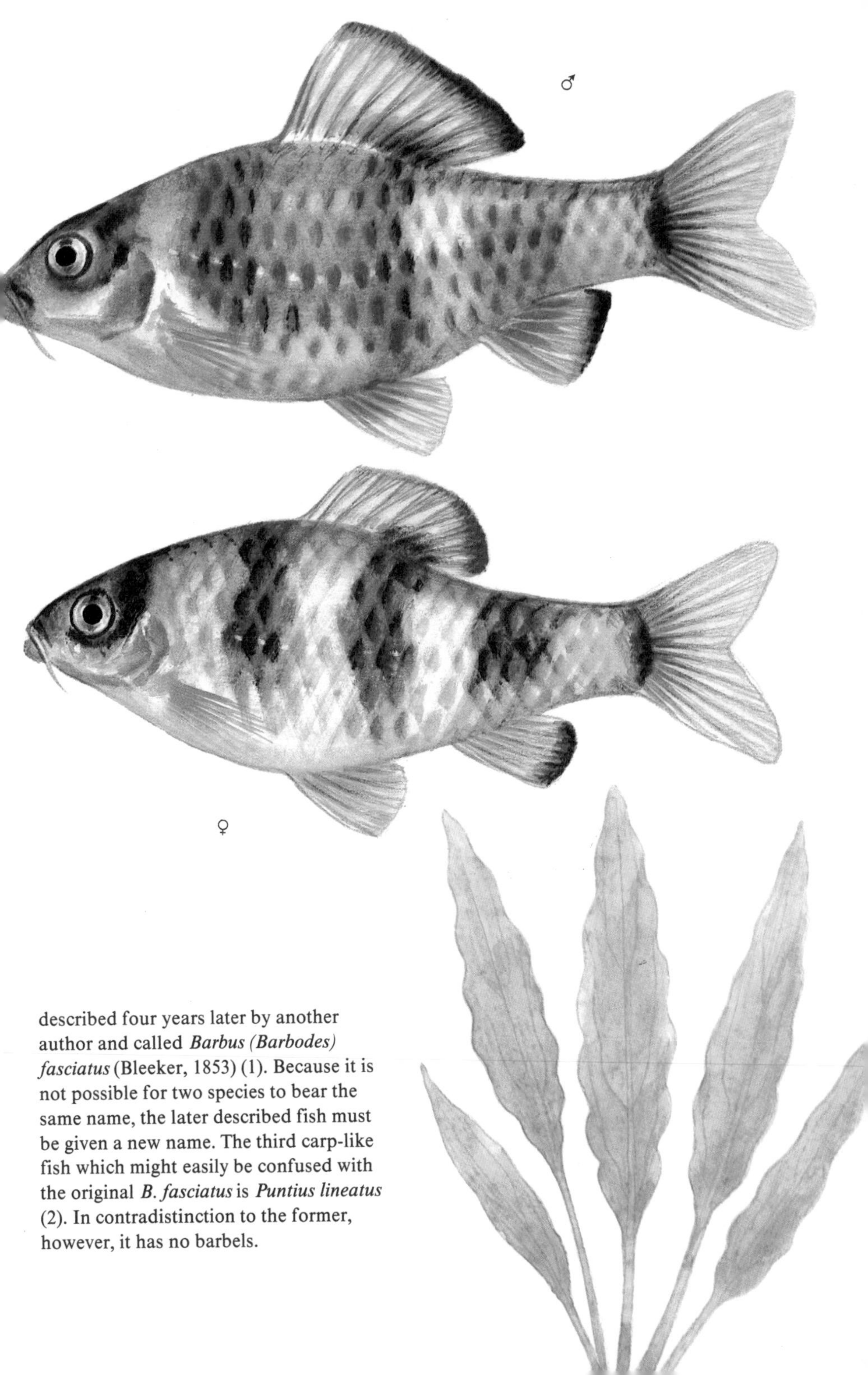

described four years later by another author and called *Barbus (Barbodes) fasciatus* (Bleeker, 1853) (1). Because it is not possible for two species to bear the same name, the later described fish must be given a new name. The third carp-like fish which might easily be confused with the original *B. fasciatus* is *Puntius lineatus* (2). In contradistinction to the former, however, it has no barbels.

Zebra, Zebra Danio or **Striped Danio** Cyprinidae

Brachydanio rerio (HAMILTON–BUCHANAN, 1822)

In nature this fish occurs in the waters of the eastern parts of India. Since 1905, when it was imported for the first time, probably to Germany, it has lost nothing of its popularity among aquarists. The males are slim with a golden hue; the silvery females have a markedly fuller ventral region. The fish grow to a length of 5 cm.

The tank used for spawning should have a capacity for 10—50 l, and a protective grid should be placed on the bottom. Boiled tapwater at 22—24°C with a pH of 7.0, up to 10°dGH and up to 2°dCH will prove sufficient. Before spawning, the females are separated from the males for 7—14 days. The fish are set up in the ratio of two males to one female, but it is possible to set up several dozen fish together. The more fish are about to spawn, the larger the tank must be. The fry usually appear in great numbers, one female being capable of laying as many as 2,000 eggs. The fish are set up in the evening, before switching off the light. Spawning takes place in the morning hours, usually on the following day, and is very vigorous. Immediately after spawning, the fish are removed, the grid is taken out and 50 % of the water is replaced by fresh water of the same composition and temperature. The eggs are treated with methylene blue. The embryos hatch in 96 hours at 23°C and suspend themselves on the tank walls. The fry are capable of free-swimming on the seventh day after spawning; being very small, they are given the finest possible food. An ideal nourishment is an infusorian monoculture or fine wheel-worm 'dust'. If necessary, they may also be offered hard-boiled egg yolk or good artificial fry food mixed with a drop of water and made to fall into the tank over a dense net. In a week's time the fry are already capable of eating brine-shrimp nauplii.

The Zebras (1) are ideally suited for life in mixed aquarium communities. They require fresh water and plenty of space to move in. They are always kept in larger shoals. Old aquaristic literature depicts them as children of the sun, which is quite justified. In 1963, Meinken described *Brachydanio frankei* (2) as a separate species with a hitherto

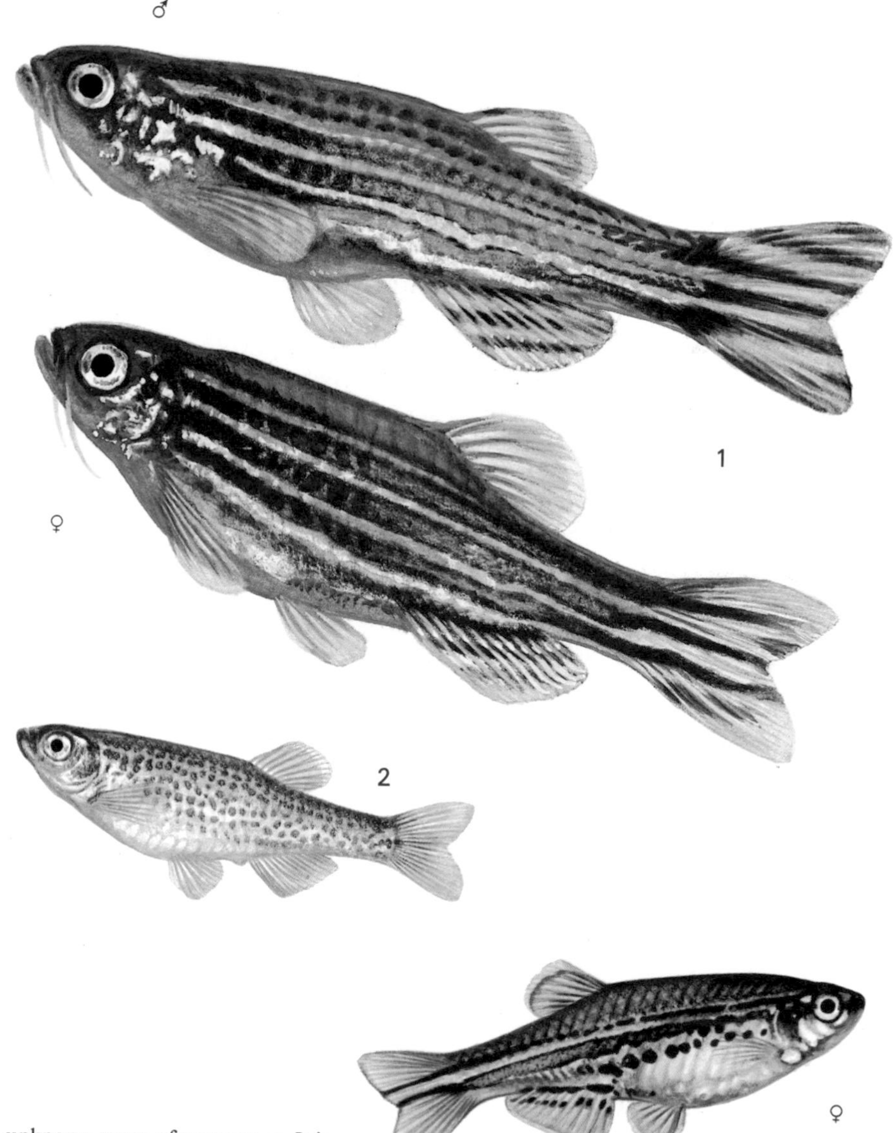

unknown range of occurrence. It is therefore assumed to be a mutant of the species *B. rerio*. In captivity *B. rerio* and *B. frankei* fuse into common shoals and interbreed; their progeny is fertile. Strains with veil-shaped fins have been produced in both species. The Zebra also crossbreeds with other species, e.g. with *B. nigrofasciatus* (3).

Giant Danio
Cyprinidae

Danio aequipinnatus (McCLELLAND, 1839)

The pure running waters of the western coast of India and Srí Lanka are rich in shoals of mobile fish, including the species *Danio aequipinnatus*. It has been kept in the containers of European aquarists since 1909. The maximal length it may attain is 12 cm. The females are fuller in their ventral region than the males. For spawning, larger aquariums are used (50—200 l). Their bottom is covered with a protective grid. A cluster of plants and an aerator will complete the equipment of the breeding tank. Water of the values 23—26° C, pH 7.0, 10° dGH and up to 2° dCH provides the best environment for the successful development of eggs. The fish are set up for spawning in a group, the ratio being two males to one female. Spawning usually takes place in the morning hours of the following day. Eggs are produced in great quantities. After spawning, the breeders as well as the grid are removed, and a third to a half of the water is replaced by fresh water of the same composition and temperature. The water is slightly coloured with methylene blue. At a water temperature of 26° C, the embryos hatch in 30 hours and subsequently suspend themselves from the glass sides of the tank with the aid of a sticky secretion from cutaneous glands. In their first days of life the fry are fed on the finest live or artificial food. After three days they may already be offered brine shrimps (fine sort). Several young slugs (genus *Ampullarius*) are used to keep the bottom of the tank clean.

Since the time they were first imported the fish have been known under the erroneous name *Danio malabaricus;* all the fish reared in aquariums definitely belong to the species *D. aequipinnatus* (1). *D. malabaricus* is more similar in shape to the species *D. devario* (2); hence it has probably not been imported for aquaristic purposes at all. The Giant

Danio is a vital, hardy and mobile fish species. The fish form shoals and love sunshine and freedom of movement. For this reason only large tanks with sufficient space for swimming about are found suitable. In polycultures they are reared together with fish that have similar properties, in particular with species of the genera *Danio* and *Esomus (E. lineatus* [3], *E. danrica* [4]). In danger or when frightened the fish try to save themselves by long jumps above the water surface. Therefore, aquariums should be provided with a protective net or a glass cover. At the beginning of June young fish may be placed in garden pools where they can stay until mid-September.

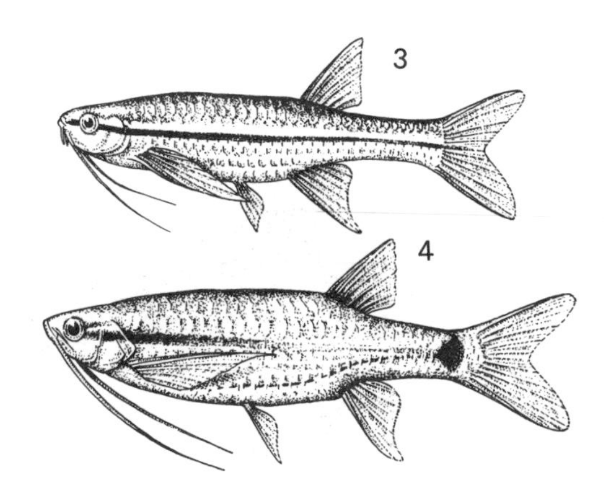

Tiger Barb or **Sumatra Barb**

Capoeta tetrazona tetrazona (BLEEKER, 1855)

Cyprinidae

The Tiger Barb inhabits Sumatra, Thailand and Kalimantan (Borneo). Since being imported to Europe in 1935, it has always been kept in aquariums until now. It grows to be 7 cm long. In the males the paired ventral fins are completely dark red, the upper part of the snout is reddish and the dorsal fin bears a vivid red rim. The females have a fuller ventral region; their colours are duller, their ventral fins are edged with a transparent rim.

The fish spawn in pairs, in 6—10 l tanks with a protective grid at the bottom. During the act of spawning the pair seeks support in the foliage, and this is why a tuft of Java moss or of another fine-leaved plant is inserted into the tank. The water has a temperature of 26° C, pH 6.5—7.0, up to 5° dGH and up to 1° dCH. The eggs, 1 mm in diameter, are yellowish and sticky. The embryos emerge after 36 hours and need several days to consume the yolk sac. Free-swimming fry are fed on brine shrimps or copepods. They grow rapidly; in a fortnight they attain a length of 1 cm and are conspicuously striped.

In 1957 L. P. Schulz tried to overcome the lack of systematic unity in classifying various species of carp-like fish. On the basis of a number of morphological characteristics, including the length and the number of barbels, he distinguished four genera: *Barbus, Barbodes, Capoeta* and *Puntius*. Fish belonging to the genus *Capoeta* have two barbels.

The Tiger Barb (1) is a school fish. In polycultures it is kept together with motion-loving fish. It tends to attack peaceful, often even much larger fish and nip off their fins. When resting or sleeping, the fish assume their characteristic position with their head downwards. They live on a mixed diet.

In 1975 an interesting mutation called 'Mossy Barb' (2) made its appearance on the market. It originated most probably in Asian breeding enterprises, where variously coloured albino strains of this species have also been developed.

One of the easily discernible features differentiating between related and similar fish is the arrangement of stripes in the species *Barbodes pentazona pentazona* (3), *B. pentazona kahajani* (4), *B. pentazona hexazona* (5) and *Capoeta tetrazona partipentazona* (6).

Rosy Barb

Cyprinidae

Puntius conchonius (HAMILTON–BUCHANAN, 1822)

This modest carp-like fish has become a regular inhabitant of aquariums since as early as 1903. Its original habitat is the north of India, Bengal and Ásam. In nature it grows to be 15 cm long but in an aquarium it is somewhat smaller. Fish growing up under unfavourable conditions from a very young age are rather stunted and reach sexual maturity already when about 4 cm long. The courting attire of males is purple, while their dorsal, ventral and anal fins are black. Females are an inconspicuous silvery colour and their productivity is very high. The size of the tank is chosen according to the size and the number of fish prepared for spawning (from 20 to 100 l). The basic breeding unit consists of two males and one female. The bottom of the tank is covered with a protective grid; this, however, can only partly protect the eggs owing to their stickiness. Yet the losses caused by cannibalism are negligible in proportion to the large quantity of eggs. The water should be 24° C, pH 7.0, 10° dGH and 2° dCH (boiled tapwater). When spawning is over, the breeders are removed and half of the water is replaced by fresh water of the same qualities and temperature. The glassily transparent eggs are treated with methylene blue. The fry break through the eggshell in 24 hours and learn to swim freely three days thereafter. They are intensively fed three to four times a day on copepods or brine shrimps; high-grade artificial fry food may be added. The yolk of hard-boiled eggs can also be used if necessary. A regular addition of fresh water is beneficial to the young fish. In sufficiently spacious tanks the fry grow rapidly.

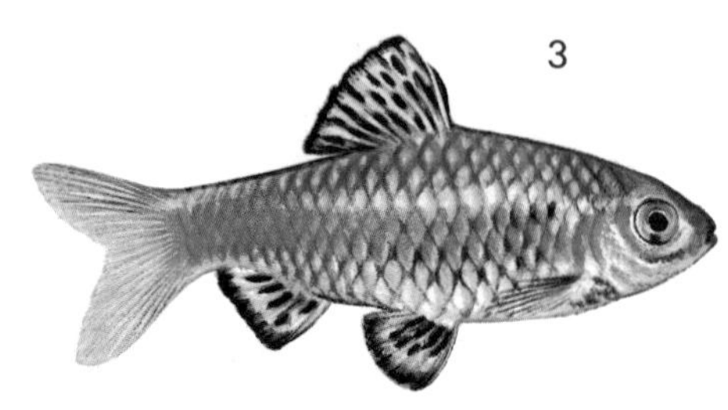

3

The Rosy Barb (1) is reared in large-sized aquariums, always in greater numbers, co-existing with species of similar demands and sizes. The optimal temperature ranges between 18 and 22° C. From June till September the fish can also be kept in garden pools.

The Rosy Barb likes to nibble delicate species of aquarium plants. This can be prevented by regularly adding plant food.

In recent years, gold-coloured strains (2) adorned with veil-shaped fins have been developed. Cultivated strains are usually smaller. The Rosy Barb is widely used in various ichthyological laboratory studies. Picture 3 presents the so-called 'Odessa Barb'.

Black-spot Barb

Cyprinidae

Puntius filamentosus (CUVIER ET VALENCIENNES, 1844)

The Black-spot Barb is a barbelless, carp-like fish which in nature and in roomy aquariums grows to a length of approximately 15 cm. It inhabits the water systems of India, Srí Lanka and Burma and was imported to Europe in 1950. In males the rays of the dorsal fin terminate in a pectinate elongation, and a conspicuous spawning rush appears on their upper-jaw snout (1). Young fish bear a typical juvenile colouring (2) substantially different from that of the adult fish (3). This colouring fades out at the age of about 7 months; the third cross band is transformed into a blotch characteristic of the adult fish. The fish reach sexual maturity when approximately $1\,^{1}/_{2}$ years old. Two males and four females are set up for spawning in large tanks, 200 l being optimal. Appropriate water values are temperature 26° C, pH 7.0, 8° dGH and up to 1° dCH (boiled water). A protective spawning grid is inserted at the bottom and plant tufts are located on the surface. Spawning takes place in the plants right below the surface and is very vigorous. The eggs are relatively small, yellowish and only slightly sticky. After spawning, the adult fish are removed and 50% of the water may be replaced by fresh water of the same composition and temperature. The water is slightly coloured with methylene blue. The fry emerge from the eggs in 48 hours. In their first days of life they are fed brine shrimps. Later the young fish are distributed among more tanks to promote their growth. The size of the fish makes it easy to introduce artificial spawning; this is particularly helpful in experiments connected with interbreeding piscine species.

The Black-spot Barb is a peaceable school fish suited for large aquariums only. The fish, being relentless swimmers, must be given sufficient space for motion.

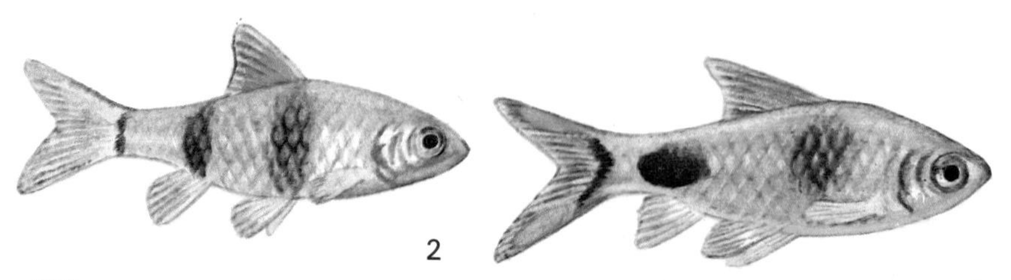

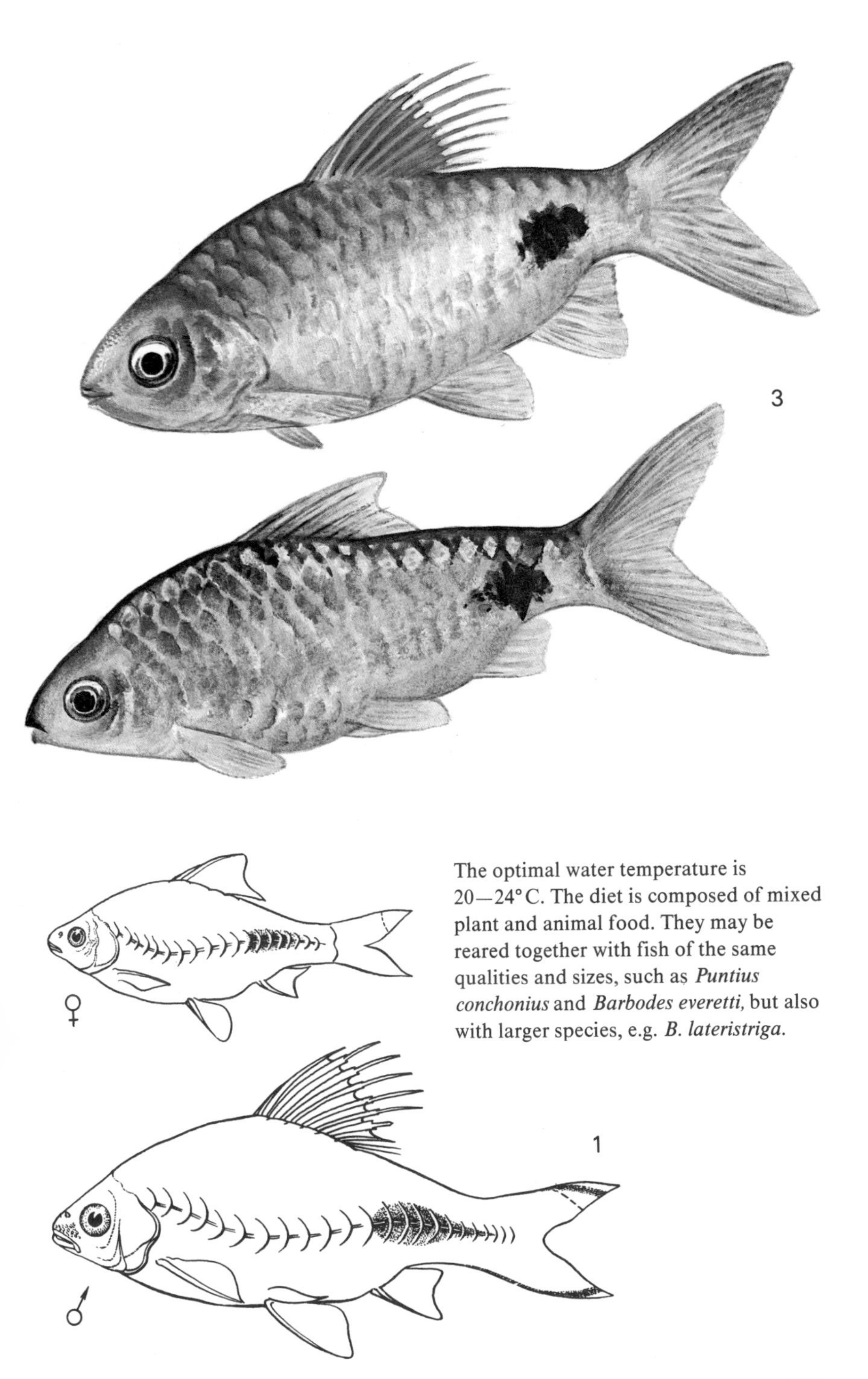

The optimal water temperature is 20—24°C. The diet is composed of mixed plant and animal food. They may be reared together with fish of the same qualities and sizes, such as *Puntius conchonius* and *Barbodes everetti,* but also with larger species, e.g. *B. lateristriga.*

Harlequin Fish, Rasbora

Rasbora heteromorpha DUNCKER, 1904

Cyprinidae

The Harlequin Fish comes from the Malay Peninsula, Thailand and eastern Sumatra. Ladiges presents an exact picture of the swamps in the vicinity of the city of Medan: 'The water surface is overshadowed by the vault of the surrounding jungle, the bottom is covered with decaying vegetation, branches and trunks of fallen trees interwoven with a dense thicket of aquatic plants. Open surface areas are scarce. The temperature of air measured here was 32°C, that of water was 20°C. The water was found to contain iron and its hardness was 2.4°dGH.' The Harlequin Fish was imported in 1907. It grows to be 4.5 cm long. In the males, the anterior lower tip of the wedge extends as far as the medium belly line. The females are fuller-bodied and their wedge tip is obtuse. If there is a sufficient supply of suitable water available and it is not necessary to prepare the water elaborately for spawning, as many as 50 fish can be set up simultaneously in a large tank. If the water has to be prepared the fish are set up in pairs in 3—6 l tanks. 10—14 days before spawning the females are separated from the males and the fish supplied with abundant food. They have a particular liking for red midge larvae. The water should have a temperature of 26—28°C, pH value of 6.5, 6°dGH at most and 0°dCH. The water should be enriched with a peat extract so as to make it amber-coloured. The females stick the eggs on the underside of large-leaved plants, mostly of those belonging to the genus *Cryptocoryne.* Since during the act of spawning some eggs fall to the bottom, it is advisable to use the spawning grid. The Harlequin Fish is a zealous egg-eater. The fry emerge in 24 hours and hang themselves from the plants. After five days they start swimming freely and are relatively large in size. In the first days of life they are fed on brine shrimps.

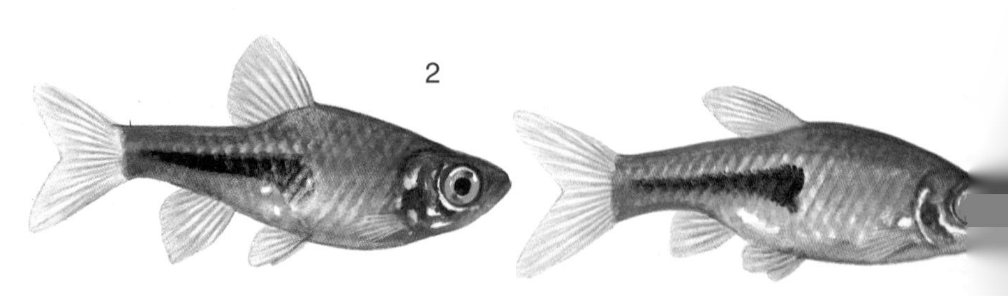

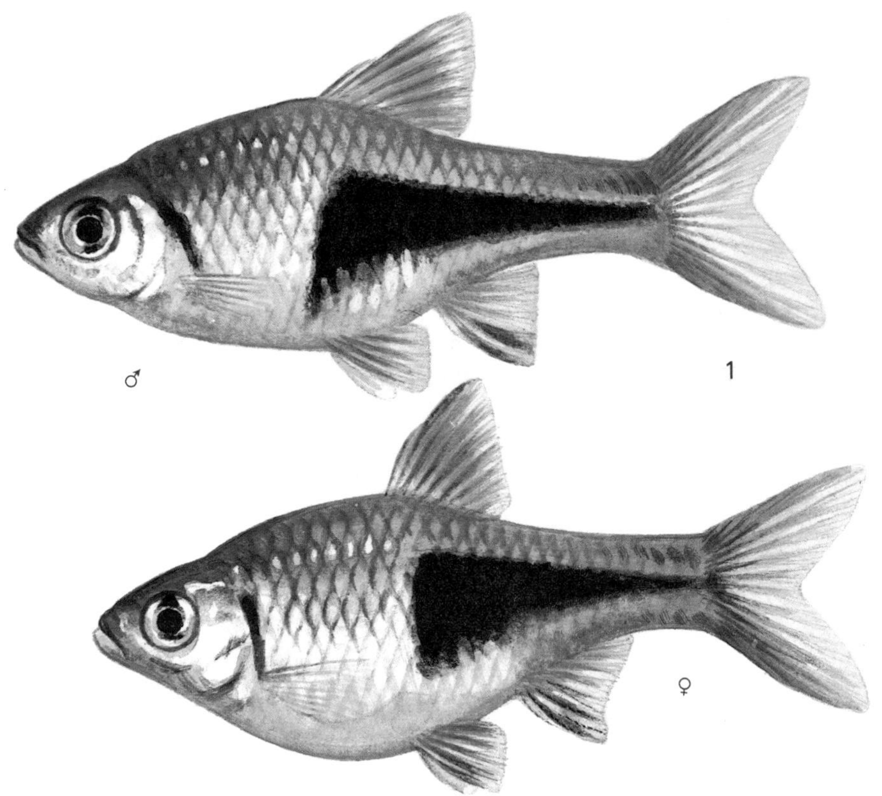

It follows from the reports of ichthyological expeditions that the localities inhabited by species belonging to the genus *Rasbora* are, as a rule, overgrown with plants of the genus *Cryptocoryne,* along with the plant *Blyxa echinosperma*. The genus *Cryptocoryne* includes many beautiful species differing in size, in the shape of leaves and in colour; here nature itself instructs us how to plant an aquarium for the Harlequin Fish. The general appearance of the tank may be complemented by petrified wood from peat bogs. If packed filters are used, they should contain peat packing. The Harlequin Fish (1) is always kept in a shoal, sometimes together with other small Rasbora species.

In 1956 Meinken described a similar Rasbora, *R. hengeli* (2): this is smaller, slimmer and has a narrower wedge blotch.

Spotted Rasbora or **Dwarf Rasbora** *Rasbora maculata* DUNCKER, 1904

In the territory of the Malay Peninsula, East Indies and Sumatra, as well as in the neighbourhood of Singapore, countless shoals of small fish not exceeding 2.5 cm in length can be found in rapidly flowing waters, but also in pools and small ditches. These belong to the species *Rasbora maculata,* one of the smallest representatives of the family Cyprinidae. On the Malay Peninsula it was often observed in the company of large shoals of the Sumatra Tiger Barb. Although it was brought to Europe two years earlier than the Harlequin Fish (in 1905), it has failed by far to become as popular among aquarists. Males are smaller, slimmer and more vividly red; females have a markedly plumper ventral region. Prior to spawning, the females are separated from the males and fed richly. As soon as the females are ready, the fish are set up in 1—2 pairs in 3—6 l aquariums at a water temperature of 26—28° C. The optimal composition of water is the same as for the Harlequin Fish. Tufts of fine-leaved plants are inserted into the mating tanks and the bottom may be provided with a protective grid. The lighting in the mating tanks should be subdued. During spawning, the female produces 30—200 eggs. After all the spawn has been expelled, the breeders are removed. The fry hatch in 24 hours and four days later they learn to swim freely. The fry are light-shy, keep near the bottom and may easily be overlooked. They feed on a fine sort of copepods or brine shrimps. The fish grow quickly, and at the age of 2 1/2 months they become sexually mature.

The Spotted Rasbora (1) is an ideal fish for small, maybe only 20 l aquariums. In large aquariums it is kept in shoals consisting of at least 20—30 specimens. It looks well in company with the

Harlequin Fish. Just like all the species of the genus *Rasbora,* it eats both live and artificial food. In both shape and size it resembles two other species: *R. urophthalma* (2), 3 cm in length, imported to Europe in 1913, and *R. axelrodi.*

R. axelrodi (3) is a new species described by Dr M. R. Brittan in honour of Dr H. R. Axelrod who discovered it in the containers of a Singapore dealer. It has apparently not yet been brought to Europe.

Goldfish

Cyprinidae

Carassius auratus auratus var. *bicaudatus* (LINNAEUS, 1758)

The Goldfish lives in Tonkin, China, southern Manchuria, Korea, Japan and on the islands of Hainan and Taiwan. In China its ornamental strains have been reared since as early as 960 AD. The main strains known today were cultivated in several stages in the years 1547—1925. Thus the Shubunkins, Veiltails (1), Tiger-veiltails, Telescope Fish, Comets, Eggfish, Black Telescope Fish (2), Lionheads, Skygrazers and Nymphs have come into being. In Chinese breeding establishments also strains unknown in Europe are available (3).

For the purposes of the so-called natural spawning, selected fish are set up in the tank either in pairs or in a group where males predominate. The spawning rush on the opercles is a conspicuous sexual characteristic of the males. The tank bottom is covered with willow roots, fir branches or artificial brush pads; the surface is interspersed with floating plants that have powerful root systems (e.g. the water hyacinth *Eichhornia crassipes*). Thanks to the adaptability of these fish, the water composition is of no importance. The eggs are small and very sticky. At a temperature of 25° C the fry hatch in three days. They are fed on brine shrimps and artificial fry food and, later, on plankton, chopped tubifex, granulated and flake feeds.

Artificial spawning is made use of by professional breeders for the purposes of effective and controlled breeding.

The Goldfish, including all the strains (breeds), are cold-water fish. They are destined primarily for reservoirs and pools in gardens or parks. They hibernate at temperatures slightly exceeding 8° C (without taking food). If they are kept at higher temperatures they must be fed throughout the winter. The plant component must never be lacking in their varied diet.

In exhibitions, the classical dimensions of veiltails, shown in Fig. 4, are often subjected to valuation.

2
4
1

Red-tailed Shark or **Red-tailed Black Shark** Cyprinidae
Labeo bicolor SMITH, 1931

The warm, shallow streams of Thailand and the East Indies are the habitat of the superbly coloured Red-tailed Shark. In nature these fish can be found primarily in places with a heterogeneous substrate composed of broken stones, tree trunks, branches and roots covered in sessile organisms. It is exactly here that the fish find a 'richly laid table', and their mouth is excellently adapted to this way of taking food: it is subterminal and forms a suctorial organ provided with horny ridges and tubercles for scraping off benthic growths and algae from the substrate. The Red-tailed Shark grows to a length of 12 cm. In Thai breeding establishments, these fish are reproduced semi-artificially in large quantities in small ponds situated in the neighbourhood of the farm. It is probably from here that the fish was taken to Europe for the first time in 1952.

Breeding and rearing are very difficult from the purely aquaristic point of view; this may be because the fish are extremely demanding as regards space. Aquariums with a capacity for 500—1,000 l, and also roomy, heated glasshouse reservoirs are used for breeding. The substantial features of a suitable environment are soft water at 24—26°C, with less than 1°dCH, subdued light, and many hiding-places. Control of breeding fish in large tanks or in pools is rather problematic. The development of eggs takes 30—48 hours. In five days the larvae learn to swim freely and actively take fine 'dust' food.

Already when small, the fish take part in violent territorial struggles, and their roughness increases with age. The Red-tailed Shark (1) prefers narrow fissures to large-sized cavities. The fish seem to draw a feeling of security from the immediate contact with the surrounding crevice walls. Here they stay in various positions, head upwards or downwards. As soon as they catch sight of an intruder's signalizing red caudal fin within the bounds of their territory, they dart forth to an aggressive attack. Sometimes they launch assaults also upon other red-coloured fish, while fish of different colours are left unnoticed.

The species *L. erythrurus* and *L. frenatus* (2) are reared more frequently. The African species are represented by *L. variegatus* (3), *L. wecksi* and *L. forskali.*

White Cloud, White Clouds or **White Cloud Mountain Minnow**

Cyprinidae

Tanichthys albonubes LIN SHU YEN, 1932

This small, 4 cm long fish comes from the neighbourhood of Canton in the territory of southern China. It was imported to Europe in 1938. Since it readily reproduced, and also due to its lovely colouring, it has kept its position in the aquarists' tanks until our time. Also its veil-finned strain was produced (1). The fish may be set up for spawning in pairs, or, better still, in small shoals. The White Cloud likes sun-flooded tanks, fresh water at 20—22° C, with a pH of 7.0, 8—10° dGH and 2° dCH. Small sprigs of fine-leaved plants are inserted into the breeding tanks; their bottom is covered with a protective grid, although the White Cloud usually does not consume its own eggs. The males are slimmer and their dorsal and anal fins are more prominent and more vividly coloured. In 72 hours small larvae burst out of the tiny, slightly yellowish eggs and attach themselves to the plants and aquarium walls. In a further three days they start swimming freely. Subsequently, high-grade fry food is mixed in a little grind-dish with a drop of water, and several drops are put into the aquarium through a dense net to produce a 'mist'. This is repeated three to four times a day. Several small slugs will eliminate superfluous food. After 12—14 days it is possible to feed the fry on a fine sort of copepods and brine shrimps and eventually on wheel-worm 'dust'. Longitudinal bands glistening with a neon sheen belong to the juvenile colouring and disappear in the more advanced stages of development. From May till October the fry may be left to grow up in garden pools.

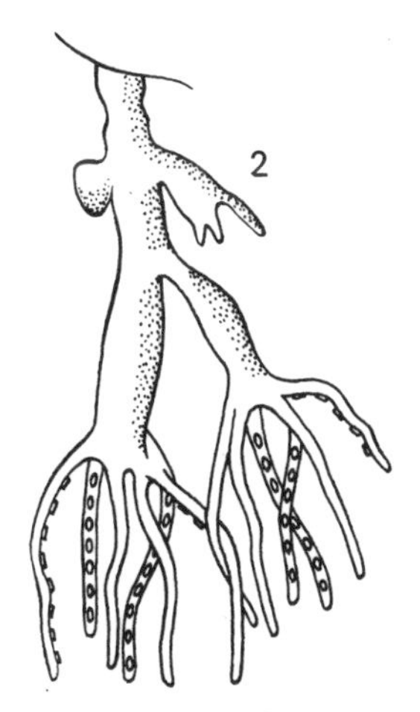

The White Cloud looks its best in a shoal in spacious aquariums which are exposed to sunlight from time to time, richly overgrown with plants, and provide sufficient room for swimming. The diet of the fish consists of various foods. Although the preferred water temperature is 19—21° C, the fish are able to survive temperatures falling as low as 5° C or rising up to 30° C.

The linedrawing shows the Hydra (2), a dangerous fry pest which is usually introduced into the tank with plankton.

Malayan Halfbeak

Dermogenys pusillus (HASSELT, 1823)

The live-bearing Malayan Halfbeak is abundantly distributed in both fresh and brackish waters of Thailand, Malaya and through to Indonesia. It lives in brooks and rivulets with pure water, but also in stagnant, muddy waters of swamps and bow lakes. It was imported to Europe for the first time in 1905. The dorsal and anal fins are situated further back than usual, enabling the fish to make sudden and violent assaults upon the prey. The Malayan Halfbeak is a surface fish living mostly on insects flying close to the surface. Its lower jaw is immobile and elongated. The upper, shorter jaw, being flexible, facilitates hunting on the surface (1). The fecundating organ of the male, markedly different from the gonopodium, is called the andropodium (2). It is formed by the first rays of the anal fin. The male grows to 6 cm and the female to 7 cm in length.

A shallow tank with a broad, open surface area is used for breeding. Thickets of floating plants are fastened along the circumference of the tank, and it is from here that the fry are regularly obtained. In breeding cages and in small tanks the females break off the beaklike projection of their lower jaw. The water conditions should be: temperature 24—28° C, pH 7.0—8.0, rather hard, and with one spoonful of sea or kitchen salt added for each 10 l of water. In the wild the fish are exposed to intensive solar radiation which fosters the production of vitamin D. This is what they lack in captivity. They must therefore be offered vitamin D twice a month with their food. Its lack causes the premature birth of insufficiently developed young. The interval between each delivery is 6—8 weeks; the number of 1 cm long baby fish usually does not exceed 50. At first the fry are given brine shrimps or small copepods; they grow very quickly.

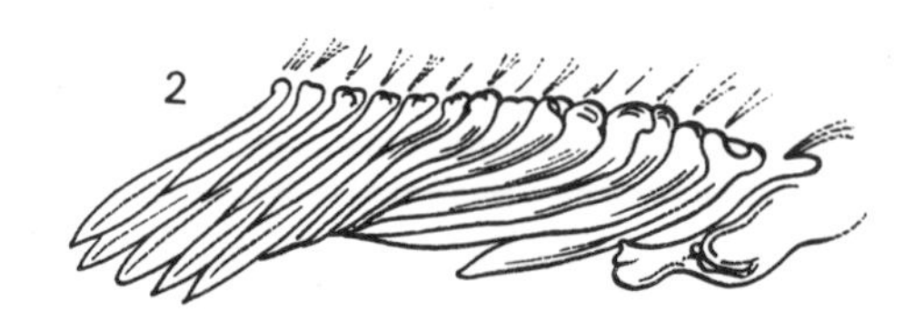

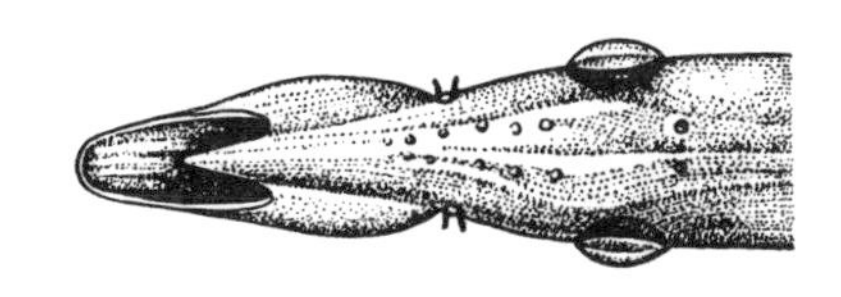

1

The Malayan Halfbeak suitably complements the surface zone of warm and rocky tanks. It may be kept with small fish that require similar water. Specimens reared in captivity are less vividly coloured (3). Natural populations are more colourful but their wide geographical distribution gives rise to differences in the colouring of fish coming from various localities.

The diet of fish living in captivity consists of zooplankton. Fruit flies, aphides and small swept-up insects are offered as supplementary food. Food falling to the bottom is unsuitable.

The related species *Dermogenys sumatranus* and *Nomorhamphus celebensis* (4), with an imperceptibly elongated lower jaw terminating in a fleshy excrescence, are reared less frequently.

Glass Catfish

Siluridae

Kryptopterus bicirrhis (CUVIER ET VALENCIENNES, 1839)

The Glass Catfish inhabits the waters of the East Indies, of the Greater Sunda Islands; it may be found on Java, Sumatra and Borneo. Although it is abundantly imported and sold, little is written about this fish in professional literature. Since 1934, when it was first brought to Europe, its way of life and especially its reproduction have been veiled in mystery. Its maximal length is 10 cm. Observation in nature indicates that, during the rains, mature fish migrate into the surrounding flooded jungle where they spawn. As soon as the water starts to recede, the adult fish, accompanied by shoals of their young, return to their regular waters.

The Glass Catfish is sometimes classed among the group of Ghost Fish. Generally, however, the term Glass Catfish is used to cover a vast range of water-coloured species. In nature, such colour affords effective protection against enemies. Besides its transparency, the Glass Catfish is characterized by a long anal fin, a pair of long, thin barbels on its upper jaw, a stunted dorsal fin (with the exception of a single fin ray) and a tilted stance with the head turned upward to the surface.

Other Catfish with a similar way of life are *Kryptopterus macrocephalus* (1), *Ompok bimaculatus* (2) and *Silurichthys phaisoma* (3). They always live in shoals, inhabiting middle water stretches, preferring gentle currents; they are diurnal fish and never excavate. When isolated, withdrawn from their shoal, these fish wither away and ultimately die. An acceptable environment for them is a spacious aquarium with enough room for movement, but also sufficient vegetation and peat roots providing shelter and dispersing sharp light. The optimal water temperature ranges between 22 and 25°C.

The most favoured food is

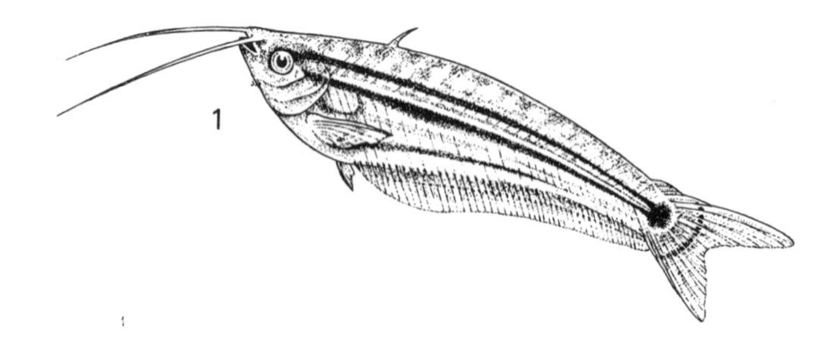

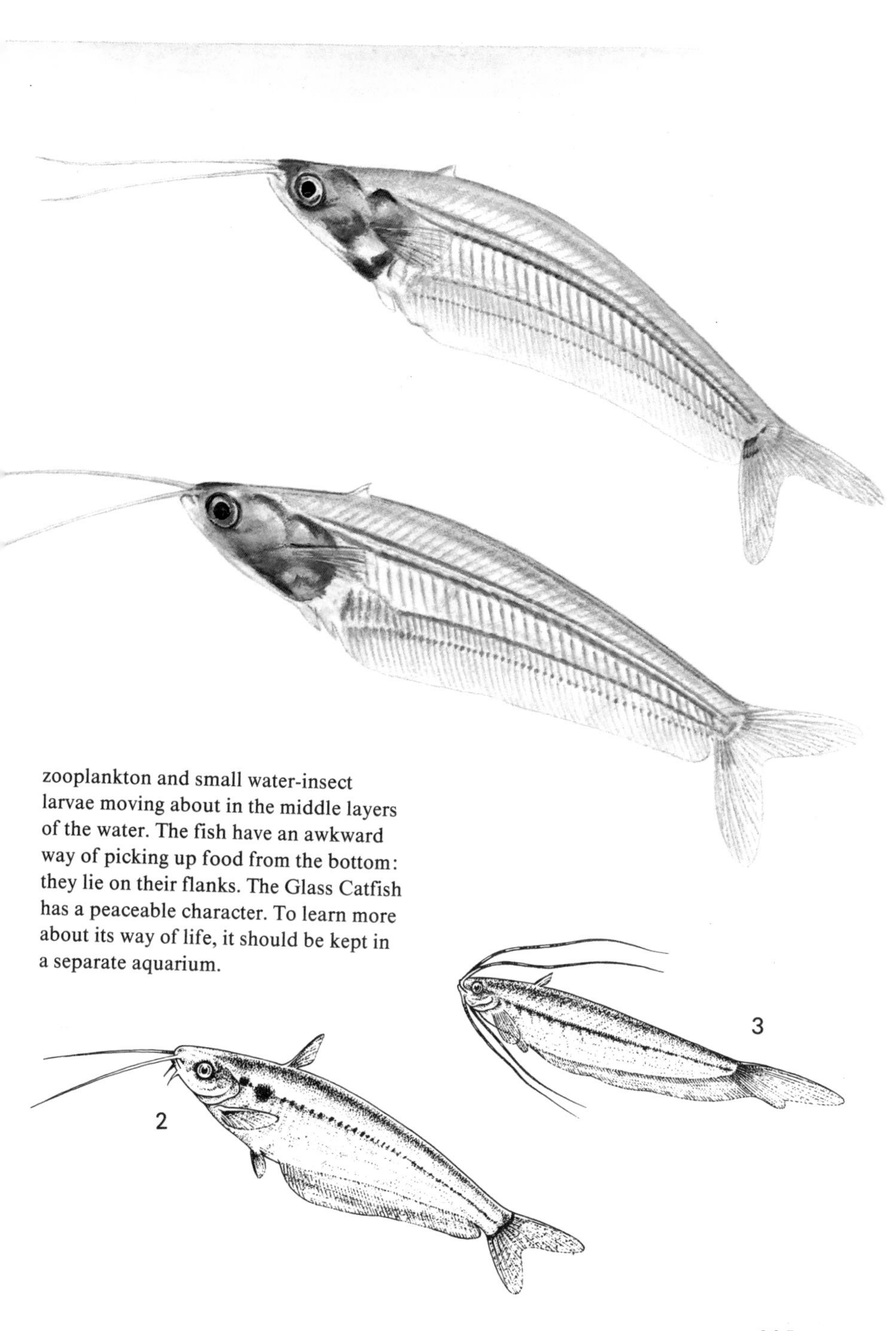

zooplankton and small water-insect larvae moving about in the middle layers of the water. The fish have an awkward way of picking up food from the bottom: they lie on their flanks. The Glass Catfish has a peaceable character. To learn more about its way of life, it should be kept in a separate aquarium.

Chinese Algae-eater

Gyrinocheilus aymonieri (TIRANT, 1883)

Mountain brooks in Thailand and on Kalimantan are inhabited by the Chinese Algae-eater which, in a way, resembles the Gudgeon *(Gobio gobio)*. Since 1955, young fish of this species have been imported to Europe in large numbers. This is indicative of the fact that the Chinese Algae-eater is a prolific fish occurring in nature in large shoals. In spite of this, however, no reports are available as to its reproduction in captivity. Of course, it would not be right to exclude the possibility of its reproducing in spacious, warm pools. Observations made in the large pool of the Botanical Garden in Prague tend to suggest this. The fish grew to be 15—20 cm long and were evidently approaching sexual maturity. However, the subsequent emptying of the pool and the transfer of the fish into exposition aquariums prevented further examination. The likelihood of the reproduction of these fish in a pool is backed up with the fact that the Chinese Algae-eater is a prolific fish which, moreover, inhabits both mountain brooks and stagnant waters of various types in the lowlands where it may attain a length of 15—30 cm. Females are larger and stronger; males have spawning tubercles on their head. Characteristic of this species is an ingenious device (two gill openings enabling the water to flow through and wash the gills) making possible the exclusion of the mouth from the respiratory function and its full utilization in scraping off algae growths attached to the substrate. The broad lips encircling the mouth are endowed with a sucking capacity and provided with coarse ridges.

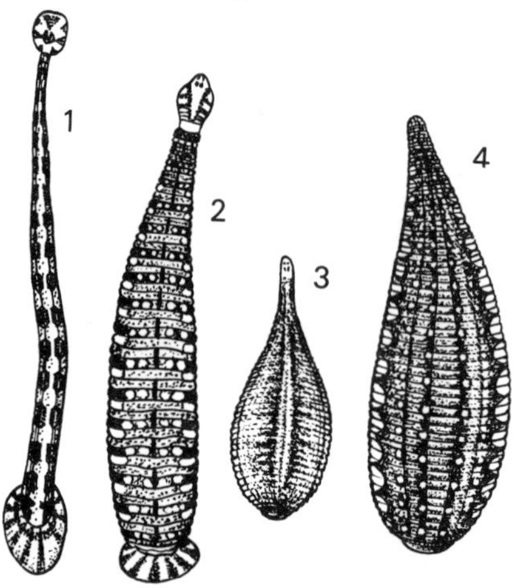

The Chinese Algae-eater is kept in light, sufficiently aerated tanks bathed in sunlight, at a temperature of 25° C. Besides the usual live food and flake feeds the diet should include spinach purée, scalded lettuce leaves, etc. Young fish are peaceable and keep the aquariums free of algae. Older fish mostly stop being careful glass cleaners.

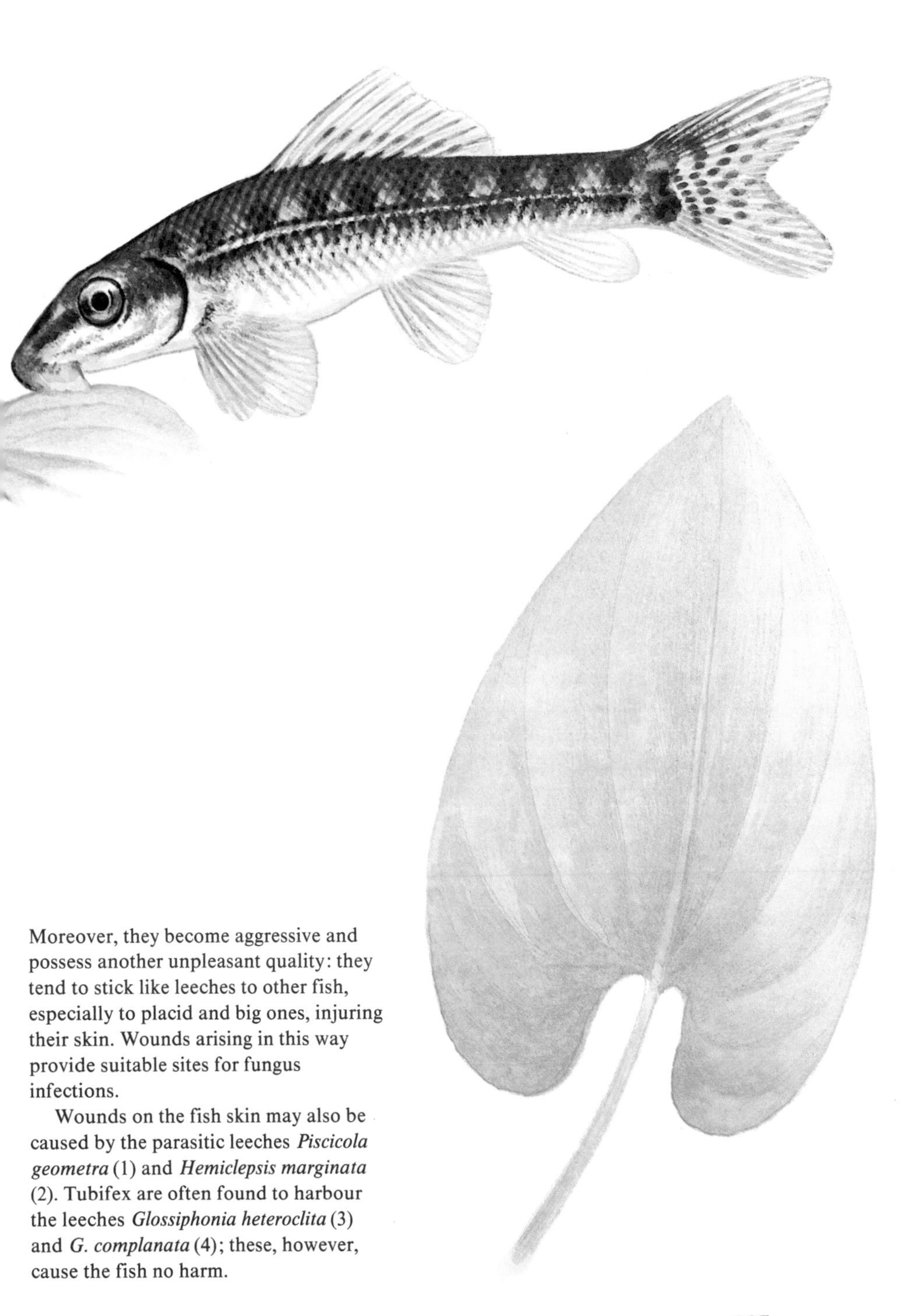

Moreover, they become aggressive and possess another unpleasant quality: they tend to stick like leeches to other fish, especially to placid and big ones, injuring their skin. Wounds arising in this way provide suitable sites for fungus infections.

Wounds on the fish skin may also be caused by the parasitic leeches *Piscicola geometra* (1) and *Hemiclepsis marginata* (2). Tubifex are often found to harbour the leeches *Glossiphonia heteroclita* (3) and *G. complanata* (4); these, however, cause the fish no harm.

Clown Loach

Cobitidae

Botia macracantha (BLEEKER, 1852)

The Clown Loach is a native of the waters of Sumatra and Kalimantan. The maximal length it attains is 30 cm. Next to nothing is known about the way of life of these fish. However, there exist reports about successful reproduction of them in the USSR, where also hybrids between *Botia macracantha* and *Misgurnus fossilis* have been obtained with the help of gonadotropic-hormone injections, but the vitality of hybrids produced in this way was said to be low. Because these results have not yet been published officially, it can only be said that both sexual distinctions and the manner of reproduction have hitherto remained unknown. Due to the fact that the Clown Loach belongs to the most beautiful representatives of the genus, it has often been imported and offered for sale on the market since 1936. All the fish concerned were caught in nature.

The Clown Loach has four pairs of barbels; its eyes are not covered with a protective skin. An erectile double-pointed spine is situated below each eye. Relatively soft water at 24—26° C, free from nitrous substances and rich in dissolved oxygen, is recommended for breeding. The fish are kept separately in a small group of 5—6 specimens in large, dimly illuminated tanks with plentiful hiding places. Essential facts concerning the hitherto mysterious life of these fish can be disclosed only under the condition that they will be allowed to live in an optimal environment and that serious efforts will be exerted to discover what they are lacking in captivity.

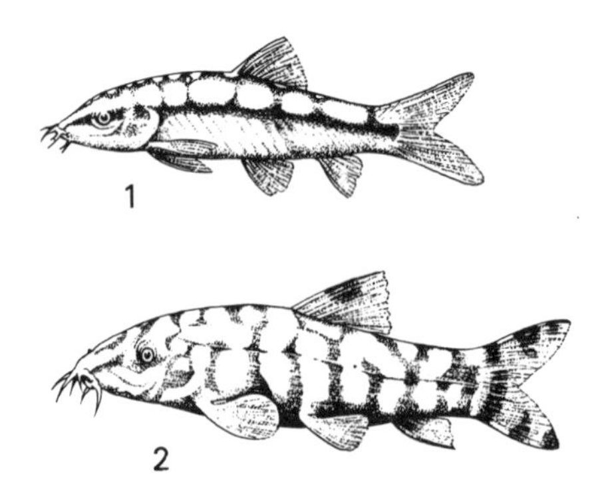

While the young fish unite in large schools, the adult fish form only small groups. Some individuals are aggressive and pugnacious and threaten weak fish. Some ichthyologists hold the opinion that, in nature, the adult fish migrate against the current to the sources of rivers where they spawn in shallow waters along the banks. Later they return with the current.

Besides the Clown Loach, other species such as *B. sidthimunki* (1), *B. lohachata* (2) and *B. modesta* (3) are imported. All these species of the genus *Botia* are fish of the water bed where they also love to forage for food in the form of worms and insect larvae. In captivity they take both live and prepared food. They are sensitive to infestation by the ectoparasitic infusorian *Ichthyophthirius multifiliis*.

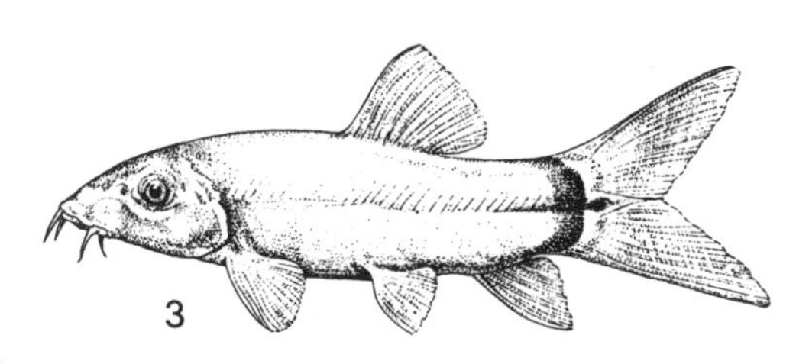

Slimy Myersi

Acanthophthalmus myersi HARRY, 1949

Fish of the genus *Acanthophthalmus* are abundant in the waters of southeastern Asia. The genus includes numerous species and subspecies often greatly resembling each other. A characteristic feature of these fish is a serpentine, strongly laterally compressed body and three pairs of barbels around the mouth. Below the eye there is an erectible spine.

The Slimy Myersi inhabits the waters of Thailand and grows to a length of 10—12 cm. The males are slim, while the females have a more robust ventral region with green ovaries showing through. It was not until 1975 that the first successful breeding was achieved in the USSR after injecting gonadotrophic hormone into the fish. The fish spawn below the surface, side by side, in a gliding motion, with such speed that whirlpools and waves are created on the surface. Having expelled the sexual products, the fish fall to the bottom in a vehement manoeuvre, producing a multitude of air bubbles. This is repeated at intervals of 5—10 minutes for 2—4 hours. The water temperature should be kept at 26°C, with pH 6.5, 8°dGH and up to 1°dCH. Greenish eggs, 1 mm in diameter, are produced in great abundance. The females sometimes spawn spontaneously by rubbing against the plants. At short intervals they literally shoot out more than 100 white (not green) eggs in one spurt. After fertilization of the eggs the embryos emerge in 24 hours. They are provided with auxiliary fruticose gills which disappear within a fortnight. Brine shrimps are suitable as the first fry food.

Large, oblong tanks are advisable for rearing purposes. The Slimy Myersi (1) and other related species suitably complement community aquariums where they enliven the bottom zone. They

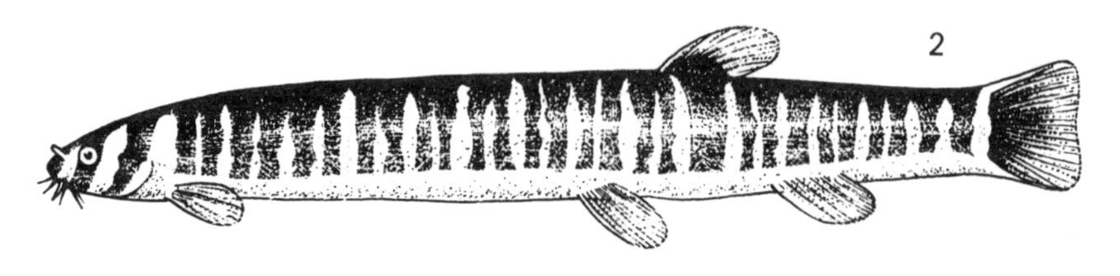

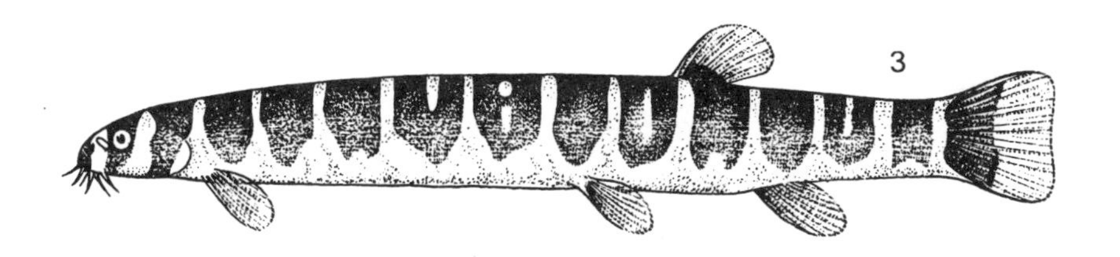

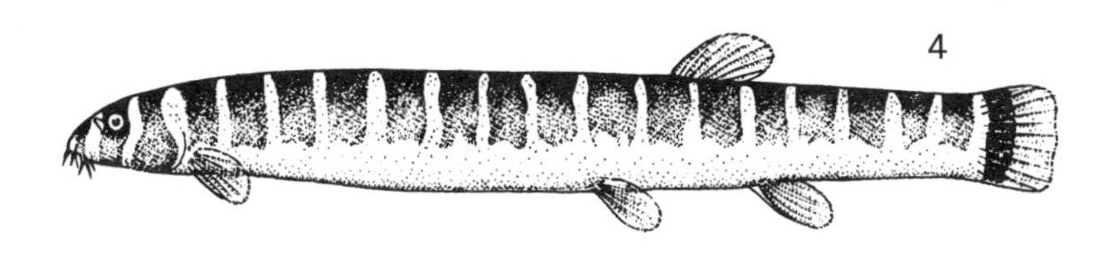

like dim lighting and hiding places. A soft bottom of fibrous peat is preferable to too sharp sand which might cause them harm. They react to changes in atmospheric pressure by restlessly swimming along the aquarium panes.

They are partial to tubifex and insect larvae but will also take animal and plant remains. The following species have structural differences: *Acanthophthalmus kuhli kuhli* (2), *A. kuhli sumatranus* (3) and *A. robiginosus* (4).

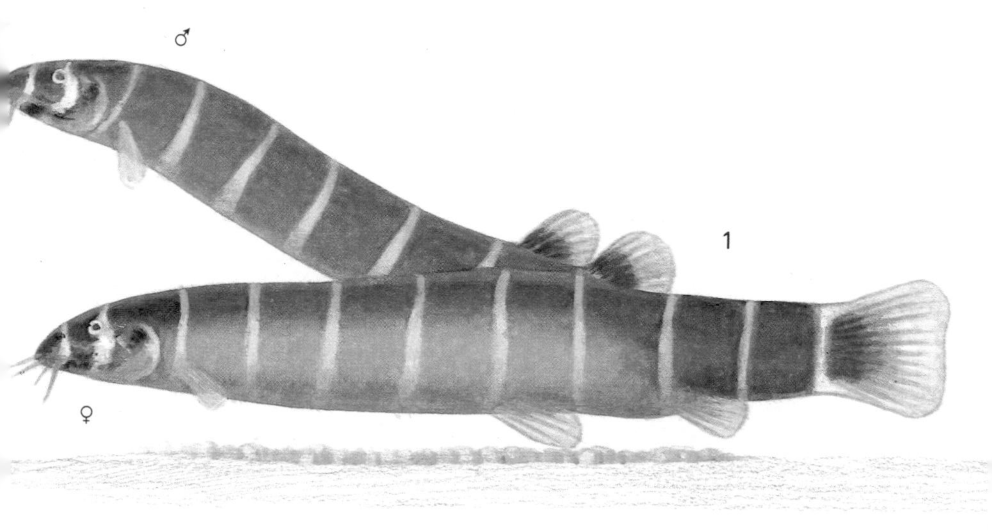

Bumblebee Fish

Gobiidae

Brachygobius xanthozona (BLEEKER, 1849)

The aquarists call it 'bumblebee' owing to a certain resemblance to this insect. It inhabits both brackish and fresh waters of river estuaries in the territory of Sumatra, Borneo and Java. In 1905 it was brought to Europe but has not become particularly widespread. The fish grow to a length of 4.5—6 cm. Although the females have a somewhat fuller ventral region, there is no conspicuous sexual dimorphism. Several specimens are kept together and the arising pairs are gradually segregated. For the actual spawning the fish are set up in pairs in elementary tanks holding 20 l with tapwater containing one spoonful of sea salt per 10 l; kitchen salt can be used if necessary. The suitable water temperature is 26—30° C. A base-less flowerpot is placed at the bottom of the tank, or flat stones are arranged so as to form overhangs and cavities. The female deposits 100—150 circularly arranged eggs, one beside the other, on the upper surface of the cavities. The drop-shaped, whitish eggs, 1 mm in diameter, adhere to the substrate by their narrower end. The male literally sits on the eggs, wriggles among them and stirs them. The female can be removed. The fry emerge on the fifth or sixth day and are 2 mm long, transparent, and may easily not be noticed. They have no yolk sac and immediately start taking food. At this stage also the male can be removed. Newly hatched brine-shrimp nauplii of the finest sort and, better still, copepod or wheel-worm 'dust' should be used for feeding the fry. The immobile fry stay in the medium layers of water near the tank walls. They grow very slowly and need three weeks to attain the length of 5 mm; they remain transparent and slowly descend to the bottom where they afterwards live permanently.

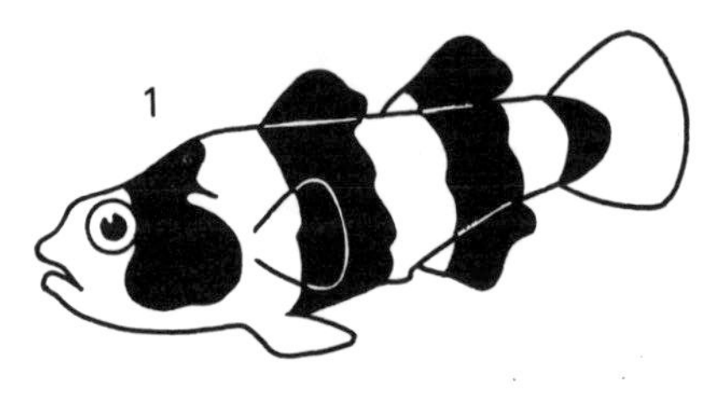

In view of the specific natural environment, it is inadvisable to keep the Bumblebee Fish in community aquariums. The fish should be kept separately in tanks with a stony substrate. The water must be crystalline pure, free of nitrites. Sea salt is regularly added with each water replacement.

Characteristic of the family of Gobies (Gobiidae) is the partial or complete coalescence of pelvic fins. This forms a sucking disk enabling the fish to cling firmly to the substrate. The Bumblebee Fish (1) and the related species *Brachygobius nunus* (2) and *B. aggregatus* (3) are distinguished according to the stripe design. All the same the visual specification of the species is extremely difficult with regard to the great colour variability involved.

The diet of these fish consists predominantly of live food. It includes tubifex, cladocerans, copepods, brine shrimps and other small live food.

Green Puffer Tetraodontidae

Tetraodon fluviatilis (HAMILTON–BUCHANAN, 1822)

The greater part of piscine species belonging to the family Tetraodontidae are sea-dwellers. The musculature of these fish and, in particular, their sexual glands and their viscera contain poisonous tetradotoxins. The ovaries of some species living along the Japanese coast contain a strong poison called 'fugu' which allegedly accounts for a great number of suicides. The poison causes a paralysis of the blood-vessel and respiratory nervous systems.

Some species prefer fresh and brackish waters. One of these is the Green Puffer. Its area of distribution is vast: India, Srí Lanka, Burma, Thailand, the Malay Peninsula, the Sunda Islands and the Philippines. Adult fish grow to a length of 17 cm. In 1905 it was imported to Europe. The Green Puffer feels content in brackish water (with one spoonful of sea salt to 10 l of water), but does not like sea water. It can have great colour variability. No traces of sexual dimorphism are apparent. These fish have already been bred with success, yet there are very few reports on the subject. The fish have the same manner of spawning as the Cichlids. The female deposits 200—300 eggs on stones. After spawning is over, the male takes care of the eggs and literally sits on them. The fry hatch in 6—8 days and are transferred by the male into prepared sand pits. Feeding the fry in the first days of life is difficult for they are very choosey; brine shrimps seem to be the most suitable food.

The fish require water temperatures ranging between 23 and 28° C. Their diet consists mainly of slugs and lamellibranches; they like earthworms, midge larvae, meal grubs, but also beef, heart and liver. For crushing shells, which can be heard far away, the fish use their strong jaws equipped with sharp tooth plates. The dorsal and pectoral fins are admirably suited to locomotion, enabling the fish rapidly to change their movement in all directions, including backwards.

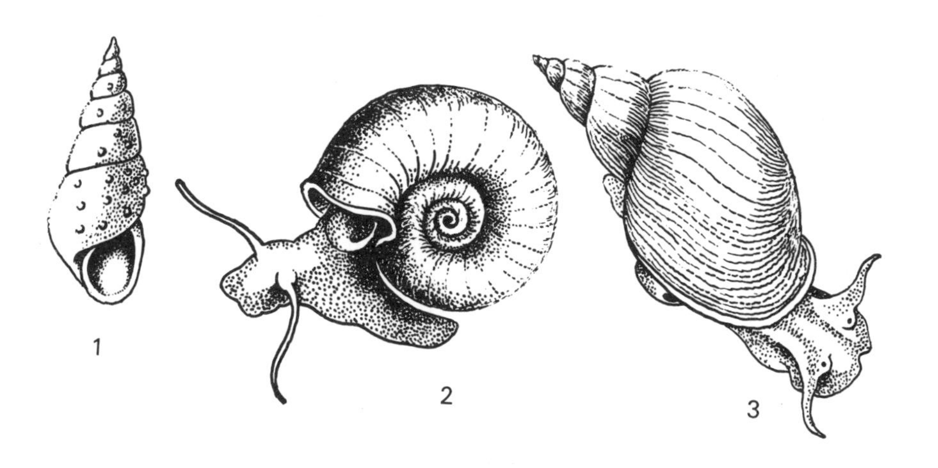

Ventral fins are absent. In danger the fish are capable of inflating with water (or with air if taken out of water) into a spherical shape, and simultaneously erecting the dermal spines. The water or air taken in may be puffed out at once.

They feed on slugs currently occurring in aquariums, e.g. those belonging to the genera *Melanoides* (1), *Planorbarius* (2) or *Lymnaea* (3). Having attained maturity the Green Puffer becomes a biting and intolerant fish.It needs roomy, specific aquariums and is unsuitable for community tanks.

Nutrition of Fish

Tropical fish living in the wild do not always enjoy an abundance of food, hence they are able to endure long periods of hunger. They make up for it when the supply is plentiful. This is usually in the rainy periods. At this time the gonads of the fish ripen and spawning takes place. Thus the hatched fry are sure to attain sexual maturity without suffering privation. It is the aquarist's basic task to offer the fish substitute food in place of their natural diet. To find an adequate food structure one must know how to class fish into the following three groups:

a) fish living on plant food (herbivores);

b) fish living on small aquatic animals, zooplankton and benthes, as well as on plant food (omnivores); and

c) fish living at first on small and later on larger aquatic animals and fish (carnivores).

In a natural environment abounding in foods, the respective fish species can choose its nourishment according to its requirements. In captivity, however, the fish are entirely dependent on what they are given. This is why, among aquarists, it is often heard that some fish species or another has become accustomed to atypical food. This, of course, is extremely misleading, for the fish may accept such emergency food when suffering hunger. Constant habituation may result in various health disorders at a later date. Valuable and regular nourishment is of paramount importance for young fish and for breeders. Natural food contains the necessary proteins, glycids, fats, mineral substances and vitamins. This is not the case with artificial food, which is slowly but surely gaining the upper hand in the nutrition of aquarium fish. It is advisable to learn from the producer the composition of the food mixture concerned.

The most important food components are proteins, which are irreplaceable by any other nutriments. They condition all the functions of life, especially growth and reproduction. The sources of proteins are not only plankton organisms but also beef, liver, heart and egg yolk. Glycids are the main source of energy. Due to the organism's capability to produce glycids from fissionable protein products and from fats, they are not absolutely necessary as food components. Fats represent a store of energy and play an important part in the absorption of vitamins A, D and E. Fats can be produced from glycids and proteins, consequently they need not be contained in the food. Mineral substances represent an important food component, particularly the trace elements involved in the functioning of the sex organs and in the formation of the skeleton, blood, muscles and, in predators, of the gastric muriatic acid (chlorine). They include calcium, phosphorus, sodium, potassium, magnesium sulphur, chlorine, iron, copper, cobalt, iodine and manganese. Vitamins are biologically effective substances necessary in small doses for the healthy development of the organism. A lack of vitamins in food leads to serious health disorders known as avitaminoses.

It is not advisable to underestimate the value of good nutrition and, for reasons of convenience, to give the fish an unbalanced diet. Let us now compare the main sources of natural food in nature and in aquariums.

Plant food taken by the fish in nature in the form of algae, soft aquatic plants, seeds and fruits, as well as in the form of semidigested unicellular algae contained in the digestive tract of zooplankton, are replaced in captivity by spinach purée and scalded leaves of lettuce, turnip-cabbage, cabbage, dandelion and nettle.

'Worms' are a valuable and significant fish-food component. In aquariums they include mainly wheel worms (Rotatoria), tubifex (Tubificidae), white worms (Enchytraeidae) and earthworms (Lumbricidae). In nature they include various animals inhabiting the bottom regions (benthos).

Molluscs are appropriate food for quite a number of species, while in specialized species they form its basic component. Calcium contained in the shells is important for the development of the skeleton of the fish.

Crustaceans, which in nature populate fresh waters as well as brackish and sea waters, are the most widespread food of fish living in captivity. In aquariums the most commonly used crustaceans are cladocerans (Cladocera), copepods (Copepoda) and gill-foots (Anostraca), especially their nauplius stages known to the aquarists as brine shrimps.

In the tropics, insect larvae and imagos (adults) form a rich food supply. In aquariums the fish are fed larvae of mosquitoes (Culicidae) and midges (Chironomidae), as well as imagos of the fruit fly *(Drosophila)* cultivated for feeding purposes. An appropriate food for larger and predatory fish are predacious dragonfly larvae (Odonata) and larvae of some aquatic beetles. Small fish serve as nourishment for numerous piscine species; they also often play an important part in initiating spawning (genera *Astronotus, Serrasalmus,* etc.).

Substitute foods in the diet of fish can take the form of dried and lyophilized food prepared from natural raw materials, or chopped, ground and scraps of beef or ox heart. Mixed liver and spleen are thickened with agar. Also sea-fish and shrimp spawn form appropriate substitute food. Ox hearts were found to contain a ferment that breaks down vitamin B, leading ultimately to a deficiency of this vitamin in the fish organism. It is therefore better, when feeding the fish on ox hearts for a longer period of time, to mix them with the vitamin preparation B-komplex, or regularly to add spinach purée.

Schematic Illustration of Spawning:

1. Breeding cages are particularly appropriate for live-bearing fish species. The cages are suspended in medium or large-sized breeding tanks where the fry are to grow up. The fry escape from the mother fish through the cage netting.

2. For fish with non-sticky eggs that fall freely to the bottom it is advisable to cover the bottom of breeding tanks with a grid; the gaps in the grid must be such as to allow the eggs to fall through without difficulty. In this way the eggs are protected against their parents' cannibalism.

3. Sticky eggs or eggs provided with filaments are deposited among aquatic plants which also serve as supports for the spawning fish. In some species the eggs are protected against cannibalism by a grid, but only in part.

4. In the fish kingdom spawning outside water is a unique phenomenon, yet well-known to aquarists in the species *Copella arnoldi.* In captivity the eggs are attached to the glass cover; in the wild, they are deposited on leaves extending over the surface from waterside plants. Spawning is effected by a simultaneous jump by the pair, side by side, to the substrate. The males then keep close to the spawning site and, from time to time, moisten the eggs by spraying them with water using their caudal fin. The hatching larvae fall into the water, which brings the male's care to an end.

5. Eggs are laid on a firm substrate on the bottom (stones, branches). In the majority of cases, such species take intensive care of both eggs and fry; this may involve both members of the pair or just one of the partners. In some species the eggs are assembled in the mouth (mouthbreeders), where their further development takes place. In the case of species or pairs with cannibalistic tendencies the substrate with the eggs is transferred into another tank, or the fish may be removed after they have finished spawning.

6. As in 5 above, the breeding pair seeks a firm substrate but in a slanting or vertical position, such as the glass tank sides, branches, large leaves or plant stems (of the genus *Pterophyllum*). Here too, the eggs may be extracted, either on the substrate or by being swept off it with a fine brush into a net.

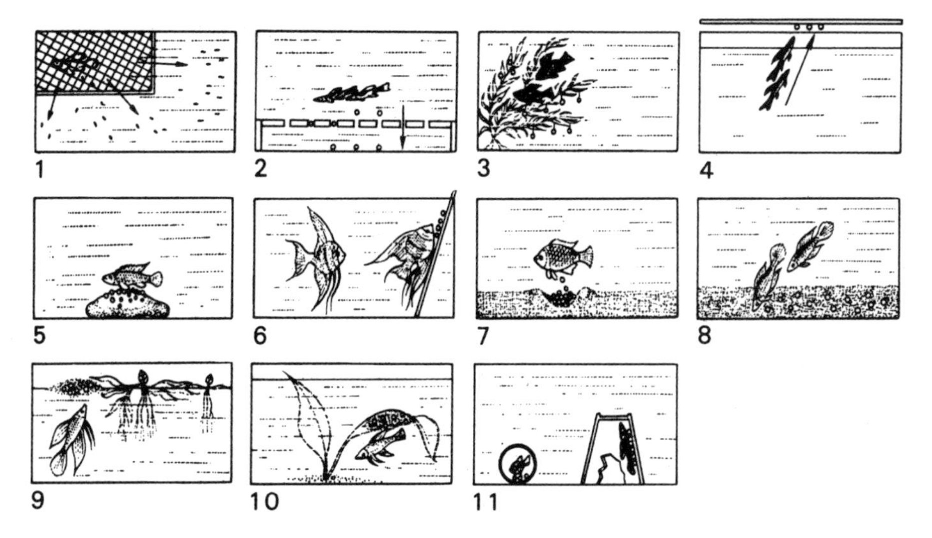

7. Eggs are deposited into pits hollowed out in the ground. In some species the spawning site is guarded by one or both partners.

8. Some fish species, particularly those inhabiting periodic waters, deposit their eggs in the soft substrate of the ground which protects them against desiccation. Here the eggs can survive the unfavourable living conditions in dried-up reservoirs, while the adult fish die. When the reservoirs are replenished with water, the development of eggs is concluded and the fry hatch. In these fish, growth and sexual maturing are very rapid.

9. Eggs are laid in bubble nests on the surface, mostly anchored in the foliage of aquatic and paludal plants (labyrinth fish), or on the underside of broad, floating leaves of water lilies and similar plants (catfish). Instead of broad leaves, dummies are used in the form of suspended plastic plates turned upside down. In both the above cases it is the males who build nests and take care of the eggs and later of the larvae until the latter have consumed the yolk sac and become self-sustaining.

10. As in case 9 above, eggs are deposited in bubble nests. These are built under the surface or in the medium layers of water and attached to the underside of plant leaves or in the top parts of rocky overhangs.

11. Some fish species seek spawning sites in cavities and crevices. Such an environment can be simulated by well-placed flowerpots or pipes. Even here, easy handling of the substrate and eggs is possible. The spawning site is usually protected by both partners or by one of them, most often the male.

Piscine Diseases

Just like other living organisms, fish too are exposed to danger in the course of their life from the ever present microorganisms. It is necessary to mention, in general at least, some fish diseases and their causes, because a timely diagnosis of the illness and its rapid elimination will prevent unnecessary losses among the reared fish. This is all the more true in places where fish are kept in large numbers, i.e. in shops or wholesale establishments. It is exactly here that various infections and diseases threaten to break out, often exacerbated by prolonged starvation and exhaustion due to travelling.

Environmentally induced diseases. The temperature of water, its chemical reaction, the oxygen content in water, all play a significant part in the health of fish. A violation of the optimal environment may result in a disease or poisoning of the fish.

The life of most freshwater fish is endangered if the pH rises above 9.0 or falls below 5.5.

The decomposition of organic matter gives rise to the poisonous ammonia and nitrates. These substances are capable of poisoning fish even in relatively clean aquariums containing stale water. Neglected filters are a particularly serious source of danger. The health of fish is further imperilled by incorrect application of medicaments or by the contact of water with poisonous substances (nicotine, paint diluents, copper, etc.).

A fall in oxygen content is liable to occur in tanks overstocked with fish, with decomposing organic matter (superfluous food, decaying plants), in tanks densely overgrown with plants or algae during night hours (unlit plants absorb oxygen and give off carbon dioxide), and also in cases where the atmospheric pressure falls suddenly. Well-fed fish require more oxygen than hungry ones. A contrary phenomenon, less frequent but equally detrimental, is the overoxidization of water. This may be brought about by an exposure of algae and plants to intensive sunlight or by introducing compressed oxygen into the water. Also intensive water replacement and mixing of warm and cold water in a flow heater may result in a sudden release of oxygen and the formation of fine bubbles (white mist), which is very dangerous for the fish because the gas enters their blood stream. The danger is heralded by the formation of subcutaneous gas bubbles all over the body, but especially in the fins. The fish die as a consequence of heart embolism.

Diseases ensuing from wrong nutrition may be caused by inappropriate or stale food or an unbalanced diet. Digestion disorders manifest themselves by gastric and intestinal inflammations (mucous excreta, enlarged body cavity, protruding scales, etc.). An unbalanced diet lacking certain vitamins results in avitaminoses causing serious disorders in the organism of fish.

Growth disorders and hereditary diseases are represented, first of all, by growth anomalies originating already in the development of the egg or during the growth process of young fish. They arise as a consequence of injury or illness; in this case pathological changes in the organism are referred to. In other cases congenital (inborn) defects are involved; these are sometimes made use of in the cultivation of interesting morphological deviations from the original species on the basis of purposeful selection.

Viroses and bacterioses. Hygiene, strict quarantine for new fish and an optimal living environment are some of the precautionary measures that will prevent the outbreak of these diseases. Also the timely removal of ill or dead fish forestalls the spreading of the disease. In fish breeding, infectious dropsy, furunculosis, tuberculosis and bacterial fin rot are the most common diseases. Most effective in fighting these are antibiotics, sulfonamides and methylene blue (remedies are offered as a part of food or may be applied as long-term baths).

Fungus diseases occur mostly as secondary diseases affecting the damaged tissue of weakened fish in an unfavourable living environment. They are caused by fungi of the genus *Saprolegnia* and *Achlya.* The fungi generally attack dead eggs, and the resultant mycelia grow through and destroy sound eggs. If left uncured, the fungus disease exhausts the organism, floods the body with toxines, and the fish dies. To combat the fungi therapeutic means are used on the Trypaflavine (Acriflavine) basis as long-term baths in combination with kitchen salt and methylene blue.

Invasive diseases may be caused by unicellular parasites (e.g. of the genus *Amyloodinium*) living on the fish body. They are introduced into the tank with natural food on the one hand, and with infected fish on the other. The typical symptoms usually appear in mass in many fish belonging to species prone to the disease (labyrinth fish, spawnrich tooth carps and, above all, some carp-fish species). The body surface and the fins are covered in a brownish 'semolina' visible only under a particular light refraction or in irradiating the fins. If the fish are strongly affected, it becomes especially apparent in their dorsal regions. The fish, particularly the young ones, are spent, their fins flutter and stick together, and, if not given medical aid, they die. The treatment consists of long-term or short-term baths in preparations made from blue vitriol (copper sulphate, $CuSO_4$); yet these remedies, being very toxic, kill all species of invertebrate animals, and cannot be applied to some fish species due to their sensitivity. This is why they are used with great care and strictly according to the instructions. They can be applied only where the pH value is equal to 7.0! Good results are achieved by a short formaldehyde bath (1 ml 40% formaldehyde per 4—6 l of water for about 30—60 minutes). This bath is also applied in treating fish attacked by the ciliate *Ichthyobodo necatrix,* which produces a fine, fluttering, bluish grey lining and reddish cutaneous hematomes on the bodies of the affected fish, or by the infusorian ichthy *(Ichthyophthirius multifiliis)* causing a whitish 'semolina' to appear on the fins and skin of the fish. This infusorian is sensitive to malachite green, thanks to which it has been eliminated from aquarium breeds. Malachite green is to be applied in compliance with the instructions issued for the respective preparations. In contrast to methylene blue, malachite green is toxic if overdosed.

Further causes of invasive diseases are external and internal parasites of the worm group; for example, sucker worms of the genus *Dactylogyrus* and *Gyrodactylus* usually parasitize fish gills. The symptoms of the disease may include fimbriated fins, atypical movements and difficulty in breathing. To kill the parasite completely it is necessary to give the fish an ammonia and trypaflavine bath: 100 parts of 10% ammonia (NH_4OH) are mixed with one part of a 2.5% tripaflavine solution and diluted in the ratio 1:1,000. Duration of bath: 1 to $1^1/_2$ minutes. Prior to mass treatment it is advisable to apply the bath to several experimental fish of the respective species.

Parasitizing leeches of the genera *Piscicola* and *Hemiclepsis,* capable of transferring blood parasites and other infections, can be introduced with natural food. They are removed mechanically (by a pair of tweezers); in case of mass occurrence in a large number of fish, a short (five seconds) Lysol bath is applied: 2 ml of Lysol to 1 l of water. The bath must be tried out first on several experimental fish.

Parasitizing articulata, mostly carp lice (genus *Argulus*), attach themselves to the fish to suck their body fluids. They are usually introduced into aquariums with zooplankton. The adults of carp lice are mechanically removed with a pair of tweezers. Under favourable conditions, however, the carp lice will reproduce in aquariums and in heated reservoirs. Their larvae are invisible and so these parasites recur despite the mechanical treatment of the fish. In such cases again the Lysol bath must be used. After the bath the fish should be placed in a perfect environment; the contaminated tank should be left to dry out or should be disinfected with chloramine, and then rinsed.

In conclusion it is necessary to point out that it is much easier to prevent diseases than to cure them. A regular and careful cleaning of tanks, adequate food and temperature and the placing of new fish in quarantine are the best aids in the prevention of fish diseases.

Index